The Infielders

A Novel

Lewis Segal

Butternut Books

ISBN: 978-1-0688525-1-0 print

ISBN: 978-1-0688525-0-3 e-book

For Rosemita
Ma chère amie

For Barbara and Ted
For kindness

Prologue

Friendship is such a beautiful thing. It gives pleasure. It gives comfort. It is a refuge in times of distress. It provides solutions to vexatious problems. It is a cure for loneliness. It provides a sense of place in a tangled world. It is always there when you need it.

But friendship is such a fragile thing. It must be nourished. It must be protected. It must be given attention. It must be a priority. It must be precious. And yet, and yet, no matter how precious it may be, how much attention it is given, how loudly the friends proclaim their friendship, a friendship remains a fragile thing. It still can fade away or even crash and burn.

Part One

Boys and Baseball

The Season of 1947

Chapter 1

The Heights

The friendship among the four young men who were selected by Coach McCullough to be the George Washington High School infielders for the 1947 baseball season began in earnest in the summer of 1946. Living within a few city blocks of one another in the Washington Heights neighborhood of New York City, Sean Flaherty, Aram Petrosian, Dino Russo, and Bernie Heller were casually acquainted with one another since their earliest years in elementary school. But they were not yet what you could properly call friends. And they had no way of foreseeing whether the friendships they might form would bring them pleasure or end in pain. In the Heights—as everyone called the neighborhood—friends were guys who "went up one another's houses."

In the argot of Washington Heights, a "house" was one's apartment. If you "went up" a friend's house and got lucky, his mother would welcome you and serve you hot chocolate in winter and lemonade in warm weather. Or, if your friend was Bernie Heller, his older brother might show you playing cards with pictures of naked women, a "French deck."

The houses in the Heights were all in apartment buildings. They were homes to tens of thousands of people, most of whom moved to the Heights from older neighborhoods in New York and considered themselves fortunate to live in what they believed to be a quality area. Each building had a super who lived with his family in a basement apartment and served as the maintenance and repair person, the absentee landlord's representative, and a sort of concierge who cared for the building and its occupants in almost a proprietary manner. Most of these superintendents were Negroes (the polite term for African Americans in the 1940s). Almost everyone else who lived in Washington Heights was white.

Notwithstanding the uniformity of color of the population, there was a dizzying ethnic diversity within the neighborhoods of the Heights. The towering structure of Yeshiva University, with its distinctive Moorish architecture, commanded the area on Amsterdam Avenue between 185th and 186th Streets. The presence in the neighborhood of this center of Modern Orthodox Judaism gave notice to the world that "Jews live around here." St. Spyridon Church on Wadsworth Avenue between 179th and 180th Streets made the same statement about Greeks as did the Holy Cross Armenian Apostolic Church on 187th Street about Armenians. The beautiful Gothic-style St. Elizabeth Roman Catholic Church at the corner of Wadsworth Avenue and 187th Street served the religious needs of the neighborhood's substantial numbers of Irish and Italian residents. Congregation Gates of Israel, with its massive columns fronting 185th Street, was where most of the Jewish boys at PS 189 went to afternoon Hebrew school.

Virtually everyone was a first-, second-, or third-generation American with European origins that continued to echo in the apartments and on the streets, contributing texture and a distinctive mixture of tones, characters, and cultures to the area. It was a cliché in films about World War II that each foxhole contained an Irishman, an Italian, a Jew, and a "regular" American sergeant. What was a cliché in the movies was real life in Washington Heights. The neighborhood around PS 189 would have been empty but for the Irish, Jews, Italians, Greeks, Armenians, Slavs, and sprinkles of other ethnic groups who lived there.

Chapter 2

Up the Houses

In Aram Petrosian's house, you would discover that his mother always wore a black dress and that she couldn't speak English. Her treat for Aram and his friends was typically a bowl of fruit. The Petrosian house was on the fourth floor of a building that had a lobby that looked like the entrance to the RKO Coliseum—ornate, carpeted, richly furnished with upholstered chairs and gilt trim—really "fancy" for an apartment building in the Heights. It had an elevator operated by an elderly man in a faux military uniform. Aram's house, on Laurel Hill Terrace, was by far the most elegant the boys had ever seen.

At the other end of the spectrum was Sean's house. The entrance to his building was not a lobby but merely a stairwell, and it stank of urine. It was obvious that Sean's family was poor, although that was not a subject that particularly engaged the attention of the boys. None of them were rich—with the possible exception of Aram, but that did not seem to be a matter of importance to any of them, either. However, the boys never went to Sean's house, and that placed Sean at the margins of the boys' friendship.

Bernie Heller's father worked as a butcher in a kosher meat shop on St. Nicholas Avenue. This shop had a virtual monopoly on kosher meat for the significant segment of the Jewish population of the Heights who observed their faith's dietary laws. Mr. Heller didn't own the business; he just worked there. Bernie was born in Germany, as was his older brother, Werner. The Heller family immigrated to the United States in 1934 when Bernie was four years old. His parents never called him Bernie; to them his name was Bernd. He quickly learned English and spoke without an accent, except the accent of the streets of Washington Heights. Eight years older than Bernie, Werner spoke English poorly and had a heavy German accent. Bernie was too young to share with his family the sense of trauma and displacement their flight from their native country instilled in them. To the joy of his otherwise grim and humorless parents, Bernie was innately happy, playful, funny, friendly, and good-looking.

Mrs. Heller rarely greeted Bernie's friends. Her English was weak, and, as she once disclosed to Bernie, she disliked and distrusted gentiles ("goyim," as she called them). But Bernie's intuitive sociability made him a natural host to his friends.

Dino's apartment was in an old building on Amsterdam Avenue. Almost all the tenants in that building and in the equally old and decrepit adjoining building were families of Italian immigrants. Notwithstanding the shabby character of the building that housed the Russo family, Dino's house was a magnet for his friends. His mother was an ebullient and cheerful woman who was delighted by visits from Dino's many friends. She prided herself on her skill and virtuosity in cooking Italian food, and she invariably insisted that any friend of Dino who came "uppa my house" had to sample her cooking. Usually they did, con gusto.

The religious and ethnic diversity of the people of Washington Heights was no cliché.

Chapter 3

Serious Baseball Playing

The four boys began to spend a great deal of after-school time with one another when they reached the age when playing with a ball in the streets was what boys their age did. Sean's natural athleticism provided him entry into the nascent friendship circle of the boys who would become the Infielders.

Stickball became the predominant afternoon and weekend activity of most of the boys in the neighborhood. And then, when stickball evolved into baseball shortly before the boys entered high school, baseball or—as it was generally called, "hardball"—became the principal activity and the unifying element in the lives of the four boys. That was in the summer of 1943. They spent hours every day from late March through September on the high school baseball field, practicing fielding ground balls, throwing, batting, and playing pickup games. Eventually, they formed a neighborhood team called the Royals, and they played against other neighborhood teams in the Police Athletic League. Baseball became the bedrock of their friendship. They became good at it.

They tried out for the George Washington High School baseball team, and all were selected. But for the most part of the seasons of '45 and '46, they sat on the bench and only occasionally got into a game as a substitute. Sean could hit a baseball further and harder than any kid in the neighborhood, but he struck out much too often. Bernie and Dino were inconsistent hitters but outstanding and graceful fielders. Aram was the least talented ballplayer of the four boys. But he played with such intensity that he won the respect of the other three boys and—equally important —of Coach McCullough, who recognized that Aram could make an important contribution to the team. He selected Aram to be the team's starting second baseman in 1947.

Chapter 4

1947

S pring arrived late in Washington Heights in 1947. That meant the start of baseball practice had to take place in chilly weather. Neither Coach McCullough nor the players were pleased about that, but they had to get ready for the opening game against Theodore Roosevelt on March 24 and the first road game two days later against DeWitt Clinton. The coach called the first practice session for the afternoon of March 10. The team had the nickname of the Trojans for reasons no one could explain.

The George Washington High School baseball field's configuration was dictated by the topography of the Heights. It was situated on one of the highest points on Manhattan Island, flush against the edge of the cliffs leading down to the Harlem River on the east and the Inwood neighborhood on the north. A ten-foot-high chain link fence enclosed the outfield. Because the playing field was squeezed into the area surrounded by the cliffs beyond the outfield, the baseball field was shaped like a football field— more of a rectangle than a diamond. Consequently, the distance from home plate to the right field fence was only about two hundred forty feet, while the corresponding distance along the left field fence was nearly four hundred feet. Inevitably, many more home run balls were hit over the right field fence than the left field fence. This was a great advantage for a strong left-handed hitter like Sean Flaherty. It was doubtful that any of the right-handed batters in the Trojans' lineup could actually hit a ball as far as the left field fence.

A brisk wind was blowing in from the northeast on the first day of practice. It stung a player's hands when he caught a hard-hit ball or a strong throw. It stung even worse when a batter hit an inside pitch. Players standing still in the outfield shivered. It was simply not a day for baseball. After all, baseball was a summer sport, and the weather on that first day of practice was more like that of a winter day. Coach McCullough wouldn't let the pitchers throw hard for fear of injuring their arms. He seemed to have less concern for the fielders, who he thought should be tough and resilient, not fragile like pitchers.

Notwithstanding the adverse weather conditions, the four infielders played like a perfectly synchronized unit. Each of them was always positioned precisely where he should have been. Their throws were like well-aimed darts, unerringly hitting their targets. The coordination between Dino, the shortstop, and Aram, the second baseman, as they practiced double plays was a meticulously choreographed pas de deux. Watching Bernie fielding a bunt with his bare right hand and, in an unbroken motion, throwing a bullet into Sean's glove at first base was a treat—a superb athlete executing a difficult gymnastic maneuver. Coach McCullough knew that Sean's nonchalance at first base was not a sign of indifference but an indication of confident command of the position.

The entire team watched the four infielders at practice with admiration. They drew enthusiasm for the team's prospects from the beauty and strength of the infielders.

However, the infielders were an uneven bunch as batters. Sean could hit with power, and he was the linchpin of the offense. But like many power hitters who could swing a bat with ferocious intensity, he was prone to striking out.

Bernie was a productive hitter, especially in clutch situations. Coach McCullough slotted him third in the batting order just before Sean, the cleanup hitter.

Dino, fifth in the batting order, was a consistent line-drive and power hitter, but that distant left field fence was simply too far for Dino to reach with even his best shot. He hit many fly balls to left field that would have been home runs in other ballparks but were caught for outs at the GW field. Dino was smart enough to adjust his batting at home games to not swing for the long ball. He clearly would be an asset to the team's offense.

Aram's hitting improved somewhat with constant batting practice. Still, he would always be a weak spot in the batting order— where he batted ninth, behind the pitcher.

"He's too smart to be a good hitter," Sean observed one day during practice. "He reads too much to be able to keep his eyes on a pitch" was another of Sean's diagnoses of Aram's hitting weakness. Aram's steadiness in the field at second base kept him in the starting lineup.

Coach McCullough knew he had a good team. There was something about this team that Coach McCullough had never previously observed in his many years of coaching. There was a spirit, an enthusiasm, a unity that could be the foundation for great team performance. The players seemed to like one another in a way that no team he had ever coached had. He hoped that friendship, that closeness, would last until the end of the season, perhaps even longer. It would seriously damage the team's prospects if it fell apart during the season.

It was Dino Russo, he thought, who was the glue that held this team together and the inspiration for the way it would perform. He named Dino to be the captain of the team. When he announced that in the locker room on the last day of practice, the other players applauded and cheered.

Chapter 5

1947

Part 2

The first game of the season was against Theodore Roosevelt High School, nicknamed, naturally, the Rough Riders. It was played at the GW field on a day when spring finally arrived—as it should have weeks before. The day was warm, the sky was cloudless, and there was just a hint of a breeze coming from the south. When the Rough Riders arrived for the game, they immediately began to taunt the George Washington players.

"We know why you guys are called the Trojans. You know what Trojans are—they're scumbags."

"That's what we're going to call you guys, the scumbags of Washington Heights."

This derisive shouting started before the game and continued almost to its end. Coach McCullough tried to get the opposing coach to instruct his team to stop this behavior, but he refused to do so.

"They're just kids having fun, showing off their team spirit. Relax and enjoy the game," the other coach responded.

Coach McCullough did enjoy the game—very much. It was a

rout. The Trojans defeated the Rough Riders by the lopsided score of twelve to one. Every player in the Trojans' lineup except Aram got at least one base hit. Sean hit two towering home runs over the right field fence that probably traveled far enough that they would have cleared the more distant left field fence if Sean had hit in that direction. Aram reached first base once—when he was hit by a pitch.

This was the game that clinched Aram's friendship with Sean, when Sean—the star of the game—made a point of comforting and consoling a distraught Aram—the game's least productive player.

"You played a strong game at second. Even major league players don't get a hit in every game."

It is impossible to overstate the importance of Sean's gesture to Aram.

Bernie sparkled in the infield, making a spectacular backhand stop of a hard-hit ball behind the bag at third base and throwing the runner out with a sizzling throw across the diamond. He also had three sharp singles, a stolen base, and two runs batted in. A stellar performance. Dino played a flawless game in the field and also had two base hits. Even the pitching was effective for the Trojans as they launched their championship season.

In the locker room after the game, Coach McCullough complimented his players. "Not only did every one of you play with skill, you played with spirit and teamwork. We'll always be winners if you keep on playing as you did today. I'm also proud of you that you didn't let that disgusting shouting from the Theodore Roosevelt bench get under your skin. Keep up the good work, men."

Aram wondered whether the coach intended to include him in this praise. He decided that he was included. Sean and Dino made him think that way.

Chapter 6

Aram

As the players celebrated the last out of the game, Dino put his arm around Aram's shoulder and said, "Everyone has a bad game from time to time. That's why a season in the majors is 154 games. Now, smile. We won. Next game, you'll be the star."

With that small gesture, the long and warm acquaintance of Aram and Dino that began in the second grade suddenly blossomed into a friendship with the potential to last more than nine innings, perhaps more than the season, even possibly for a lifetime.

Aram was an excellent student, something that mattered a lot to Dino, who was a good student himself. Aram went on to finish at the top—first!—of the junior year of the class of 1947. Aram quoted his mother's joyful response to the news of Aram's achievement.

She spoke in Armenian and said, "You even finished ahead of those two Jewish boys." She was referring to Larry Epstein and Morris Feldman, ranked second and third in the class.

Coach McCullough had faith in Aram and kept him in the

starting lineup for the rest of the season. Although Aram's performance improved after his dismal first game, as Dino had predicted, he never became a star. But he became a valued friend.

Some friendships are born in an instant. Others ripen slowly over time. It's not clear which will survive longer.

Chapter 7

Sean and His Father

I t didn't make much of a difference that Aram was a mediocre player. The 1947 George Washington High School team was a powerhouse, with a strong lineup and two fairly good pitchers. Sean's performance in game after game was superb. He hit with consistent power. He played flawlessly at first base. His performance was so outstanding that, later in the season, Sean was approached by scouts for the New York Giants and the Boston Braves. He also received a baseball scholarship offer from New York University. The other infielders were happy for Sean and pleased that their teammate had earned opportunities he would not have had but for the baseball team.

It was good that Sean's life looked promising because it had been clouded by misfortune. An older brother whom he idolized had been killed in the war in 1943. His home life could be fairly described as dysfunctional. His father fancied himself to be a poet. An authentic Irish poet. He had two collections of his poems published by a company in Dublin, but his royalties from the sale of those books had dwindled to virtually nothing. He submitted his work to publishers, poetry magazines, newspapers—anyone who might pay him any amount for a poem. His income ranged from zero to negligible, yet he worked full-time writing poetry. The long, bitter, and painful poem that he wrote following the death of his son in combat at Guadalcanal was published in the *Journal of Modern Poetry* and was commented upon favorably by a number of reviewers.

But even if Mr. Flaherty had been a genuinely talented poet—and he might have been—there isn't much money to be made writing poems. Notwithstanding, Mr. Flaherty worked diligently at his poetry. He brushed his children aside whenever they approached him and said things like "Don't you see that I'm working? Do you think my poems write themselves?" Especially to Sean, he said hurtful things like "Why can't you get it through your thick head that I cannot tolerate interruptions when I'm writing poetry. Your brother, God rest his soul, he understood, and he loved my poems. You, on the other hand, can't tell the difference between a poem and a shopping list."

Mr. Flaherty spoke with an Irish brogue, far deeper and more intense than it needed to be. He had lived in the United States since he was twelve years old. The accent was initially an affectation, but its constant use caused it to become a habit. It reinforced his image of who he was.

Mrs. Flaherty supported the family by cleaning other people's houses during the day and working as a barmaid at night. Sean and his surviving siblings—three younger sisters—were virtual orphans. He rarely saw his mother except when she dragged him to mass at St. Elizabeth Church on those Sundays when Sean didn't manage to escape from that duty (something he became increasingly skillful at doing during his high school years). Baseball—at which he was gifted—became his religion. And his teammates, especially the other infielders, gradually became a substitute family.

Sean had the body of an athlete—tall, hard, and slender. He was good-looking, although the other infielders probably didn't take note of that or attach any importance to it. The girls did, however.

Aram intuitively understood that Sean's low self-esteem resulted from his family situation. It was an irony that Sean, the son of an Irish poet, often had difficulty expressing himself effectively. When he reached out to Aram, in a gesture of friendship, after Aram's poor performance in the game against Theodore Roosevelt, he said, "It was really brave of you to get hit by that pitch."

Aram knew Sean was groping for a way to say something about the game that Aram would appreciate. Aram meant it when he responded, "Thanks. We all try to do our part for the team. Let's go find Bernie and Dino."

"I'd rather go up your house for a while," Sean said.

Sean admired the appearance of Aram's apartment but didn't quite know what to say about it, so he said nothing. Moments after the boys sat down on the comfortable sofa in the living room, Mrs. Petrosian appeared carrying a bowl of grapes and some napkins. She said something to Aram in Armenian, smiled shyly at Sean, and left the room.

"I didn't understand what your mother said," Sean said.

"Of course not. She was speaking Armenian. She said she's glad I have a new friend."

"Do you always speak Armenian at home?"

"My mom doesn't speak much English, so it's usually in Armenian when she and I talk."

"That's amazing, you know a foreign language."

"Actually, I spoke Armenian before I could speak English."

After a long pause in the conversation in which it appeared that Sean was contemplating the remarkable thing he had just learned about Aram's language abilities, Sean said, "Aram, I want to ask you something."

"What's that?"

"I'm having trouble in a couple of subjects in school, and I was hoping you might help me."

"I'd be happy to do that. What subjects?"

"Algebra and French. I don't suppose you know French, but if you could help me with algebra, I'd really appreciate it."

"Actually, Sean, I know French quite well. I'm now taking French 8. That's the highest level course in French, and I'm sure I'll get at least a ninety-five in it."

"You are unbelievable. I'll be happy to pass French 4 with a sixty-five. That's what I got in French 3, by the skin of my teeth."

"Well, we've got some work to do. When do you want to start?"

Sean went up to Aram's house almost every day. Aram was a diligent tutor, and Sean was a grateful student. Together, they also ate a lot of fruit.

Some friendships develop with ease and with grace. Others are stumbled into and take hold almost by accident.

Chapter 8

Bernie and Sean

As diverse as the infielders were in economic circumstances, ethnicity, and religious backgrounds, no two were as different from each other as Bernie and Sean. Bernie was brash, confident, sassy and fun-loving. At times, he was crude, coarse, or profane. Sean had none of those traits and tended to be offended by them. And yet, there was something that drew them together. Bernie was a Jew, and Sean, a Roman Catholic. Neither of them gave any attention to that. The fact was they enjoyed one another's company. Sean was often amused by Bernie's antics, and Bernie had a thoughtful and a kind interior concealed beneath his cocky public persona. Several years before they became teammates, they had a conversation one day when Sean met Bernie outside of Bernie's apartment building across the street from the schoolyard of PS 189. Bernie was returning from a rare attendance at Hebrew school carrying a book written in Hebrew. Sitting on a stoop in front of Bernie's building, this was their conversation.

"Hey, Bernie, can you read that book?"

"More or less, but I can't understand a word of it."

"That's funny . . . When I go to mass and pick up one of the books in my pew, I look at it . . . I can read it, but it makes no sense to me."

"Looks like neither of us knows much about religion. Hey, Sean, there's something I've been wanting to talk to you about."

"What's that?"

"My father told me you had a brother who was killed in the war. I was sorry to hear that."

Sean's face fell. "I think about him every day. He was smart. He did good in school. Much better than me. He joined the Marines as soon as the war started."

"You really miss him? I don't think I'd miss my brother. There's something wrong with him. I think he's crazy."

"I miss Paddy so much that sometimes I just want to cry because he's dead. I want to cry right now because we're talking about him."

"If you feel like crying, you should go ahead and do it. Come up my house. You'll be safe there. No one will see you crying up there."

They were not yet twelve years old when Sean and Bernie went up to Bernie's house that day.

Some friendships connect people who have very much in common. Others involve people who have nothing at all in common except their friendship.

Chapter 9

Armenians and Jews

Throughout all the years that they were in the same class at PS 189, in all the years that they lived just a few blocks from each other in the Heights, in all the years that they played stickball and baseball together, in all the years that they knew each other, Aram and Bernie never became friends. Although they shared an interest in sports, Bernie's interest was serious, and Aram's was far more casual. Their personalities were markedly different. Bernie was flighty and fun-loving. Aram was serious and studious. There was simply no emotional connection between them.

It was Dino who brought them closer. It was his idea that the infielders were a unit, the mission of which was to be the bedrock of the team's defense. "After all," he told the infielders, "most of the times we get a guy on the other team out, that happens in the infield. We got to carry the defense on our backs. We got to work together, we got to think together, we got to be a team within the team." This was quite an insight for a seventeen-year-old, but the other infielders grasped it with enthusiasm.

The first time they were in Aram's apartment, Mrs. Petrosian brought a bowl of fruit and some plates into the living room, looking fondly at her son and his friend without saying a word.

When she left the room, Aram said, "She can't speak English, only Armenian."

Bernie felt awkward sitting on the sofa in Aram's house. The place looked foreign to him. He was curious about Armenians—about whom he knew absolutely nothing—and wanted to learn more about Aram and his family. Aram's name was strange; it was a name Bernie had never heard before. Armenians were somehow exotic and unknown to him. Bernie couldn't hold back his curiosity and began to ask questions.

"Hey, Aram, can I ask you something?"

"Sure."

"Okay. You know I'm Jewish, don't you?"

"Yep. I think everybody knows that. We have a lot of Jews in our class. But our neighborhood has quite a few Armenian families, too."

"Is Armenian a religion, like Jewish?"

"Armenians are Christians," Aram replied politely.

"Are you Catholic?"

"No. Like most Armenians, my family is Armenian Apostolic. We go to the Holy Cross Armenian Apostolic Church on 187th Street, between Audubon and St. Nick."

"I know the building," Bernie said. "I've walked past it hundreds of times. I thought it was a Catholic church. How is it different from a Catholic church?"

"Well, our services are very different. First of all, they are entirely in Armenian."

"Really? Jewish services are mostly in Hebrew which I don't understand one word of. Can you understand Armenian?"

"Yes, I can understand and speak Armenian."

"But weren't you born in America?"

"Sure, but my parents were born in Turkey. To this day, my mother really speaks only Armenian and maybe ten words of English."

At Bernie's request, Aram began to tell him the story of his family.

"My mother was five years old when the Turks massacred millions of Armenian people. Both of her parents were killed, but she somehow survived. She doesn't know how."

"Wait a minute," said Bernie. "What are you talking about? What massacre?"

"You really never heard of the genocide of the Armenians by the Turks during the First World War?"

"Honest to God, this is news to me."

"You know, that's so typical. I'm not blaming you, but it hurts me that so many people can be unaware of the mass killing of my people. Let me tell you, Hitler knew about it. Before he started murdering Jews, he said to his followers, 'Don't worry. Today, no one remembers the Armenians.' He was right about that. Maybe if people remembered what the Turks did, just maybe the Germans wouldn't have massacred your people in Europe."

Aram looked at Bernie for a reaction. Bernie just sat quietly, staring into empty space.

"Say something, Bernie. Don't just sit there."

Bernie looked at Aram, and after a few more moments of silence, he said, in a barely audible voice, "My mother's parents and my father's parents—all of my grandparents—were killed by the Germans. The only reason my mother's alive, the only reason I was born, is that my father insisted we leave Germany as soon as possible after Hitler came to power." Tears began to form in Bernie's eyes. "I never had a grandparent."

Aram put his arm around Bernie's shoulder.

Some friendships are born in happiness. Others are the offsprings of tragedies.

Chapter 10

A Kiss on the Lips

Every circle has a center. All of the radii of a circle meet at the center. Dino was the center of the circle of the infielders. It was not a role that Dino sought, nor was he conscious of the fact that he was the center of the circle, attaching all of the infielders to himself and to one another. He was simply, by nature, a leader. The players on the George Washington team unanimously supported the coach's designation of Dino as the team captain, ratifying the appointment and avoiding a constitutional dispute over appointing authority.

For certain, Sean looked at Dino as his leader. Sean took seriously every word Dino uttered. The fact that Dino treated him as a friend—that he was, in fact, a friend—was regarded by Sean as an honor. Dino valued Sean's contribution to the baseball team: his power hitting, his competent fielding at first base, and—most of all—his team spirit, the exuberance with which he played and applauded good playing by his teammates. Dino viewed this friendship as mutually rewarding even though Sean thought of it as a gift from Dino.

Because it was a fact, tacitly accepted by all of the boys, that Sean's house was not a suitable place to visit, Dino and Sean spent a great deal of time together in Dino's apartment, especially in the winter of 1947 when they expected to be in the opening lineup when the baseball season started in March. Mrs. Russo liked Sean, probably because of his modesty, his good looks, and the genuine gratitude he showed for the hospitality she offered on behalf of the Russo family.

Mr. Russo worked as a laborer in a road construction crew. In winter, he usually was home before five o'clock because work was cut short by darkness and often by snow. He always entered the apartment with a loud announcement of his presence and the unvarying question "What does a hardworking man get for supper in this house, and how long does he have to wait?" He was an amiable, gregarious, and demonstrative man, gentle and loving despite his rough and disheveled appearance and heavy Neapolitan accent. The ritual of his arrival involved a hug and a kiss on the waiting lips of Mrs. Russo followed by another hug and a kiss on Dino's lips. If any of the three other Russo children were accessible, they also received the hug and kiss treatment. The first time Sean saw Dino's father kiss him full on the mouth, he was utterly astonished. Dino was the eldest of the five Russo children.

The day he met Mr. Russo was memorable for Sean for more reasons than the kiss. When Mr. Russo saw Sean sitting shyly on the sofa, he asked Dino, "Is that big guy a friend of yours?" After Dino affirmed that Sean was his good friend, Mr. Russo pronounced, "Then he is a friend of mine. Come here, big guy." He then embraced Sean, who, while wrapped in the arms of Dino's father, worried that he, too, might be kissed. To Sean's relief, there was no kiss.

But there was a warmth that Sean had never experienced with his own father. The contrast between the two fathers was staggering. Sean's father was inaccessible; Dino's father was almost too intimate. Sean had concluded that his father was all pretense and self-absorption. Dino's father was genuine.

Sean had to fight off the thought that he wished Mr. Russo was his father instead of his real father. "Honor thy father and thy mother" was a commandment. Were his thoughts a sin? Sean was enough of a Catholic to worry about sin. But he loved being part of the Russo family, having spaghetti dinner with them, drinking red wine at Mr. Russo's insistence, having second portions at Mrs. Russo's insistence, and enjoying the rapturous adoration evident on the face of Dino's fourteen-year-old sister, Theresa.

Some friendships are as close as families. Some families are not as close as they are supposed to be.

Chapter 11

The Most Exclusive Club in the World

Thus, the infielders became more than teammates. A friendship circle was formed among four very different boys. Although those boys were at the threshold of manhood, they were still boys as their senior year at George Washington High School began in the fall of 1946. None of them had much experience with the world outside of Washington Heights. They still had a lot of growing up to do before they became full-fledged adults. And yet, they had a sense that the circle was a thing of value to each of them, that it was something of importance in their lives, and that it might be worth preserving.

One day in the late winter of 1947, the four boys were sitting on the stoop outside of Bernie's house. Bernie said, "You know we are the most exclusive club in the world. Membership is closed. Nobody else can ever join our club."

"That's right," Sean agreed. "We should have a name for our club."

"How about just calling ourselves the Infielders, with a capital *I*," Aram offered.

"That's perfect," Bernie said. "Should we have caps or jackets or shirts with the name on it?"

"I don't think so," Dino replied. "That would give away the secret of the club. Only the four of us should know we are the Infielders."

Everyone agreed, and the Infielders became the official name of the circle of the four boys.

Bernie said, "I think we need more than a name. Not jackets or caps. I mean we should agree on what it means to be an Infielder. Not only on the ball field but everywhere. And always. I think it means always helping a fellow Infielder when help is needed."

"I think Bernie's right," Sean said. "I agree we got to be there when needed."

"This is wonderful," Aram said. "An Infielder should always be on the side of another Infielder if there's trouble. I want to be sure I have an ally—three allies—if I'm ever in a fight."

Dino laughed and went on to say, "Aram, it's hard to picture you being in a fight, but you can be sure I'll be on your side in every fight you have. That's funny in a way, but I really mean it. And since it's far more likely that I'll find myself in a fight than Aram, I love the idea that I have three automatic good guys on my side."

Sean and Bernie voiced their agreement with Aram's idea.

Sean said, "You can all count on me." Bernie said, "I'm so glad we talked about this. We're more than infielders on a baseball field. We are Infielders everywhere and always. Let's shake on that."

All of the Infielders shook hands with one another.

As the weeks of the school year rolled on, the boys in the circle were together at every opportunity they had to be together. They played sports together—basketball outdoors and indoors, roller hockey (Bernie and Aram didn't play), touch football, and—whenever the weather permitted—stickball. Baseball would have to wait until spring.

But they did more than play. They had conversations. They talked about the usual things—sports, girls, female anatomy, school —and they also talked about the future, their futures, and the future of the circle. They explored the things they might do after high school and what careers they might pursue, including the question of which was more important: making money or doing something that was really interesting. Bernie and Sean voted for money. Aram wanted something challenging and stimulating. Dino couldn't decide and wondered why there had to be a choice. "Why can't we do both?"

People are innately social beings. They bond with one another. They don't need bylaws to be members of a club; they only need to be friends.

Chapter 12

Marching Toward a Championship

The 1947 high school baseball season proceeded with one victory after another. The Trojans' march toward the championship was marked by the decisive toppling of longtime rivals, all of whom fell like dominos before the superbly confident Trojans of George Washington High School.

At the end of their 16–0 regular season in June, the Trojans had to wait until a playoff game between James Madison of Brooklyn and New Dorp High School of Staten Island was played to determine which team would be the Trojans' opponent in the city championship game. The playoff game was to be played at the James Madison field, not far from Ebbets Field, home of the Brooklyn Dodgers. Coach McCullough decided to take his team to Brooklyn to watch the playoff game. The Trojans were given the day off from classes and the trip to Brooklyn in a yellow school bus was one of the happiest occasions in the lives of the nineteen boys who were on the edge of the most notable achievement of their young lives. They were reading about the two teams in the *New York Post*. Madison was called the Golden Knights, a name the boys unanimously called "ridiculous." During the season, the Golden Knights won twelve games and lost four. Their opponent, New Dorp, a school none of them had ever heard of, also had a season record of twelve and four. Notwithstanding this respectable record, New Dorp was ridiculed by the Trojans because its name sounded like some sort of joke and because the team name was the Central Cougars.

"What the hell kind of a name is that?" asked Sean Flaherty, a big grin on his face. "Why don't we become the *Grand* Central Trojans?"

"Great idea," someone yelled. "Coach, can we get shirts that say *Grand Central Trojans?*"

"No," said the coach, ending that discussion. "We're going to watch this game to see what these two teams are capable of doing and what their weaknesses might be. Let's be grown up about nonsense like team names." They may have had an undefeated season in which they played superb baseball, but the players were still just boys.

New Dorp defeated James Madison and thereby became George Washington's opponent in the city championship game. The game was scheduled to be played in Ebbets Field on Monday, June 28, when the Brooklyn Dodgers were on the road. That was just two days before all of the seniors on the team would graduate.

The idea of being one game away from the city championship layered on top of the idea of playing a game in a major league stadium, was almost too exciting for the boys to absorb. After practice on the day before the game, the four Infielders had gathered in the ice cream parlor near the subway station on 191st Street. They were drinking egg creams.

An egg cream was the name given by New Yorkers to a fountain drink that was a mixture of seltzer, chocolate syrup, and about an ounce of milk. It contained neither eggs nor cream, but it was delicious.

"Pinch me," Bernie said to no one in particular, "I want to be sure I'm not dreaming. You don't know how much I dreamed that this would happen."

Dino said, "I don't think anything compares to being city champions."

"I agree," Sean said, "but I hope it's not the best thing we'll ever have."

Then Sean continued, returning to form, "I think we'll be even happier if we beat New Dorp."

The other Infielders all smiled, expressed their agreement with Sean, and returned to their egg creams.

The days before the championship game were filled with intensive practice sessions as Coach McCullough tried to get the players—especially the seniors—to focus exclusively on the upcoming game. He knew that the imminent graduation had to be a distraction to the seniors, especially the Infielders. Dino, the leader of the Infielders, was keenly aware of the weight the championship game and graduation had on himself and his friends. A few days before the championship game, he called a team meeting. Not usually an especially articulate person, Dino made what had to have been the longest speech of his young life.

In the locker room after a rigorous practice session, he said, "Guys, we've had a lot of tests in high school. Those of us who are seniors have had the most tests of all. I want you to think about this. You had to pass a test to be on this team. If you are in the starting lineup, you had to pass a test to get there. Every ground ball that comes to me—or any infielder—is another test. Same for fly balls in the outfield. Every time at bat is another test. For our pitchers, every opposing hitter is another test. And every game we play is still another test.

"Do you guys realize how many tests you've passed to bring you—to bring us—to where we are now? We're winners, that's what we are. We have been challenged, time and time again, and we have succeeded time and time again."

Dino then addressed each of the starting players and, with remarkable insight into each one's strengths and weaknesses, he pointed out—one by one—how each player succeeded in spite of his weaknesses by drawing upon his strengths.

To Sean, he said, "You're a far better athlete than you are a student. We all know that high school has not been easy for you, but you worked hard at all your subjects, and with a bit of help from Aram, you passed all your subjects. You are going to graduate later this week. Baseball is easy for you by comparison. Bring all of your skills to Ebbets Field, and you'll pass another test."

To Bernie, he said, "My friend, sometimes I think your greatest challenge is keeping your pants on." The locker room erupted with raucous laughter.

Bernie looked around the room with a proud grin on his face and said, "Dino, you really know me, don't you?"

"Yes, I do. I also know that keeping your pants on is not one of your strengths. It's very much one of your weaknesses. But, somehow, the things about you that attract girls also make you a fine ballplayer." Everyone was listening intently to Dino's remarks, but this last one caused several of the boys to look at one another, seeking clarification. Dino continued. "It's not the size of your cock that attracts the girls. I've seen your cock in the showers hundreds of times. It won't win any prizes. The thing that attracts girls isn't hanging between your legs. It's somewhere in your brain or your heart. It's whatever gives you your amazing self-confidence. I wish I could come at every challenge I have to face in life with the same level of confidence that helps you seduce an innocent girl, or charge a ground ball, or swing a bat and hit a fastball.

Finally, Dino addressed Aram. "It's not hard to identify your weakness. You can't hit worth a shit. Don't think those two or three hits you got this season qualify you for the big leagues."

"Five," said Aram.

"Five what?" asked Dino.

"Hits. Isn't that what you were talking about, or weren't you paying attention? I made five hits, not three during the season."

"Aram, you are one of the most amazing players in the history of high school baseball. You may be one of a kind. How many starting infielders on an undefeated team—or on any team, for that matter—have also finished first in their class and been accepted to Harvard? I'll bet none, not one. So, you got classroom smarts; how does that help us win ball games? Because you bring your brains with you when you get on the field. You never make a mistake. You make sure no one on your team makes a mistake—or at least too many mistakes. When we're nervous, you calm us down. When we're not paying attention, you wake us up. Your understanding of the game could make you a major league manager. Aram, please bring your brains to Ebbets Field."

This was followed by more applause.

Dino then spoke about himself. "My greatest weakness on the ball field is the same as my greatest weakness in everything. It's fear. It's fear of fucking up. I have a great need to do everything right and I know in my heart that's impossible. I'm not the greatest ballplayer in this room, and I'm certainly not the smartest student. But I think it's possible that I try harder than everyone here. I try harder because I'm scared of fucking up. You should know when the game starts on Friday, I will be gripped with fear. Please help me get past that by playing the greatest game you've ever played. That's what I'm going to try to do."

More applause, and then every boy in the room hugged Dino or at least shook his hand warmly.

The George Washington High School Trojans crushed the New Dorp High School Central Cougars, winning the first city baseball championship in the history of the school. Aram Petrosian got two hits, a single and a double. And that was the end of the season. For the Infielders, it was the end of high school and, in reality, the end of boyhood. The season ended in triumph.

But it occurred to Aram that the Bible teaches that for everything there is a season. He kept that thought to himself.

Part Two

Baseball Isn't Everything ...
There Are Girls, Too

In High School and Beyond

Chapter 13

Boys and Girls

I n the lives of many teenagers in the 1940s, the societal norms of the 1940s were driving them in directions that were at war with the biological directions that their bodies were demanding they pursue. Sexual relations were taboo, at least for "good" kids. This principle was not only for those who paid attention to formal religious teachings; it applied to everyone who wanted to be "good," "well behaved," and "responsible."

The incongruity between society's expectations and nature's impulses left many teenagers in the 1940s in a state of confusion. The range of experiences of the Infielders in their relationships with girls in their high school years reflected this confusing mixture of pressures and desires. That was only natural.

Chapter 14

Bernie

It was a well-known fact in the upper grades of PS 189 that Bernie Heller was feeling the breasts of Marie Ferrari under her shirt. Marie was famous for being gifted with a remarkable pair of tits as early as seventh grade. There may have been others who had access to Marie's chest, but those incidents were only rumors. Bernie's experience with Marie was openly proclaimed by him and confirmed with apparent pride by Marie.

Bernie's achievements with Marie met with a mixed reception from the other three boys. Sean Flaherty was appalled that a Catholic girl like Marie would allow such an obscenity to be performed on her God-given body. Aram Petrosian—who had not yet reached puberty in the seventh grade—was utterly confused by the whole story. Dino Russo candidly admitted he was jealous, but he had no idea how to go about accomplishing what Bernie did, either with Marie or any other girl at PS 189. Bernie strutted like a peacock, savoring every moment of his reputation as the Casanova of PS 189.

George Washington High School was a more competitive

environment for the title of leading ladies' man. But Bernie more than held his own in that competition. He had a jaunty, dashing manner and, among the girls he had known (in every sense of that word), he had a reputation for being a fun-loving and rather caring companion. However, his intimate relationships tended to be short-lived, primarily because he had an appetite for variety. But his polished technique for terminating relationships left behind more friends than enemies. Most of his former lovers viewed him as a good friend and a nice guy.

There was a girl, however, with whom this was not the case. Her name was Barbara Gordon, and she came to the high school as a sophomore from PS 157 in the nearby neighborhood of Inwood. They carried on a hot and heavy affair during the summer between their junior and senior years when neither of their families left the city on vacation. Unlike all of his previous girlfriends, Barbara was the only girl he dated during that entire summer. He really cared about her. They were together constantly during that summer. They held hands whenever they walked together. Bernie assembled a mental list of things Barbara liked: music, strawberry ice cream, Van Cortlandt Park, swimming at the Miramar outdoor pool in her neighborhood, the Fort Tryon Jewish Center (also in her neighborhood), Chinese food. He made a point of arranging to fill the summertime with these things. He saw a notice in the *New York Post* that there would be an outdoor symphony concert at Lewisohn Stadium on the campus of City College that cost twenty-five cents for admission. He asked Barbara if she would like to go. She asked who was playing. Bernie didn't have the slightest idea. He dug the newspaper out of the trash bin at home and reported to Barbara that the Cleveland Symphony, conducted by someone named Szell, would play something by Mendelssohn one evening and something else by Brahms the next evening.

Barbara was overjoyed. "Can we go both nights?" she asked.

"Of course. Let's eat Chinese before the first concert," Bernie replied as if he knew about Szell, Mendelssohn, and Brahms.

That idyllic summer was filled with such events. The only thing Bernie did that summer that wasn't on the list of things Barbara liked was play baseball. And Barbara usually came to watch Bernie play baseball.

For reasons that were not apparent to anyone who knew them, the Barbara-Bernie relationship terminated abruptly in September of their senior year. Neither Barbara nor Bernie discussed the breakup with anyone at the high school or in the Heights. They were never seen alone together or speaking to each other. Each of them seemed wistful—even sorrowful—according to a number of people close to one or both of them. In Bernie's case, that was a vivid departure from his typical buoyant demeanor.

Theories abounded to explain the breakup. "Bernie lost his temper and beat her up," someone said.

"Not possible," Sean Flaherty responded angrily, "I'll beat the shit out of you if I ever hear anything like that again from your filthy mouth."

Someone else said, "I heard Barbara is going out with a college guy, so she dumped Bernie."

"So why does she look like her mother died this morning," Dino replied. "She's obviously not happy, so I don't believe she traded Bernie for some college guy. Something else must have happened."

Aram and Dino were talking while walking home from playing basketball in the PS 189 schoolyard.

"Bernie doesn't come out after school anymore. He is a completely different guy," Aram observed. "He never smiles, he never tells a joke, he doesn't show up for baseball team meetings. I never see him after school anymore. What's up with him?"

"Obviously, breaking up with Barbara has really messed him

up," Dino said. "I'm sorry about that. She was the nicest girl in his collection. The only one I didn't think was a slut."

"Do you think we could just talk to him and ask him what happened? You're supposed to be his best friend."

"I did ask him. He told me to mind my own fucking business."

"Usually, he won't ever stop talking about his girlfriends. It's as if that was the only subject in the world that interested him. I think he needs help."

"What do you mean by help?"

Aram paused for a few moments, thinking. "Maybe psychological help."

Dino laughed. "There's as much chance of his going to a head-shrinker as there is in him becoming a Catholic priest."

"I don't think this is funny. There's something wrong with the guy, and we don't know what it is. If he was bleeding, we'd do something to stop the bleeding. Well, he is bleeding. We just can't see the blood."

"You're really serious about this, aren't you?"

Aram said, "Of course I'm serious. Did you hear Coach McCullough say that if Bernie keeps missing meetings, he might not be on the team when the season starts in the spring? Look, he's more your friend than mine. If I was you, I'd tell the coach that Bernie and his girlfriend broke up and he's not acting natural, which is why he's not showing up for meetings and workouts. And I'd ask the coach to take him aside and find out what's eating him up. That's what a friend should do."

"Coach McCullough couldn't care less about teenage love affairs."

"But he does care about his players. Talk to him. It can't hurt. Please."

———

Dino knocked on the door of Coach McCullough's office. The coach's face lit up when the young man shyly asked if he could have a few minutes of the coach's time.

"Pull up a chair, Dino. You really looked like you're in good shape. Keep it up, and I'll try to find a place in the starting lineup for you. The trouble is I have excellent players at every infield position," the coach said playfully. "Do you think you could play in the outfield?"

"Coach, I'd like to talk about something else."

The light on the coach's face dimmed as he asked, "I was just joking. Is something wrong, Dino? Tell me, and I'll try to help you."

"It's not about me. It's about Bernie. There's been something wrong with him since he broke up with his girlfriend. Aram thinks he needs some kind of help, and he may be right. Do you know what's eating at Bernie?"

"I do, but I can't tell you. Believe me when I tell you that there's nothing wrong with Bernie. He's not sick. He's not in trouble. I know he's sad about breaking up with that girl, but there's nothing wrong with her, either. That's all I can tell you. I'm hoping that Bernie will be able to return to the team soon, and I hope he will be on the squad and playing third base when the season starts in March. And . . . I want to say I'm proud of you and Aram for being so concerned about your teammate. Right now, just leave him alone."

"But Coach, now this is even more of a mystery. People are talking about Bernie. There's all kinds of stories flying around. We don't know what to do when people ask us what's wrong with him."

"Dino, there's nothing you can do about Bernie. There's nothing you can do for him. I'm sorry I've left you with a mystery.

If I could clear up the mystery, I think you know I would. Now go home and study."

It would be years before the mystery surrounding Bernie Heller and his ex-girlfriend would be cleared up. During his entire senior year at George Washington High School, he never dated another girl. And, since the breakup with Barbara, none of the boys in the circle was ever asked to come up to his house.

A girl can be a great source of joy and contentment to a high school boy. She can also be a cause of grief and bitter disappointment.

Chapter 15

Bernie

Part 2

A few weeks before the first game of the 1947 baseball season, Dino decided it was time he took Bernie Heller aside to try to learn the story behind the breakup of the relationship between Bernie and Barbara Gordon the previous September and Bernie's uncharacteristic persistent melancholy since then. It was Dino's judgment that the team would be adversely affected by having a sullen and noncommunicative third baseman. Moreover, knowing that the coach knew the cause of the problem made Dino's curiosity more of a distraction than he thought he could handle standing next to Bernie in the infield. Dino asked Bernie to meet him after Bernie finished his turn at batting practice.

"What's up?" Bernie asked Dino.

"I don't want you to blow up at me, but I have something to talk to you about. It's important, and I'm talking to you as a friend."

"Barbara and I broke up. I'm sad about that."

"I was sorry to hear about that. She's a classy girl."

"She sure is," said Dino as he searched for the right words to talk about Bernie and Barbara.

"It probably had to happen. There were probably too many family issues getting in our way."

"But she's Jewish, and so are you."

"Hey, Dino, there's other kinds of family problems besides religion."

"Well, in the Russo family it's Catholic or get lost."

"As a matter of fact, in the Heller family, same thing. It's Jewish or get lost."

"So, I don't get it. You said, 'too many family issues.' If it's not religion, what is it? Tell me, please. I'm your best friend. Is it because your family came to America as refugees? If that's the problem, I say fuck them."

"Hey, look, Dino, you know I don't want to talk about that. It's a very private matter."

"Bernie, we can have a very private discussion. I really don't want to invade your privacy, but I'm worried about you. I know Coach McCullough knows the story, but he won't say a word about it other than that you're not sick and you're not in trouble. That's what he told me and Aram."

"You spoke to him about it?"

"We did. We were worried about you. The coach didn't tell us anything other than what I just said. You trusted him, and you can trust me."

"I never told him about it."

"Well, he told us that he knew about it but couldn't talk about it. How would he know if you didn't tell him?"

"Because Barbara's father told him about it."

Dino looked stunned, and Bernie could see that. "What the hell was your girlfriend's father doing talking to your baseball coach? This sounds crazy."

Bernie stared into Dino's face and looked around to see if anyone was nearby. "Let's walk up to the top of the grandstand,

Dino, where no one can hear us. It's not gonna be easy for me to talk to you about this, and you have to swear to me, swear on your mother's life, that you will not tell anyone—not your mother or your father or your brothers or sisters, not even your priest—what I'm going to trust you with."

"I swear, Bernie."

The boys climbed all the concrete steps leading to the last row of benches at the top of the grandstand. The late March wind and the cloudy sky made both of them physically uncomfortable as they sat down on a bench in their lightweight baseball uniforms designed to be worn under the summer sun. Dino waited silently for Bernie to begin to tell him what happened with Barbara Gordon.

In a voice just slightly louder than a whisper, Bernie began to talk. "The only people who know what I'm going to tell you are my parents, Barbara and her parents, Mr. Klein—the principal—and Coach McCullough, which I didn't know until you just told me. No one else. And I don't want anyone else to know."

"You've made that perfectly clear, Bernie. You can trust me."

"A terrible thing happened. My father works in the butcher store on St. Nicholas Avenue."

"What's so terrible about that?"

"Just shut up and listen. The store is owned by my uncle, a guy named Erwin Ludwig, my mother's brother. During the war, when there was rationing, Ludwig used to sell meat to some of his customers without requiring ration stamps. When the government found out about this, Ludwig forced my father to say to the investigators that he was the one who did that. That he had taken money under the table from those customers. I really don't know whether it's true that Ludwig forced my father to admit he did it. It's possible my father's not telling me the truth."

"How could Ludwig force your father to admit to doing something he didn't do?"

"Ludwig made it possible for my family to escape from the Nazis. He gave my father a job he wasn't really qualified to do. I don't know if this is a fact, but he could have threatened to fire my father. I just don't know."

"Whatever. But why is this such a big problem?"

"My father's been under investigation, and now he's been indicted. That means charged with a crime."

"What do you mean 'crime'? Who's been hurt? The war's over. We won. It doesn't sound very serious to me," Dino said ingenuously.

"It is very serious, Dino. He could go to jail for five years."

"No way! It's just a technicality. People do far worse things and don't go to jail."

"That's what I thought when I told Barbara about it. She then went and told her father, and he had a fit. He absolutely forbids her to ever go out with me again. When she told me that, I went to their house to argue about it with him. He was so mad, I thought he was going to beat the shit out of me. He screamed at me and said terrible things."

"What did he say?"

"Stuff like 'When my kid brother was fighting on the beach in Normandy, your father, that fucking criminal, was getting rich beating the system. If I ever catch you anywhere near my daughter again, I'll break every bone in your body.' I tried to calm him down. In the first place, there's no way he could beat me up. So I told him that, and he got even madder. Barbara and her mother were trying to calm him down, and Barbara was crying her eyes out. Then, when I looked away for a second, he took a swing at me and hit me on the side of the head. Stupidly, I punched him back, and he fell to the floor, and his nose was bleeding. Mrs. Gordon screamed and said, 'Get out of our house and get out of our lives! You will turn out to be just like your father, a criminal.'"

"What's wrong with them? Whatever your father did, you didn't do it."

"You think I don't know that? It's all so fucking unfair. It's eating me up."

"I'll bet it's eating you up. It's fucking unfair. What I want to know is why it has to be kept a secret. You haven't done anything wrong, and yet this thing is burning up your insides. For sure, you won't have a good season on the baseball team because you won't really be part of the team. You can't be part of a team if you keep something as painful as this bottled up inside of you. Why does it have to be a secret, anyway?"

"My mother insists it should be kept secret until after I graduate and go away to a college where no one will know me or my family. She thinks she's protecting my reputation. The principal spoke with Mr. and Mrs. Gordon and persuaded them to keep it secret as long as I don't go out with Barbara."

"Well, Bernie, I'm just a seventeen-year-old high school kid, and I don't claim to be the smartest person in the world. But I think your mother and Mr. Klein are being stupid about this. I think they're more worried about your father's reputation than yours. That really pisses me off. You're suffering for no good reason. If everyone knew about this, the whole school would talk about what a bad deal you got because of your father. I guarantee you will feel better than you have felt all these months when you isolated yourself. And another thing—"

"I get your point, Dino. You don't need to say anything more. I appreciate what you've been trying to tell me, and I think you're probably right. In fact, I know you're right. The thing is, I promised my mother. She's got enough to deal with right now without having the whole neighborhood look at her as the wife of that 'criminal.' I just can't let the whole world know that my father's been indicted. I just can't."

"Okay, okay, I understand. Just let me tell Sean and Aram. I'll make them swear to me to keep it secret for all the reasons you just gave me. You know they'll do whatever I tell them to do."

"I do know that. Okay, do what you think's best. Sean and Aram are good guys. I can trust them, especially if you're the one who tells them to keep the secret."

Dino told Sean and Aram the whole story about Bernie, his father, his mother, Barbara and her parents, and the reason for secrecy. Sean and Aram pledged to keep the story secret, and there was no question in Dino's mind that they would faithfully do just that.

After a conversation that lasted about ten minutes, Aram said, "Let's find Bernie."

————

The three boys found Bernie sitting in the boys' locker room. He was staring vacantly into space. Sean and Aram walked over to the bench where Bernie was sitting. Sean sat on one side of Bernie, and Aram sat on the other side. They each put an arm around Bernie's shoulders.

Aram said, "Dino told us the whole story. We'll keep it a secret. We feel so sorry for you. There's no way we can know exactly how you feel, but we want you to know that we are with you the whole way. Whatever happens, we will never stop being your friends."

The sins of the fathers . . .

Chapter 16

Bernie

Part 3

A few days later, Aram came to see Bernie. "I've been thinking. The best way to solve your problem is to solve your father's problem. If your father's really innocent and somehow the indictment against him can be dropped, bingo. No more problem."

"That's easy to say, but how on earth are we going to get a federal criminal indictment dropped. We can't afford a lawyer. I don't even know the name of a lawyer," Bernie lamented.

"Please don't give up. Bernie, please try to think of this as a challenge we can meet."

Bernie laughed. "If only it was as simple as winning a ball game. But it's not. I think we knew how to be a winning baseball team. But we don't know how to deal with this. We don't have the slightest idea."

"Well, I do have the slightest idea. I talked to Dino about this. He told me he knows a guy who works in the office of the US Attorney for Manhattan. That's the office that indicted your father. And you know Dino, he can get people to eat out of his hands. He's become a friend of that guy. Dino said if you'd agree, he would get that guy to set up an appointment to talk with the US Attorney."

"That's our Dino, but I don't know where that will get us. What would we say to him? I don't think saying 'Hey, I'm very upset that my father has been indicted' will get him to drop the charges."

"Of course not," Aram replied. "Give me some credit for having a small amount of common sense. And stop being so fucking negative."

Aram's use of an obscenity brought Bernie up short. He could not recall a single occasion when he heard Aram utter the word *fuck* or any of its variations.

"Sorry, Aram. I just don't understand what we could accomplish by visiting the office of the prosecutor."

"Okay. Here's my thinking. There are a lot of Jews here in the Heights who buy kosher meat at the place where your father works. If we can find out which of them bought meat without ration stamps or paid for it under the table, we might be able to learn if your father was involved or whether it was his brother-in-law who did it."

Bernie thought about this for a few moments. "Don't you think the prosecutor knows who those people are?"

Aram replied, "Probably, but maybe not. And we don't know whether the government really pressed those people for the truth since your father apparently admitted he did it. Look, Bernie, let's stop cross-examining each other and go and find out whatever we can and then see if we can use that information. What have we got to lose? And more important, what does your father have to lose? Let's get our asses down to the US Attorney's office and find out whatever we can. Dino will come with us, and I think we should ask Sean as well."

One week later, early on a Friday morning, four Infielders rode the subway to Chambers Street in an area of Manhattan that none of them had ever visited. Walking to the building housing the US Attorney's office, the four boys were more nervous than they had ever been on a baseball field. They were out of their element, and it showed on their faces and in the tone of their voices. Perceiving this, Aram bravely asserted that he would "do the talking."

"Oh no," Bernie said, "this is about my father, so I have to take the lead. If either of you think of something I've left out, then you can talk. But this is something I have to do."

After several minutes of wandering around the building, they found the office they were looking for. A receptionist asked what she could do for them.

Bernie spoke up. "We'd like to speak with the lawyer who is handling the case of my father, Mr. Heller."

"Do you know which attorney that is? We have twelve attorneys in this office."

"The United States attorney."

"Well, all of the attorneys in this office are United States attorneys. Do you have an appointment?"

Dino jumped in. "How can we have an appointment if we don't know the name of the guy we want to see?"

Aram pushed Dino aside and said politely, "We're sorry to trouble you, Miss, but we don't know much about this office or who's in it. Our friend Bernie here," pointing to Bernie, "is terribly concerned about his father who's been indicted for some sort of violation of some law regarding selling meat without getting ration stamps. What's his first name, Bernie?"

Bernie noticed that the nameplate on the receptionist's desk said her name was Hannah Waldman, an obviously Jewish name— probably German Jewish like his family. He decided to try what might prove to be a useful tactic. He said, "His name is Albert,

Albert Heller, and it's important that we learn more about the case so my father can get a proper defense. He is a very good man, a refugee from Nazi Germany, so please let us talk to the lawyer who's prosecuting him."

The receptionist smiled and said, "Do all four of you need to see him?"

"Yes," said Bernie, "we're a team. We are the four infielders on the George Washington High School baseball team. We're good friends. We work well together, and we thought it would be a good idea for us to work together to try to help my father."

She smiled again. "The assistant US attorney who usually handles the rationing violation cases is Paul Matsakis. Let me see if he's available to see you. By the way, I went to Theodore Roosevelt. I enjoyed going to their baseball games. The boy who became my husband was a pitcher on their team. Why don't you fellows sit down while I see if Mr. Matsakis can see you."

The first thing the boys noticed when they were ushered into the office of the assistant US attorney was the American flag standing in the corner of the room. The thought occurred to them that this was no place to fool around. Mr. Matsakis, a man who appeared to be about sixty years old, pointed to the four chairs in front of his desk, and the boys quietly sat down. None of them said anything, not even "hello" or "good morning." They couldn't help but notice that Mr. Matsakis's desk was covered with papers in loosely arranged piles and file folders that might have been six inches high. This was a busy man.

"Which one of you is Mr. Heller's son?" was the question that broke the silence.

"That's me, Bernie Heller."

"Is Bernie your real name or a nickname?"

"It's a nickname. My legal name is Bernd."

"Burned . . . that's an unusual name."

Bernie smiled and said, "It's not burned like something that's been in a fire. It's Bernd, a German name." He spelled it for Mr. Matsakis, who wrote it down on a yellow legal pad he placed before him after clearing aside some papers. Bernie pronounced the name as it sounded in German.

"That's interesting," Mr. Matsakis said in a friendly tone. "My legal name is Aristotle, which is sort of a pretentious name to carry around. Everyone calls me Ari, which is far more comfortable. To me anyway, if not to my parents. They were both immigrants from Greece and I was their firstborn son. I know they thought they were bestowing a distinguished name on me. I assume your parents are also immigrants from Germany, is that right?"

"Not really," Bernie responded. "They came to America, bringing me and my brother along with them. I suppose technically we're immigrants, but really, we are refugees from Nazi Germany. Me and my family are Jewish, and we probably would've been killed if we stayed in Germany. My grandparents were killed."

"That's also interesting. But it's also troubling. Of course, you know we were fighting a war against the same Nazi Germany your family fled from. That caused those of us on the home front to experience shortages of many important things during the war— because of the war. One of the ways our government dealt with that problem was by imposing a system of rationing of many items, including meat. For that system to work and for things that were in short supply to be fairly available to everyone, people had to comply with those regulations. We think your father got around those regulations by secretly selling meat—kosher meat, I understand—to customers who didn't produce the necessary rationing documents—stamps, actually—that were required for those purchases. That's why I asked the grand jury to indict him. There was nothing personal about it. I never met your father. I suppose he's a nice man and a good father. Now, what do you want to say to me?"

"I don't know for certain, but I don't think my father did what you said."

"What makes you say that?"

"My father doesn't own the butcher store. It's owned by my uncle, my father's brother-in-law. My father just works there. He had nothing to gain by violating the rationing. We want to talk to the customers you think bought meat without stamps and ask them who sold them that meat, my father or my uncle. So, we would like you to give us the names of those customers. That's what we came here for."

"This may surprise you, but I don't know the names of those customers. The way we enforce the regulations is by examining the sales records of the retailers and comparing them with the ration stamps collected by them. We could never be able to keep track of the customers."

Aram jumped in and said, "That's exactly what we wanted to know. We'll find the customers."

Mr. Matsakis stood up and walked to his file cabinet. He withdrew several file folders and carried them to his desk, opened one of them, then another, pulled out some papers, read several pages, returned those pages to the folder, carried all of the folders back to the file cabinet, restored them to the cabinet, returned to his desk, and sat down. "Boys, don't bother to look for the customers. It's more than three years since the end of the war and more than two years since the end of rationing. I don't think there will be any useful public interest served in continuing the prosecution of Bernie's father. Bernie, go home and tell your father that the government of the country that provided refuge for him and his family has decided that, in his case, justice will be served by a small act of mercy. Tell him the indictment will be dismissed.

Also, tell him that his son and his friends are a great team, and he should be proud of them. And now, please leave because I have a great deal of work to do."

The boys tried to remain dignified, which they did until they went through the door exiting Mr. Matsakis's office. The instant the door closed behind them, they began to jump for joy. Bernie screamed, "Do you believe this? It's unbelievable. I can't wait to tell my father."

On the long subway ride back to the Heights, the celebration continued with laughter and shouting. Their joy was so obvious that from time to time, other passengers actually applauded whatever it was these well-dressed young men were celebrating. Emerging from the subway station at 191st Street, they ran as fast as they could to the Heller apartment on 189th. Bernie burst into the apartment, followed by the other Infielders. His mother appeared frightened by the sudden entrance of the four boys. Bernie hugged and kissed his mother and asked her when his father would be coming home. She told Bernie that his father was not feeling well and that he had come home early and was sitting in the living room. Holding his mother's hand, he moved quickly along the hall into the living room. The other boys followed, tentatively, as if they were uncertain whether they should be participating in this family event.

Mr. Heller was sitting in an upholstered chair, looking forlorn and deeply troubled. Bernie shouted, "Daddy, I have wonderful news. You're a free man. No more indictment!" His father looked at him, confused and cautious. Bernie embraced him as he slowly rose from the chair. He kissed his father on both cheeks and proceeded to tell the entire story, step by step, of how he and his friends had obtained a dismissal of the indictment by the government lawyer who got the indictment in the first place. "There is no more case. You're free!"

With tears in his eyes, Mr. Heller explained to his wife, in German, what he had just learned from his son. He then asked Bernie to introduce him to the three friends. He vigorously shook each of their hands.

Mr. Heller then spoke to Bernie. "Bernd, your Jewish name is Baruch, which means blessing. What you have done today shows me we gave you the right name. You are a blessing to me and your mother." He said something in German to Mrs. Heller, who then left the room. She returned a few moments later carrying a tray with six whiskey glasses and a bottle of Canadian Club. Mr. Heller filled the glasses and then announced that he was going to say an important prayer, which Jews call a *blessing*. He explained —obviously for the benefit of Bernie's friends—that he will be thanking God for enabling him to live to this day and to have this blessed moment. When he said "Amen," Sean crossed himself, Dino burst into tears, and Aram whispered to Mr. Heller, "You have a wonderful son."

Chapter 17

Sean and Theresa

There was hardly a girl in George Washington High School, including the legion of girls who succumbed to Bernie Heller's charms, who wasn't in love with Sean Flaherty. Or, at the very least, attracted to him. Sean had a handsome face. It was perfectly proportioned. His chin looked as though it had been chiseled by a master sculptor who remembered to place a small dimple directly in the center. Sean's eyes were blue, bright blue, so blue that their blueness could be seen across a room. His nose was just the right size but slightly bent to the left, its asymmetry adding to the charm of his face. His dark brown hair had a natural wave that made it look as though hours were spent grooming it, although, in truth, Sean paid almost no attention to his hairdo beyond a quick stroke with a comb. He was tall, well-built, graceful in his movements, and thoroughly masculine in his appearance.

But more important than his good looks was the undisputed fact that Sean was a nice guy. He was modest but outgoing. He was soft-spoken, but he exuded strength. He was quiet but easy to engage in conversation. He was lighthearted but serious about friendship and relationships.

How could a girl not fall in love with Sean Flaherty?

The problem for the girls at George Washington High School was Theresa Russo. One day during the summer of 1944, when she came to watch Dino play a pickup baseball game at the high school field, Dino introduced Theresa to Sean. Theresa was only thirteen years old at the time. Sean was fifteen, and he'd never had a real girlfriend. He had had a few dates on which he took a girl to the movies, followed by a visit to an ice cream parlor for egg creams, followed by a kiss at the door to the girl's apartment as they said goodnight.

But a kiss is just a kiss, especially when it is as brief, chaste, and decorous as the pecks on the lips that Sean exchanged with his movie dates. No emotions were stirred, and neither romantic passion nor sexual attraction had yet been part of Sean's life's experience. He felt awkward in the presence of girls, never really sure of how to act or what to say. Although girls approached him in droves, some quite openly, even immodestly, Sean was unable to respond to those overtures in a manner he felt was appropriate. Girls confused him.

Theresa was different. There were sparks of excitement as they looked at each other that summer day on the ball field. Dino noticed that immediately and pulled Sean aside, saying, "She's too young for you."

Sean's response was a comment that Dino found puzzling. "But she'll get older."

"I certainly hope so," replied Dino—a comment that Sean found puzzling.

It never became clear to Dino or the other Infielders exactly what the cause of the attraction between Sean and Theresa was. Theresa was not a notably attractive girl. She had a swarthy

Neapolitan complexion, frizzy black hair, and eyebrows that were almost connected above her large brown eyes. She was skinny and flat chested when she and Sean first met. Whether Sean thought there was a reasonable prospect that the flat chest might yet bloom into something worth fondling was a topic that was never discussed among the boys.

What was perfectly clear to everyone who knew them was that Sean and Theresa liked each other. They sought out opportunities to be together in school and after school when Theresa regularly came to watch baseball practice, often as the only person seated on one of the benches in the ballpark grandstand. Dino eventually became reconciled to the fact that Sean was his sister's boyfriend. Throughout their high school years, everyone who knew them knew that Sean and Terry were a couple.

Dino was satisfied that Sean was an honorable young man who would not take advantage of his younger sister. In fact, he was somewhat more apprehensive that his spirited sister might make physical advances on Sean that he wouldn't be able to resist. He spoke about that with Theresa. That was a tactical mistake. Theresa was offended that her brother was questioning her morality.

"What right do you have to give me instructions as to how to behave with my friend?"

"I'm your older brother. That's why I have that right," Dino responded.

"We have a mother and a father whose job it is to teach me about my morals. Not you."

"Oh, please, Theresa, you know they are so naïve, and it would never occur to them that their young daughter might be seducing a young man. Especially Sean, who they correctly think is a nice and decent kid. I'm not worried about him. I'm worried about you."

"Well, you can go fuck yourself," Theresa shouted. "Just leave me alone."

Dino was stunned and rendered speechless by his baby sister's vocabulary.

She wasn't finished with the conversation. "In fact," she said, "you've given me a good idea. I don't have to wait for Sean to make the first move. I can do it, and I will. And by the way, you can call me Terry from now on. Sean likes that better than Theresa."

Dino grabbed both of Theresa's wrists as she was swinging her arms around to emphasize her determination to assert herself. Having quickly subdued her, Dino said, "I like the name Terry, too. Terry, you're not an idiot, so don't behave like one. Please."

"I love him so much."

"Love is a good thing, I think. I love Mama and Papa. I love Tony and Marco and Isabella. And I love you, Theresa. Very much."

"Terry."

"I really love you all, Terry. But that's family love. It's natural. I've never loved anyone outside my family. I know there is such a thing, but I've never felt it."

"It's the best thing ever. It feels wonderful, Dino."

"I'm sure it does. But the kind of love you're talking about has to last a lifetime, or it's hurtful. You have to be careful. I know you hate to hear this, but you're only fifteen."

"I'll be sixteen in two months."

"I'm so impressed. What was I thinking? You're a fully grown woman. You know all you need to know to make a good life for yourself. I'm sorry I butted in. I thought you were only fifteen."

"Don't make fun of me."

"Okay. I'll only ask two things of you. Don't hurt my friend Sean. And please, don't hurt yourself. One more thing. Don't say 'fuck' again, or I'll wash your mouth out with soap."

"What is it you don't want me to say? Please repeat that?"

"Oh, shut up."

Sean and Terry went steady for the rest of the time Sean was in high school. For Sean Flaherty and Theresa Russo, the high school years were magical.

Chapter 18

Aram and Annette

The inventory of eligible girlfriends for Aram Petrosian at George Washington High School was severely limited. His parents made it known to him that dating a girl who wasn't Armenian was utterly unacceptable to them and was prohibited. No exceptions.

Aram was hardly the only student of Armenian descent at the school. There was a sizable Armenian population in Washington Heights centered around the Holy Cross Armenian Apostolic Church on 187th Street. In fact, the church was regularly attended by people from areas outside of the Heights, so opportunities existed for Aram to meet Armenian girls at the church who were not students at George Washington. Nevertheless, his high school years were rather arid when it came to love and roses. He blamed his parents. He blamed the church. He blamed Armenia. He blamed Bernie for making girls seem so dangerous. He blamed the time he spent honing his baseball skills. He blamed his studies, which he pursued with far more vigor than he ever pursued a girl. But, in his heart, he would have liked to have had a girlfriend.

Then, at the beginning of Aram's senior year, in September of 1946, a remarkable thing happened. A girl—the daughter of a doctor who relocated his practice from the Bronx to Inwood— entered George Washington High School as a transferee from Evander Childs High School. Her name was Annette Nazarian and she had been at the top of her class at Evander Childs. She very much did not want to move from the neighborhood where she had lived all her life or transfer from the school where she was thriving and where most of her friends were students. But her parents were adamant about there being no practical way for her to commute to school from Inwood to the East Bronx, and that ended the debate.

Sean was the first of the Infielders to notice the new girl. Theresa introduced her to him on the opening day of school. Recognizing that her name might be Armenian, he immediately began looking for Aram.

He found him in the boys' locker room. "Hey, Aram, there's a new Armenian girl in our class."

"Oh, that's thrilling news. Lead me to her, and I'll propose marriage."

"Don't be such a wiseass. Terry thinks she's very nice."

"Good. Ask Terry to tell her that."

"You know, Aram, you're not even trying to find the right girl. You don't know what you're missing. Years from now, when you're a lonely old man, you'll wonder how life passed you by without a woman by your side."

"That's an interesting thought. It's also the longest speech I've ever heard you make."

"I give up. You're hopeless."

Sean was hurt. He was trying to help a friend, and he was rudely rejected. Aram sensed this and said, to Sean's amazement, "Thanks for the information. What did you say the girl's name is?"

"It's Annette."

"What does she look like?"

"Actually, she looks a little like Terry. Dark. Somewhat chubby, not skinny like Terry. Long dark hair. Look, I'll get Terry to introduce the two of you, and you can see what she looks like better than I can describe. By the way, I've heard she's very smart."

"Then she can't be Armenian," Aram said with a smile.

"Well, I guess you're not Armenian either. You're near the top of our class."

In fact, Aram's grade average was at the very top of the class, but he never mentioned that to any of the Infielders. Somehow, that fact seemed to diminish—in his own mind—his image as a baseball player.

Eventually, Aram did meet Annette. They were in the same honors European History class. Aram screwed up his courage when the class ended, and he introduced himself to Annette. She made it easy for him by saying she was looking forward to meeting him.

"Sean Flaherty and his girlfriend, Terry Russo, spoke to me about you."

"Is that right?" Aram replied, feigning ignorance. "What did they say about me?"

"Only nice things. The first thing Sean said was that you are Armenian. Using my extraordinary brain, I put two and two together and figured out that Sean thought we might become a couple. Terry jumped in and said you were the smartest guy in Sean's class and that you also were on the school varsity baseball team. Quite a résumé, I thought."

"They didn't say anything about how good-looking I am?" Aram asked with a straight face.

Annette, not wanting to upset Aram, replied, "I think Terry said something like 'not bad looking'."

Aram laughed. "She's sweet. But I know—with absolute certainty—that I'm not good-looking. How do I know? Because my mother, my own mother, who loves me more than life itself, she told me recently. 'Aram, you don't have to be good-looking to succeed in this world,' she said."

"I like you, Aram, in spite of your looks."

"And I like you, too, in spite of your looks."

They began to hang out together. Lunch together in the cafeteria several times a week. Annette joined the school newspaper staff. Aram was editor in chief.

After a few weeks in which they got to know each other, Annette said, "Aram, I have to tell you something. I'm being absolutely serious right now. I can't go out with you until my father meets you and approves. My family is extremely old-fashioned about such things."

"It looks like I'm going to crash on takeoff. It's been a delight knowing you."

"I'm sure my father will approve of you. Don't you think it's worth a try? Come home with me after school today. It's Wednesday, and my father's office is closed. You can meet him and demonstrate why you are qualified to date the most beautiful and intelligent Armenian girl in North America."

Aram was on the verge of winning his first girlfriend and she was taking the initiative.

"Well, it's probably a lost cause," he said, "but let's give it a try. Where do you live?"

"On Payson Avenue, just off Dyckman Street. I usually walk home on nice days like this. It's a nice walk."

They agreed to meet at the front door of the school after the last class of the day. As it happened, they were both in that class—Advanced Algebra. So, they walked out of the high school building together and headed to Fort George Hill, the street that led down the steep escarpment from Washington Heights to Inwood. As they walked, excitement was building in Aram. But it was excitement that was side by side with anxiety about meeting what he assumed would be the fearsome Dr. Nazarian. Annette tried to ease his evident anxiety by saying that her father was a really nice man.

"Tell me, Annette, how many prospective boyfriends have you brought before your really nice father."

"You will be the second."

"What happened to the first guy?"

"He wasn't approved because he wasn't Armenian."

"Really? Does that mean you've never dated a boy?

"Well, I'm only sixteen. I don't think life has passed me by?"

"So, if I pass this test, that will mean I will be the first boy you've ever dated."

"Don't make it sound as if I am losing my virginity."

Aram could not think of a response to that comment, so he veered to a different topic. "I heard that you're a very good student. I don't know if you know that I have the highest grade point average in our class."

"Well, Aram, that may no longer be the case. The principal told me that my grades from Evander Childs will be carried over to GW, and my average is one-tenth of a point higher than yours."

"You have to be kidding. I won't accept that. I'm going to protest." Aram was genuinely upset, and his voice became louder and squeakier as he spoke. "I've had the highest grades in my class for three full years, and you've been here for less than a month. That is grossly unfair, and I won't accept it," Aram said emphatically, with his voice rapidly rising into the alto range.

"It looks like our relationship is off to a rocky start."

"I don't regard this to be funny. When I started at GW, I had two goals in mind. They were to play in the infield for the varsity baseball team *and* to finish at the top of the class academically. I have worked my ass off to achieve those goals, and now, in my senior year, some stranger shows up and claims to have a higher average than me. No way, no how!"

"Than *I*," interposed Annette. "Than *me is* incorrect because the pronoun is the subject of the implicit verb *have*, so what you really were saying is 'a stranger claims to have a higher average than *I have*.' You would never say *me* have. Unless you're Tarzan saying 'Me Tarzan, you Jane'."

"Have a nice life, Annette," Aram barked as he turned abruptly and began to walk back up Fort George Hill. Annette walked home alone, thinking—quite correctly—that Aram was immature for his age.

The next day, after first period class, Annette approached Aram and apologized. "Giving you a lecture on grammar was a really obnoxious thing for me to do. I was trying to be funny. I guess I have a lot to learn about humor. Please forgive me. You know I want to be your friend."

"Okay, I forgive you for the grammar, but I'm still upset about your jumping ahead of me in class ranking. I may seem silly to be so concerned about this. But I think it's unfair, and it's going to get in the way of our relationship. I think that relationship may have to die in its infancy."

"That's mean, and it really hurts. I tried my best to start a relationship with you, but the very first thing you do is say a truly ugly thing to me. It looks like it's not going to work. Let's just be casual friends and forget about yesterday." Annette walked home alone again that day. It was raining.

Aram sought out Dino after school and said he needed to talk to him. They went up Dino's house because it was closer to school than Aram's. Mrs. Russo greeted them warmly and invited Aram to stay for dinner—veal and spaghetti. Aram politely declined, saying something about his parents needing him that evening. All of Dino's siblings were in the apartment, and there was no place to have a private conversation. The presence of Theresa in the apartment complicated matters further. She tried to start a conversation with Aram about Annette which was the last thing in the world Aram wanted to discuss with her. Dino went into the kitchen and spoke with his mother.

"Mama, I need to speak privately with Aram. Please tell the kids not to come into my room while the door is closed."

"I knew there was trouble. Tell me what's the matter."

"Nothing's the matter. Can't two friends have a private conversation about something other than trouble?"

"If there's no trouble, why private?"

"Mama, please, it's raining outside, and I don't want to have to leave the house to talk with my friend without Theresa listening."

"If you and Aram need help, tell me, and I'll do whatever I can."

"Yes, Mama, I know." Dino and Aram went into the bedroom that Dino shared with his brother, Tony, and they closed the door. Aram told Dino all about his two failed conversations with Annette.

"For a smart guy, you can be a real jerk," Dino commented.

"You think I screwed up?"

"Oh no, you handled it brilliantly. A very desirable girl comes on to you like a storm, and you blow her off because her grades are higher than yours. That's the way to get ahead in the world of love and romance."

"Okay, so I screwed up. What should I do now?"

"Do you really want to date that girl?"

"Yes, I really do."

Dino walked over to the window and looked out onto the street for a few moments. He turned and looked at Aram, and then he turned again and looked out of the window. Aram sat motion-less, his hands on his lap joined as if in prayer, as he waited for a response from Dino.

Still standing, Dino looked at Aram and said, "If I was you, what I would do is find out Annette's address in the phone book, wait for the rain to stop, and walk down the hill to her house. I'd ring the doorbell and hope she—and not one of her parents—would come to the door. If she opened the door, I'd say 'I realize I've acted like a jerk, and I'm sorry.' I'll bet she'd be pleased to hear that. If one of her parents came to the door, I'd introduce myself. They've probably already heard about you. They may or may not call Annette to the door, but at least the ice will have broken, and you can find Annette at school and apologize for acting like a jerk. That's what I'd do if I was you."

"Do you think she will still be interested in dating a jerk?"

"I hardly know the girl. I can't answer you. Go and find out for yourself. You spend too much time thinking and not enough time doing. Get off your ass and woo that girl."

Aram didn't wait for the rain to stop. He walked from Dino's house to Annette's house, arriving soaking wet from head to shoes.

Annette answered the doorbell, took one look at Aram, and almost convulsed from laughter. "Come in, you idiot. Isn't that what they call someone who doesn't know enough to come in out of the rain?"

"I came to apologize to you for behaving like a jerk."

"Apology accepted. Now let me get some towels for you. I don't know what we can do about your wet clothes."

"I suppose I could take them off."

"I have a better idea. Catch pneumonia."

"Very funny."

They both laughed, but Aram began to shiver noticeably.

Annette said, "I have an idea. I'll get my father's bathrobe. It's made of the same material as a bath towel."

"Terrycloth."

"Right. You can go into the bathroom, take off your wet clothes, and hang them up as best you can. Put on the bathrobe and come back out. I'll make hot chocolate for both of us."

"Truly romantic first date."

"Remember, we can't date until my father approves you. He should be home in about half an hour."

"Oh no, I can't be interviewed by your father wearing his bathrobe over my naked body."

"Well, your other choices are to sit in our living room in sopping wet clothes or stark naked. I doubt that he would look favorably on you in either case."

"Can't I just leave and come back another time?"

"Frankly, Aram, I'm afraid you'll get sick if you wear those sopping wet clothes and walk in the rain up Fort George Hill to wherever you live in Washington Heights."

"Laurel Hill Terrace."

"I really don't care where you live. The rain is pouring down. I can't let you leave here. Come in the kitchen. I'll make hot chocolate."

Aram undressed in the bathroom and put on the robe Annette had retrieved from her parents' bedroom.

The young couple were sipping cups of hot chocolate when Dr. and Mrs. Nazarian returned to the apartment. Annette leaped to her feet and exclaimed, "This is not what it looks like."

"I'm not sure what it looks like. I've never seen anything like it in my life," said an absolutely astonished Dr. Nazarian as he removed his drenched raincoat and helped his wife out of hers. "So, tell me, what am I to understand this remarkable spectacle to mean?"

Aram looked as if he wished he could disappear. But Annette calmly rose from her chair and gently kissed each of her parents, mother first. She then explained how it happened that "my friend, Aram Petrosian" was sitting in their kitchen wearing her father's terrycloth bathrobe. Her parents couldn't help but smile and then, moments later, laugh with relish. Annette concluded her explanation by saying, "Aram came here to ask Daddy whether he could take me out on a date."

"Well, then, young man, stay where you are, and I'll pull up a kitchen chair." Addressing his wife and daughter, Dr. Nazarian said, "Annette, Emma, please leave us alone for a few minutes."

In Aram's eyes, Annette's parents looked very different from his own. Dr. Nazarian was wearing a well-tailored gray suit, a white shirt, and a perfectly knotted conservative tie. Although Aram lacked any sense whatever about women's fashions, Mrs. Nazarian seemed to be nicely dressed, certainly compared with Aram's mother's perpetual black dress. When Mrs. Nazarian remarked about how wonderful the matinee performance of *South Pacific* was that they saw that afternoon, Aram was convinced that they and his parents lived in different worlds.

Aram summoned up the courage to speak first. "Dr. Nazarian, none of this is Annette's fault. She had no idea I was coming here. I was drenched when I arrived, and she was nice to me, suggesting she could let me use your bathrobe so I could hang up my wet clothes. I swear to you, we did nothing wrong."

"I know Annette well enough to conclude that she was being kind and not prurient."

Aram had never before heard that word but quickly deduced its meaning. Then Dr. Nazarian began speaking in Armenian. It took Aram nearly a half minute to activate the Armenian language brain cells in his head. His first words, in Armenian, were, "Please repeat what you just said. I was startled to hear you speaking

Armenian." The rest of the conversation was conducted in that language.

"Don't you speak Armenian in your home, young man?"

"We do, most of the time. All of the time, when my mother is in the conversation. She doesn't really speak English."

"There's nothing wrong with that. She has a son who understands Armenian, and she should be proud of that. Anyway, the Armenian language is just one of the reasons I wanted to speak with you. What do you know about the history of our people?"

Aram actually knew quite a bit about Armenian history, including the genocide of 1915 and the fact that Armenia was likely the first Christian nation in Europe. He had been speaking for about five minutes without interruption when he paused and then asked, "Could we do this in English? This is getting difficult for me."

"Difficult because you're speaking in Armenian or because the story itself is difficult?"

"Mostly the language. But I'd like to ask you this. What does all this have to do with me and Annette?"

"As two young individuals who may or may not be compatible, it has nothing whatever to do with the two of you. As two young Armenians who have the potential to be the parents of Armenian children, it has everything to do with the two of you."

"I'm interested in taking her to the movies, not fathering her child."

"Aram Petrosian, I'm not playing word games with you, so don't get flippant with me."

"I would just like to know what the point of this discussion is."

"All right, I'll tell you what the point of this discussion is. The point is life or death—the life or death of an ancient and proud people and the glorious civilization they brought into the world. The Turks murdered nearly two million of us. There are fewer than eight million of us throughout the entire world, many of whom live in places surrounded by hostile Muslims who regard us to be their enemies. We are in danger of disappearing as a distinct people and culture. If, God forbid, that ever happens, our history will be forgotten. Our music, our literature, our churches, our language, everything we have given to the world will disappear with us. It is my personal responsibility to work to see that doesn't happen. And, Aram Petrosian, it is your personal responsibility as well. Your children must be Armenians. They must be heirs to our people and traditions. That is why you must marry an Armenian woman and father Armenian children. That is why Annette must marry an Armenian man and be the mother of Armenian children. One of the tragedies of my life is that my wife and I have been able to have only one child. The great blessing of my life is that that one child is the magnificent Annette whom you want to take to the movies. Young man, all marriages begin with a night at the movies, or coffee in a café, or dinner in a restaurant, or a drive in the country—all innocent, all benign, and all a potential step in a direction I cannot abide. Do you now understand me?"

"Dr. Nazarian, I completely understand you. But you should know I've heard that same speech from my father in English and my mother in Armenian."

"Go, take my daughter to the movies. I'll drive you home before you catch pneumonia. And because I want my bathrobe back."

Dr. Nazarian went to Aram's apartment with him. While Aram was taking a hot shower and getting into dry clothes, Dr. Nazarian had a serious discussion in Armenian with Aram's parents. In a conversation that grew directly out of ancient Armenian tradition, they explored the possibility of arranging a marriage between Aram and Annette. Dr. Nazarian described his interrogation of Aram and his conclusion that Aram would be a suitable partner for his daughter. He told Mr. and Mrs. Petrosian about Annette, describing her in glowing terms and urging them to ask Aram to bring her to meet with his parents. When Aram finally entered the Petrosian living room in dry clothing, he saw three smiling people. Dr. Nazarian demanded the immediate return of his bathrobe.

All girlfriends come with baggage. Sometimes that baggage is just who she is. Sometimes it is her history, her culture, her ethnicity, her religion, her family, the values imposed on her, or the values chosen by her—things she can't opt out of. Sometimes, this type of baggage can be too much to bear.

Chapter 19

Dino

Because of his strikingly handsome appearance, Sean Flaherty was definitely the most popular boy in his class among the girls at George Washington High School. However, Dino Russo was the target of a smaller—but some might say a higher quality—contingent of girls. These were girls who were attracted to Dino not only because he was good-looking, not only because he was the star shortstop, but because he was *nice, cool, thoughtful, kind, bright, considerate,* and *funny*—all of which adjectives were in common use among Dino's female followers. He genuinely had all of those qualities, but, remarkably, he was also truly masculine. He did everything a typical male high school student might be expected to do. He hung around with guys, telling dirty jokes and real or imagined stories of their successful experiences with girls, discussing sex with the obsessive interest that investors might be expected to have in the movement of the stock markets. And he played sports with skill and enthusiasm.

Although not as strong a student as Aram, Dino was serious and diligent about his studies and earned consistently high marks.

Dino liked to study side by side with Aram—something Aram enjoyed as well—and the two of them did most of their studying and homework together. They also talked frequently about college and careers.

Unlike Bernie, whose passion for girls became the defining interest of his life—at least until the breakup with Barbara—and unlike Sean, whose infatuation with Theresa was all-consuming, Dino was not obsessed with girls. He had a typical high school boy's curiosity about girls. He was gratified by the fact that he seemed to attract girls, some of whom seemed appealing to him. He was somewhat clumsy in his responses to the advances some girls made toward him. He wasn't sure what he was looking for in a girl. And, most discomfiting of all for Dino was the fact that he wasn't sure he knew how to kiss. For someone who was kissed every day of his life by his father and every other day by his mother, Dino wasn't sure how to kiss a girl. He knew with certainty that the thousands of kisses planted on his mouth by his father were family kisses, not romantic kisses. One night, in his sophomore year, while standing in the darkened hallway outside of Frances Connery's apartment after a pleasant evening of a movie and ice cream sundaes, Dino drew close to Frances, placed his lips carefully against her mouth, and was stunned when Frances opened her mouth and stuck her tongue between Dino's lips. His first instinct was to turn around and run down the stairs. Two thoughts occurred to him within the next fraction of a second. One was that running away would be infantile behavior. And the other, interestingly, was that Frances's tongue in his mouth was an extremely pleasant experience. And within the remainder of that second, he reasoned that inserting his tongue in Frances's mouth might be reciprocally pleasant for her and additionally pleasant for him. He did it, and the two of them continued kissing for several minutes before Frances used her tongue to tell Dino that she had a great evening but it was past her curfew, and she needed to go into her apartment where her father was likely to yell at her. That was a Friday night.

The next night, Dino had a date with a girl named Arlene Kurtz who he thought was uncommonly attractive. Saturday night dates were, by common understanding, the night for more serious dates. He wore a freshly ironed shirt and a striped tie to go with his sport jacket and neatly pressed slacks. He even shined his shoes for the first time in months. Arlene said that she really wanted to see *Anchors Aweigh* with Frank Sinatra at the RKO Coliseum. That happened to be the film that Dino had seen the previous evening with Frances, but he told pretty Arlene that he wanted to see that movie, too. Throughout the film and the second feature of the double bill, Dino's thoughts were almost entirely about kissing Arlene using the exotic technique taught to him by Frances. When they finally arrived at the door to Arlene's apartment, she thanked him for a lovely evening, immediately unlocked the door, and went inside. No kiss. Dino was bewildered. He was convinced he would never understand girls.

It is entirely possible that Dino never attained an understanding of girls, but he certainly eventually mastered the techniques of dating and romancing, much of which was taught to him by the girls he dated, such as Frances Connery's lesson in advanced kissing. He rarely spent a Saturday night without a date, and as each week passed, especially in his senior year, Dino experienced increasingly vivid romantic adventures with a succession of girlfriends, complete with necking and heavy petting, terms that were fully understood in the 1940s. Unlike Bernie Heller, Dino didn't broadcast reports of his conquests. He did, however, confide in Aram, who listened to Dino's accounts of his encounters with fascination and more than a little envy. And the more Dino told Aram, the more Aram wanted to hear.

Dino began dating a girl named Rachel Schechter, a sopho-more in the high school who was in many of his classes because she was in an honors program. She lived on Fort Washington Avenue. The area where Rachel lived was sometimes called the "Fourth Reich" because many of the families that lived there were Jewish refugees from Nazi Germany—the Third Reich. Rachel was born in Germany. Her parents had the foresight—or, perhaps, just good instincts—to decide to leave Germany after Hitler came to power and began the persecution of German Jews. Rachel was just four years old when they arrived in New York. Her most persistent memory of Germany was not that of a place but of the atmosphere of persistent anxiety surrounding her parents that trickled down into the life of a little girl. She vividly remembered the voyage across the Atlantic on a crowded ship. She was the younger of two children of loving and protective parents.

At the time she began to see Dino, her father was a physician on the staff of the Columbia University Medical Center, where he practiced orthopedic surgery. Her mother was a mathematics teacher at Hunter College.

Rachel was an extraordinary student, and she was exception-ally poised and mature for someone not yet sixteen years old. She was not particularly pretty, but she had what was called an *interesting* face—long eyelashes, the slightly slanted positions of her eyes, the tiny shovel at the end of her prominent nose, and the sharply angular edges of her chin. She was popular with the many friends she made at GW. Dino was one of those friends. They were friends before they began to go out on dates together. They were part of a group of good students who had lunch together in the school cafeteria. Aram was part of the group. Rachel thought it was "nifty" that two seniors and "star" baseball players were part of her group of good friends. She was especially attracted to Dino, whom she saw as somewhat exotic, a boy from a different culture than hers—a Catholic from a working-class home with many siblings, Italian with a trace of an accent that was unfamiliar to her, a boy with a strange name, and an athlete.

She never told her parents that Dino existed, much less that he was a close friend. There wasn't the slightest doubt in Rachel's mind that her parents would forbid her from dating Dino.

Nevertheless, they became boyfriend and girlfriend. They met surreptitiously on Saturday nights at the White Tower hamburger place at the corner of Fort Washington Avenue and 181st Street. At first, they would go to a movie at the Coliseum or go bowling with friends. Dino would always walk Rachel home, stopping about a block from her building where they would embrace passionately, kissing à la Frances Connery, a girl long forgotten but for her memorable introduction to what Dino later learned was called a French kiss. Dino and Rachel quickly became very fond of each other. It was even possible, thought Dino, that they were in love. If so, it was a love fraught with obstacles and difficulties. He was seventeen, and she was even younger—a few months shy of her sixteenth birthday—far too young to appreciate the full magnitude of those obstacles and difficulties. They were aware enough of the problems facing their romance to know it had to be kept hidden from their parents and all but their closest and most discreet friends. And even those friends didn't know everything about the affair that blossomed between them.

After their first five surreptitious dates, they began to go to Rachel's apartment after school, confident that Rachel's parents wouldn't return home until early evening. Dino remembered the long-buried story of Bernie Heller and Marie Ferrari and Bernie's explorations under Marie's shirt. He delicately began his own exploration of Rachel's chest, to which she responded passionately, throwing off her shirt and bra and enjoying, with Dino, a genuine sexual adventure. After a few such blissful afternoons, Dino removed Rachel's skirt, and Rachel needed no prompting to remove her panties. Lying on her bed with the naked Rachel Schechter was the most thrilling experience of Dino's life.

But always in the deep background of Dino's mind was the terror that, in the recklessness of an unguarded moment, Rachel might become pregnant, and both of their lives would be devastated. Dino never had an orgasm when he was with Rachel. She did, but not him. He would return home as darkness gathered on those autumn afternoons, and he would masturbate until spent with exhaustion.

Then, on a Friday afternoon in January 1947, Rachel told Dino that her parents were going to leave before noon to go to a matinee at the Metropolitan Opera the next afternoon and that they planned to have dinner after the performance at a fancy Midtown restaurant. This meant the young couple would have the Schechter apartment to themselves for many hours on Saturday.

Dino told his parents he was going with his friends to a New York Knicks afternoon basketball game at Madison Square Garden, after which they would get pizza and go bowling. Mr. Russo said to his son, "Have a good time. It's good to be young now that the war is over."

You have no idea, Papa, how good it is, thought his son.

Dino practically ran all the way to Fort Washington Avenue and arrived breathless at Rachel's apartment. "Look at you," she said, "and we haven't even started."

Dino said, "First, I need to have a conversation with you. I know more about your body than about you, Rachel Schechter, the person. We are now in a serious relationship. The experience I had with you was amazing. But I want our relationship to be more than sex. Please don't think I don't like sex with you. I love it, and I want more, lots more. Here's a question I've been wondering about. You know I play baseball. What do you do after school when we're not together?"

"The thing I like best is watching you play baseball."

They both laughed.

"Rachel, are you a good student?"

"Pretty good, eighties and nineties."

"Sort of like me. But I'm mostly in the eighties."

Rachel then asked, "Do your parents know you're dating a Jewish girl?"

"Oh no! They'd have a fit if they knew."

"My parents, too. You're Catholic, aren't you? Is what we're doing a sin?"

"It sure is."

"Do you care?"

"Of course I care," Dino said.

"Is it a worse sin because I'm Jewish?"

"I don't know the answer to that. How about you? A sin?"

"I have no idea. My parents aren't religious, and I've had no Jewish education."

"If they're not religious, why would they have a problem with you dating a Catholic?"

"Oh, Dino. That's such a complicated question. You sure you want me to try to answer it."

"I am one hundred percent sure."

"Well, here goes . . . the way my parents explained it to me. Judaism is not just a religion. It's also sort of a nationality, like Italian. Except Jews no longer live on their own land. We are scattered all over the world. We are a very small part of the population of the world. Just a few years ago, Germany under Hitler killed about six million Jews in Europe. I'm told that was about one-third of all the Jews in the world. They would have killed my parents, but they managed to escape. I was born on the ship that brought my parents, my older sister, who's now married, and me to America. My parents believe it is their responsibility, and mine, to prevent intermarriage so Jewish people can continue in the world."

"I think I get it," Dino said. "You sure were right when you said it's a complicated matter. But just because we can't get married, there's no reason we can't have a little fun now."

Rachel threw her arms around Dino's neck and wrestled him down to lie on his back on the sofa. After several minutes of passionate embraces and Rachel disrobing almost casually, she began to unbutton Dino's shirt and then his pants.

"What do you think you're doing?" he said, uncertain whether he thought this was a good idea.

"It's not fair," Rachel said. "You know all about my body, and I can only imagine what yours looks like. Don't you think it's time we evened things up a bit? Sort of tit for cock."

"Not funny," he said, amazed at how clever she could be at a moment like this. *How can she be so calm about this? My heart is beating like a jazz drum. Is this really happening?* He began to help her unbutton his fly. He removed his shoes and socks and stood next to the sofa wearing only his undershorts. Rachel reached around him and pulled his shorts down to the floor. Dino was embarrassed that his erect penis seemed gigantic.

Rachel stared at his nude body for a few moments as if she was studying it. "You're not circumcised, are you," she asked.

"No," he answered shyly, almost apologetically.

Rachel stood up, put her arms around him, and kissed him. She took a step back and put her hand around his penis. Dino could restrain himself no longer. He had a monstrous orgasm and ejaculated all over Rachel's hand and belly. After a moment in which she seemed not to have understood what happened, Rachel began to laugh. She laughed so hard that tears ran down her cheeks. "So that's how it works," she managed to blurt out between guffaws. "It's a good thing I was so close to you, or it would be all over the wall and the ceiling and the living room furniture."

"I'm sorry, Rachel. I couldn't help it."

"I know I'm sexy, but I never dreamed I was that voluptuous."

"I'm so embarrassed. Ashamed. First time."

"For me, too. I don't know whether to wash this stuff off me or put it in a bottle and save it as a precious souvenir."

"Please don't joke about this. It's not funny to me."

"I'm sorry, Dino. I'd love to wait awhile until you're ready and start over."

"Are you telling me you want to go all the way?"

"Why not, we're practically there."

They snuggled on the sofa, each of them trying to contain the mounting excitement of the moment. They relaxed, and Rachel actually dozed off for a few moments into a light and blissful sleep. Dino moved so he could look at her face. He gazed at her and kissed her forehead.

To Dino's astonishment, Rachel reached under a pillow and produced a little packet containing a condom. Unsure of how to do it and hoping to do it right and pleasurably to the other, they began, clumsily, to have sexual intercourse.

They had just begun when the apartment door opened and closed. The lovers heard nothing. Footsteps could be heard walking into the apartment, but not by the lovers. Dr. and Mrs. Schechter walked into the living room and saw Dino's naked body atop their daughter. Mrs. Schechter screamed. Dr. Schechter ran to the sofa, where he violently pulled Dino off Rachel and threw him to the floor. He kicked Dino twice and shouted, "Get your clothes on, you scum, you filthy bastard, you rapist."

Rachel ran out of the room, and her mother followed her.

Dino didn't remember where his clothes were. While curled on the floor in a fetal position, he espied his undershorts protruding from under the sofa. He crawled toward them, reached out, and pulled them toward himself. He sat up, leaning his back against the sofa, and—still sitting on the floor—he clumsily pulled the shorts over his legs and up to his waist. He still had not looked at the person who was standing over him.

"How long do you plan to sit on the floor of my living room?"

Dino looked up at Rachel's father and without standing, said, "I didn't rape your daughter. You had no right to call me a rapist. The other things, okay. I understand. But not rapist. Rachel wanted it as much as I did."

"Stand up, filthy bastard."

Dino stood up. They were about the same height. They were face to face.

"How old are you?" Dr. Schechter asked.

"I'm seventeen."

"How old do you think Rachel is?"

"Sixteen."

"Wrong. She is fifteen—a minor. You screwed a minor. Now you're screwed. She can't give consent. Too young—she's still a child. That's called rape. Statutory rape. If you so much as look at my daughter again, I'll turn you in for rape. You will go to prison. Your life will be ruined. I am going to take her out of that high school. If I hear you so much as send her a message, you're finished. Now, you have two minutes to find your clothes and get out of my house before I break your neck. Rapist."

Dino found his trousers and shirt but only one shoe. Those are the only items he wore as he dashed out of Rachel's apartment and, with profound regret, out of Rachel's life.

In the bitter cold of the evening of that winter day, Dino Russo, clad in corduroy pants, a long-sleeved cotton shirt, and one shoe without a sock, made his way from Fort Washington Avenue down to and across Broadway, along Broadway for seven blocks to the bottom of 187th Street, up that steep hill to Wadsworth Avenue, along 187th and across St. Nicholas, across Audubon, to Amsterdam, and along Amsterdam for two long blocks to his building near 185th, then up the four flights of stairs to the Russo apartment where he found the door locked. He had no key. He had no choice but to ring the doorbell. He was grateful that his sister Theresa, and not his father or mother, opened the door.

As soon as she saw her brother shivering, Theresa pulled him into the apartment, retrieved a blanket from one of the beds, and wrapped it around him. She led him to the bedroom he shared with their brother Tony, who was not at home, and shoved him onto his bed. She sat on the foot of the bed and asked him what happened.

He didn't answer. His teeth were chattering. Theresa waited as Dino lay with his eyes closed. After a few minutes, with his eyes still closed, Dino mumbled. "Don't tell Mama or Papa."

"Don't worry. I'll never tell. But you have to tell me what happened. For heaven's sake, where's your other shoe?"

Dino opened his eyes. He said, "I'm so glad you opened the door. Thank you. You saved my life, for whatever that's worth. Theresa, I need to try to sleep. In the morning, I'll tell you as much as I can, but now I need to sleep."

"Okay, but you can't sleep in these clothes. Where do you keep your pajamas?"

He sat up and said, "They're under this pillow." He pulled the pajamas from under the pillow and began to take off his shirt. "Don't look, Theresa, I need to get undressed."

She left the room saying, "Sleep well, if you can."

When Dino pulled down his pants, he realized the condom was still on his now flaccid penis. He didn't know whether to laugh or cry.

Chapter 20

Dino

Part 2

Dino hardly slept at all. The word *rapist* kept tormenting him. He repeated that word. He called up visions of what her parents were doing and saying to Rachel. When he did sleep, fantastic dreams filled his head. He had never had a worse night of sleep.

Early the next morning, Theresa knocked gently on the door of his room. He sat up and realized that Tony had come in during the night and was asleep in the other bed. In order not to disturb him, Dino walked to the door and quietly opened it. He whispered to Theresa, "We can't talk here." She signaled to him to follow her, which he did. It seemed to him the rest of the family was still asleep.

In the living room, Theresa quietly asked him to explain what happened to him last night. During the night, in a lucid moment, he had decided not to invent a story to tell Theresa but to trust her to be discreet. Leaving out most of the details, he told his sister that he was "making love" with—*with*, not *to*—Rachel Schechter when her parents surprised them.

"Oh, shit," said Theresa.

"I didn't even have time to say 'oh shit' before her father attacked me. He pulled me to the floor and kicked me in the ribs. He cursed at me and called me a rapist."

"A rapist?"

"That was my question. But he told me Rachel is still fifteen and screwing a fifteen-year-old is statutory rape—a crime—and he'll turn me in to the cops if I ever see Rachel again."

"Is that true?"

"I'm afraid it is."

Theresa seemed to be mulling over that information. Finally, she said, "Well, wait until she's sixteen, and then screw her all you want."

"My dear sister, you'd make a lousy lawyer. I already committed the crime. It doesn't get erased when she gets to sixteen."

"Oh. So, what are you going to do?"

"Well, during the night, I considered committing suicide. Rejected that, for Mama's sake. Running away with her. Rejected that 'cause it'd never work. Making a sincere apology and asking for forgiveness. Rejected that. I'd get beat up again. Joining a monastery. No way. Sending you to get the rest of my clothes. My problem is not the clothes. Theresa, I just don't know what to do."

"My advice is just forget about her and get on with your life."

"Easy for you to say. I'm in love with her."

"Bullshit. You're a guy, and you're in love with her body. Every girl has a body. Pick a new one."

"Thanks for your advice. I mean it."

Dino found some warm clothes and another pair of shoes and got dressed. He intended to go out for a walk but was intercepted by his mother, who insisted that he needed a good breakfast before he went to mass with the family. All seven of the Russos had breakfast together. His mother noticed that Dino was unusually quiet. She asked him about it, and he said he was thinking about his difficulty with trigonometry. He knew his mother would not pursue the conversation.

Dino was not thinking about trigonometry. He was thinking, *Now I'm lying to Mama. What a great person I am, a liar and a rapist. And she wants me to go to church today. I'll stink up the place.*

He didn't stink up the place. He saw Sean and his mother in their regular pew, and, with his father's permission, he went and sat next to Sean.

"Good to see you, my captain," Sean said. "I've missed you lately."

Those words comforted Dino. Although Dino knew that he was going to be in a period of his life that would be filled with bitterness, regret, loneliness, anger, and other negative feelings and thoughts, Sean reminded him that he was an Infielder and would therefore never be alone.

Chapter 21

Boys and Girls

Together and Not Together

By the time they reached their senior year in high school, each of the boys had had at least one important girl in his life. Two of those relationships remained intact throughout the year and, thus, throughout the baseball season.

Sean's romance with Dino's sister, Terry, retained its full intensity with no signs of abating. Aram and Annette remained together, more as extremely close friends than as boyfriend and girlfriend. They saw each other frequently, both in school and outside of school, but almost always in the presence of other friends and students. Occasionally, they had a real date in which Aram would call upon Annette at her apartment, where he would be greeted by her parents and admonished not to stay out too late. Those dates were tame in comparison to the torrid affairs that the other Infielders had, but they were not without warmth and a gentle intimacy. They kissed but did no more than kiss. It was almost as if their relationship was a romance in gestation.

Both Aram and Annette continued to excel academically. They both received outstanding marks—all over ninety and several ninety-five or higher. However, Annette's marks in the first semester of senior year were lower than Aram's—more nineties than ninety-fives—resulting in Aram having a higher four-year average than Annette. This pleased him greatly, and it didn't seem to matter at all to Annette. Dino secretly believed that Annette "shaved points" in order for Aram to finish first in the class.

It was likely that Annette was more committed to the relationship than Aram. At his parents' request, Aram brought Annette home one evening. They spoke with her in Armenian, to Mrs. Petrosian's utter delight. Afterward, she told her son that his girlfriend was beautiful and perfect.

Bernie remained "in the market," as Dino put it. For the remainder of their high school careers, Bernie remained locked in an unrequited love for Barbara Gordon. *I really messed up the situation with Barbara. I had one conversation with her after we got the indictment dismissed, and she said I gave her father a bloody nose. "Big fucking deal," I said to her. "Did you hear what he said about my father? It's too bad I didn't break his nose." How could I be so stupid? She slapped my face and walked away. It didn't have to end that way. All my fault.*

Bernie had no more than unsatisfying, desultory dates with a number of girls and had no serious connection with any girl. Dino remained the most eligible teenage bachelor in Washington Heights, but his interest in girls seemed to have disappeared. He ignored both the subtle and the more aggressive advances that were made toward him by girls of all descriptions. Pretty girls, bright girls, buxom girls, sexy girls, girls known to "put out," nice girls, Italian girls who would have pleased his mama . . . simply every girl. None of them was Rachel. The irony that neither of the two Infielders who had been most successful in relating to girls was in a serious relationship with a girl was not lost on either of them.

On a Saturday morning in early March, Bernie decided to deal with that subject. He went to Dino's house and was welcomed by Mrs. Russo with an offer of a plate of leftover lasagna that he eagerly accepted. Both of them ignored the fact that it was ten o'clock in the morning.

"Didn't you eat breakfast?" Dino asked.

"Let the boy eat," Mrs. Russo said.

"I'm still a growing boy," Bernie said.

"You see," said Mrs. Russo, addressing her son. She had off-loaded her entire inventory of Friday night's leftover lasagna, enough for at least two grown people. Bernie scarfed it down as if he hadn't eaten in days.

When Bernie finally finished the last atom of the leftover lasagna, the two young men went into Dino's bedroom. Dino sat on his bed, and Bernie sat on Tony's bed.

"What's up?" Dino asked. A lot of conversations started like that.

"There's something wrong with both of us."

"That's a fair comment. And you and I know what it is. No girlfriend."

"Close," said Bernie, "but I would put it a bit differently. I would say 'no sex'."

"Bernie, I have to tell you something you never can tell anyone else. Can I have your word on that?

"Of course."

"I had a terrible experience with sex."

"I have no idea what you're talking about. You're not impotent, are you, or queer like your kid brother?"

"Please don't call Marco 'queer.' He's a homosexual."

"I promise."

"It's too hard for me to tell you. Let's forget about it."

"Dino, how the fuck can I help you if I don't know what's

wrong? I'll tell you what's wrong with me. I'm still in love with Barbara Gordon—or I should properly say the fiancée of Eric Rosen of Forest Hills, Queens. Every time I talk to a girl or look at a girl, Barbara's face pops up, and that's all I see. You did a great thing for me when you helped get my father's indictment dismissed. But it was too late. The damage was done. Barbara was gone. She didn't love me enough to wait for me. That's my problem in a nutshell. What's yours?"

"Same thing. Rachel. Different story, same outcome. Maybe my outcome is worse." Dino stood up, walked a few steps, and straightened a framed picture on the wall near the door. Then, abruptly, he sat next to Bernie on Tony's bed and said, "Promise me you won't spread this around."

"You shouldn't even feel you have to ask me that."

"Rachel's father caught me having sex with her."

"Fucking?"

"Yeah. He beat the shit out of me. Worse yet, he told me she wasn't sixteen and I was a rapist and if I ever came near her again, he'd send me to prison."

"He can't send you to prison. Only a judge can do that. But that explains why she's never in the cafeteria. He's technically right. It's called statutory rape. I'll deny this, but I can tell you. I've done it twice. But not in front of a father. I'm so sorry to hear that, Dino. That is a terrible experience. Terrible bad luck."

They sat looking at each other. Neither knew what, if anything, to say to the other. After several minutes of uncomfortable silence, Bernie said, "It's so weird that both of us lost the girls who meant the most to us because of something to do with fathers. In my case, my father and the rationing stamps and in your case, her father."

"So, what am I to do with that?" Dino asked.

"Nothing, it was just a thought."

"A pretty worthless thought," Dino said with a clear tone of annoyance in his voice.

"Shit, Dino, I'm here trying to help you deal with a helpless situation. Don't get pissed off at me."

"I'm sorry, Bernie, it's just that I'm hurting real bad. I didn't tell you that I ran away from Rachel's father all the way from Fort Washington Avenue to here wearing only my shirt and pants and one shoe without a sock. I almost froze to death."

"You left your other clothes behind?"

"Yeah, I was afraid he'd kill me or, even worse, call the cops."

"You poor guy." Bernie looked pensive for a few moments and then said, "I have an idea. In school on Monday, during lunch in the cafeteria, let's each pick a girl to go out with us next Saturday night. We'll have no trouble getting some girl to happily say yes when we ask for a date. We can take them up my house after a movie. My parents go to sleep real early. Let's see what we can accomplish."

"That may work for you, Bernie, but not me. Your problem is you're horny. Mine is I'm heartbroken. Good luck with your plan. I'll see you at the baseball meeting on Friday."

They shook hands, and Bernie left. At that moment, Dino entered into a long period of celibacy. He might have descended into a serious encounter with depression but for baseball, but for shortstop, but for captain, but for city championship, but for the Infielders. His self-awareness was sufficiently acute that he consciously realized that baseball and friendship saved his sanity, perhaps his life.

Chapter 22

Undying Friendship . . . Perhaps

Graduation was not just a ceremony; it was a gate through which you exited from the familiar and the comfortable into the unfamiliar and the uncomfortable. This was true whether you were a boy or a girl, whether you hated or loved high school, and whether you looked forward with eager anticipation or with foreboding to life after high school. If puberty was the biological transformation of a boy or girl to an adult man or woman, graduation was the emotional transformation of a boy or girl to a young man or a young woman. Each transformation was both thrilling and frightening.

After throwing their tasseled caps in the air at the end of the George Washington High School graduation ceremony, the four Infielders found a private corner near the left field fence in foul territory. They gathered there wearing their graduation robes, full of the knowledge that this was likely the last time in their lives that they would be together as a circle of boys who were bound in a special friendship. They would always be the Infielders of a champion baseball team. They could be certain of that. It was in the record books. But there was little else of which they could be certain, and that made this a somber moment.

They hugged. They pledged undying friendship to one another, knowing in their hearts how fragile those pledges would be in the unknowable lives they were about to enter.

Part Three

The Adventures of Becoming Grown-Ups

The Ten Years Beyond High School

Chapter 23

Sean

To Play or Not to Play

For several weeks before his graduation, Sean pondered whether he should accept an offer from the Boston Braves to play for its minor league affiliate, the Fort Lauderdale Braves, in the Class B Florida International League.

Sean's alternative was to attend New York University, a school that offered him a baseball scholarship. Coach McCullough urged him to go to college instead of playing professional baseball. McCullough had played in the minor leagues for several seasons, and he told Sean that it was a miserable life. The pay was ridiculously low, living conditions were deplorable, travel by bus from city to city was boring and exhausting, and, most importantly, the chance of making it to the major leagues was remote. Sean listened to this advice attentively, and he was discouraged by it. Continuing in school at the college level—even though he knew that he wasn't going to be expected to become a great scholar—was terrifying to Sean. He had very little confidence in his academic ability. He attributed his passing grades in high school to the help—and encouragement—given to him by Aram Petrosian, help and encouragement that would not be available to him at NYU while Aram was far away at Harvard.

He discussed his dilemma with the other Infielders. Aram and Dino urged him to accept the NYU scholarship. They argued that a college education at a good school like NYU would provide a better foundation for a successful life. Dino even went so far as to point out that staying in New York would give Sean the opportunity to continue to date Dino's sister, Theresa.

Bernie, on the other hand, advised Sean to seize the opportunity to play professional baseball. He pointed out that Sean was much more skilled at baseball than he was as a student, a point that Sean understood perfectly. Bernie—who was going to attend City College in New York—said that he would love to be in Sean's position, playing baseball and getting paid for it. He emphasized how much fun one could have in a place like Fort Lauderdale. "Life doesn't get any better than that," Bernie argued. "Playing baseball for pay and living in Florida and getting to go to Havana a couple of times a season. I would trade City College for that life in one second if I had the chance."

For one of the few times in his life, Sean decided to consult his father for advice on the issue of whether to play minor league baseball or go to college.

Patrick Flaherty was not a bad man. True, he was a poor and inconsiderate husband. True, he was a neglectful and distant father. True, he had a misplaced vision of himself as the next William Butler Yeats, bringing the beauty of Irish poetry to the world. True, this vision crowded out any sense of responsibility as a husband and a father. True, he was an especially dismal father to Sean. But he was not a bad man. He was a man whose grief at the death in combat of his firstborn son was unremitting. It enveloped him. It defined him. If he taught anything to his younger son, Sean, it was how to grieve. Sean understood his father more than Patrick

Flaherty understood himself, and Sean forgave his father's delin-
quency. He understood its source.

In the Flaherty apartment on Amsterdam Avenue, Patrick
Flaherty was sitting at his desk, an old, stained, and scratched
piece of furniture set against the wall beneath a window that
looked out into an alley. He was staring vacantly at the brick wall
opposite the window.

Sean approached his father with a mixture of fear and hope.
Sean tapped him gently on the shoulder and said, "Da, I need to
speak with you about something very important."

"Have you been thrown out of school?"

"No, Da, I'm going to graduate next week. Parents can come to
the graduation."

"You're going to graduate from high school? Now there's a
miracle."

"I need your advice about what I should do after I graduate."

"Get a job. That's my advice. Now leave me alone."

"Please, Da, I need to make a decision, and I want you to help
me to decide which way to go. I've got an offer from the Boston
Braves baseball team to play for one of their farm teams. I also have
an offer of a full scholarship to New York University."

"Why on God's earth would a university give you a
scholarship?"

"Because I'm a good baseball player, and they want me to play
on their school team."

"What a fookin' strange country this America is. They want
you to play on their baseball team? A university has a baseball
team, and they want an eejit like you to play on it?"

"Da, I'm not an idiot, and neither is New York University. It's
a fine school, and I can be a student there. That's a reward for
being a good player."

"You're not handing me a load of shite, are you?

"No, I'm asking for your help. I don't know which offer to accept."

"Somebody in Boston wants to pay you to play baseball?"

"It would not be in Boston, at least not this year. I would play for a team in Florida."

"And you want me to tell you what to do? How in hell would I know?"

"Please, Da, let's talk about it."

And for the first time in Sean's memory, he and his father had an almost civil conversation.

Mr. Flaherty began by saying, "You know, son, that your brother, Patrick Jr., God rest his soul, was my favorite of my children."

"I know that, Da. He was my favorite, too."

"He was beautiful—as you are—but he was also smart, and he had a love of poetry. Did you know that he wrote poems?"

"He showed me some of them."

"They may not have been very good, but they were a good effort. And if those fookin' Japs hadn't killed him, he might have become a fine poet. But he was smart in other ways, too. He loved to read fine literature, and he and I spent precious hours talking about books and writers. He was the joy of my life."

"I know that too, Da, and I know that I can't give you what he gave you. I just can't be Paddy. As much as I loved him and as much as I miss him, I can't be him."

"And he could do maths. Geometry and algebra. And he knew about politics and history and geography. He knew about Ireland and County Galway, where his people came from. And he was a brave soul. You know he enlisted in the army the day after those fookin' Japs bombed Pearl Harbor?"

"I know that too, Da."

"But we need to talk about you. When I think about you—and

I do think about you—I am always reminded of a story told about Joe Louis, that colored man who's the heavyweight boxing champion of the world. They make a hero out of a teacher he had in school—as if she was a great genius—because she told him that he would earn his livelihood with his hands. Well, he did do that, using his hands to knock the shite out of other boxers. But the teacher, she was no great visionary who could see that the child would go on to fame as a boxer. All she could see was a dimwitted kid who could hardly read and write, and she knew that if he ever was to earn a dime in his life, it would be with his hands and not his head. It makes me laugh the way people think she was a prophet.

"Now, why am I talking about Joe Louis and his teacher? Because, when I think about you—my son who is not Paddy—I worry that you won't make your way in the world using your head, that you will need to use your hands. Now, it's clear to me that you have a better head than Joe Louis. Look, you're going to graduate from high school. That's far more than that boxer or your Da ever did. Don't think that I don't take some pride in you for that. I do. I truly do.

"May God forgive me . . . I've not been a good father to you. I knew you were not made like Paddy, and I resented you for that. What kind of a father resents his son for being what nature made him? And worse yet, you're a better boy than I ever gave you credit for being. And now you come to me for advice. What an honor you pay me. And I call you an eejit. God forgive me. Will you forgive me?"

"Sure, Da. Thanks for saying all of that."

"You're kinder than I've ever been. I know you didn't learn kindness from me. Perhaps your mother, poor woman, perhaps you learned kindness from her. Now let me give you the advice you came to me for. I think that university is not the place for you.

You've got brains, but you're not cut out to be a student. They'll use you to win baseball games for them, but they won't try very hard to make an educated man out of you. They'll use your talent, and then they'll throw you away. Your time there will be a waste. God gave you skilled hands. Use them the way Joe Louis uses his. Be a baseball player and give it all you've got."

Chapter 24

Sean

Decision-Making

Sean and his father shook hands, and Sean walked downstairs to look for Aram. He walked up Amsterdam Avenue to 189th Street, turned left, and walked past PS 189 to see if Aram might be in the schoolyard. Bernie was there, playing softball, but Sean really wanted to speak with Aram, who was not in the schoolyard. So he walked up Audubon Avenue toward the high school ball field. Again, Aram wasn't there. Sean turned around and walked back to Amsterdam Avenue, heading toward Aram's building on Laurel Hill Terrace. When he entered the lobby, he was recognized by the elderly elevator operator, who knew from Sean's numerous visits to Aram's apartment for tutoring that Sean would be going up to the fifth floor.

"You guys won the city baseball championship," said the elevator operator.

"Yes, we did."

"I'd love to hear all about it. Congratulations."

Sean didn't really want to chat with the old man. He was deep in thought about his conversation with his father, all of it, not just the part about playing professional baseball. It had been a remarkable experience for Sean to have had that conversation, and since shaking hands with his father, he had been playing it back in his mind, over and over, as he walked the streets of the Heights looking for Aram. There was no one home in the Petrosian apartment. Sean was left with no one to talk to about the critical decision he had to make.

Suddenly, a thought came to him. He slapped the side of his head and said, out loud to no one but himself, "Where are my brains? Why didn't I think of talking to Terry?" It took Sean a few moments to realize that he was standing outside the Petrosians' building, and it was several blocks to the building where the Russos lived, near 186th Street. He started to run as fast as he could. He wondered how he could have talked to everyone, including his father, and neglected to discuss his dilemma with Terry? He ran up the stairs to Terry's house, rang the doorbell, and was delighted when Terry opened the door.

"My parents are home, and so is Dino," Terry said in a whisper.

"That's okay, I didn't come to make out. I just want to talk with you. Can we do that?"

"Sure. Come on in."

"Who's that," Mrs. Russo called from the kitchen.

"It's just Sean, Mama."

"Hello, Sean," said Mrs. Russo, walking from the kitchen to greet him. "So, this has been some big week. The big game and then graduation. That's a lot for one week. That's all Dino ever talks about. You know Dino's been accepted to City College. I think me and my husband are more excited about that than Dino is. His mind is still on a baseball game, something you play and then it's over. But college. No one in my family or my husband's family ever went to college. Did you know my sister's son wanted to go to college in Brooklyn, but he didn't get in. His marks weren't good enough. But my Dino—"

"Mama, Sean came to talk to me, not you."

"My Dino," Mrs. Russo continued, ignoring Theresa, "Not only the captain of the baseball team but good marks. So, Sean, are you also going to college?"

"Well, Mrs. Russo, I'm not sure. I got a scholarship to NYU, but I also got an offer to play professional baseball. I'm not so sure which way to go. That's what I wanted to talk about with Theresa."

"With Theresa? What does she know about such things?"

"Mama, basta! I know more than you think. Go back in the kitchen and let Sean and me talk."

Still ignoring her daughter, Mrs. Russo continued addressing Sean. "Have you talked to Dino about this? I would trust what he says. He's very smart, you know."

"I did talk to Dino. He said I should go to NYU. But then I talked to my father, and he said I should play baseball."

"Oh, I see the problem," Mrs. Russo said. "A boy should listen to his father. But how can you make a living if you're playing baseball all the time?"

"It's professional baseball."

"I don't know that word."

"Mama," Theresa interrupted impatiently and sharply, "it means he gets paid to play ball."

"Somebody pays you to play baseball? To play a game? Why do they do that?"

"I can't stand this anymore!" Theresa shouted. She took hold of Sean's arm and said, "Let's get out of here. She's driving me crazy."

Sean now had another dilemma. It was contrary to his nature

to be rude, to turn his back on Mrs. Russo, a nice woman whom he liked and who was showing a genuine interest in him. But Terry was literally pulling him toward the door leading out of the apartment. It took him a moment to sort out the priorities. Then, "Terry, please, give me a minute to explain to your mom what the baseball thing is about." He disengaged his arm from Terry's grip and, with an embarrassed smile, said to Mrs. Russo, "The reason they would pay me to play is that the owner of the team expects to make money by selling tickets to the games. It's a business—an entertainment business—and they need people like me who can perform the entertainment. That's all there is to it."

"Thank you, Sean. Now I understand." She gently patted his arm where Terry had been gripping him. "You're a nice boy, but I can't help you decide what to do. Theresa can't help you either. But go with her anyway. She likes you."

The young couple left the apartment, walked out into the dimly lit stairwell, and descended into the brightly lit sunshine of a June afternoon. Sean was annoyed with Terry, and he told her so. She snapped at him and called him a "goody-goody boy."

He sighed deeply and said, "Maybe this is not a good time to have this conversation."

"No, I think we should talk now. This is important. I'm smarter than my mother thinks, and I know you much better than she does." Silently, they walked east along 186th Street to where it ended at Laurel Hill Terrace. They knew there were benches there overlooking the wooded escarpment descending to the Harlem River. They had sat on those benches many times.

They sat down, and Terry took Sean's hand, raised it to her lips, and kissed it. "Okay," she said. "Let's talk. If you play baseball in Florida, what will happen with us?"

"We'll stay in touch, write letters, maybe talk on the phone sometimes. I'll come back to New York when the season ends. Even if I went to NYU, we would be seeing less of each other than if I was still in high school. That's the way things are."

"You'll find another girl in Florida."

"No, I won't. You're the only girl in my life, and nothing will change that."

"Then let's get married."

"Terry, what are you saying? I just turned eighteen, and you're only sixteen. You have two more years of high school to go. How can we possibly get married?"

"You could get me pregnant, and then we'd have to get married."

"Are you crazy?"

"I thought you loved me."

"I do love you. But . . ." He stopped, not knowing what to say. Then he thought of something good to say. "Terry, I love you. Someday, I want to marry you. But only if you are a virgin. That's that. That's according to our religion, and that's the way I think. I also think you are too young—no, *we* are too young—to be talking this way. If you can't trust me to come back to you because I spend six months playing ball in Florida, then maybe we shouldn't even think of getting married."

"I'm just afraid I'll lose you."

"I don't want to hear about that anymore. You'll just have to trust me, or we have to think about breaking up now."

"Oh, God, no. Sean, don't ever say that. Don't even think that. Come, kiss me."

They kissed, and then Sean walked Terry home, not having received any useful advice from her about baseball or college. He found the entire experience with Terry that day to have been upsetting, from the scene with her mother to her extraordinary suggestion that he get her pregnant to talking about marriage to her turning the entire subject of baseball versus college into nothing more than a discussion about their relationship. For the first time ever, Terry wasn't a joy for him. He wondered whether he had screwed up somehow.

Chapter 25

Sean

The Decision

Coach McCullough invited the entire team to his home for lunch to celebrate the championship and to pose for a team picture wearing their baseball uniforms. Sean had hardly slept the night before and was anxious to see Aram as soon as possible. Sean was the first player to arrive at the coach's apartment. Mrs. McCullough asked him to sit in the living room and wait until everyone was there for the lunch that she was preparing in the kitchen. The players began to arrive, one by one. Each time the door opened, Sean hoped to see Aram. Most of the players crowded into the living room of the McCullough apartment, and still, Aram had not arrived. Sean realized that not only Aram but also Dino and Bernie were missing. That was unusual and disconcerting to Sean.

"Everyone into the dining room for hot dogs and hamburgers," the coach called. "You, too, Flaherty, what are you waiting for?"

"Do you know where Aram, Bernie, and Dino are?" asked Sean.

"I'm just the coach, not the babysitter. You can have lunch without your good buddies. Into the dining room. Now."

Sean walked into the dining room and stood in line, looking over his shoulder for his friends as Mrs. McCullough passed out plates of appetizing food. He was the only Infielder in the coach's apartment. Sean felt as if he were lost, standing in the wrong place.

He looked around, trying to get his bearings. He walked back into the living room. Coach McCullough was on the telephone. The coach motioned to Sean to take a seat and wait. A few moments later, the coach sat down next to Sean. He said, "Flaherty, you are one hell of a lucky guy."

"I know, Coach, but what's going on?"

"First of all, you have three of the best friends that anyone in the world could possibly ask for."

"You mean Aram, Dino, and Bernie? Where are they, anyway?"

"Listen to this. Aram Petrosian called me at my home last night. It's a complicated story, and I'm not sure I got it all straight. After that call, he and Russo and Heller came to my home about nine o'clock last night. Dino told me that you were having a really difficult time with the idea of going to Florida to play pro ball and that your girlfriend, Dino's sister, was terribly upset that you would be so far away from New York. He asked me if there was anything I could do about that. I know that those three infielders are smart and serious kids, and they wouldn't ask me to do something if it wasn't very important. So, I called this guy I know in the Braves organization, their chief scout in this part of the country. Higgins is his name. He's the guy who saw you play a few games and recommended that the Braves make you an offer. I told him that Florida was a problem for you. He said he'd see what he could do and that he'd call me in the morning. That's today. Russo,

Heller, and Petrosian came to my house before six o'clock this morning. I was still in my pajamas. My wife made breakfast for the four of us. Your friends ate like they had been starved for a month. Finally, about an hour ago, Higgins called. He said that the Hartford Chiefs, the Braves' farm team in the Class A Eastern League, need a first baseman who can hit. That could be you—if you accept their offer today and report to Hartford not later than next Monday. So now it's up to you. Your friends and your coach have done all they could."

"This is hard to believe."

"You'd better believe it. I need to call Higgins before noon today. Now, you know, I recommended that you take the baseball scholarship to NYU, but Bernie told me, in no uncertain terms, that you really wanted to play pro ball. Let me tell you that when you walk onto the field to play for the Hartford Chiefs, you will feel as lost and lonely as you did on our field the first time you played for GW. It's your decision to make. No one can make it for you. Now, go to Aram's house, where your friends are waiting for you. Aram's mother has prepared a special lunch for the four of you. Sean, I want you to know that we couldn't have won the championship without you.

"Thanks, Coach, but I have one question. Where is Hartford?"

Chapter 26

Aram

Harvard or Home

The name Harvard had a kind of mystical meaning in Washington Heights. People knew that it was a college like NYU, City College, Fordham, or those football colleges named after states. But Harvard was something different. Different the way fine bone china was different from the plates and cups on their tables. Harvard was remote, existing in a sphere that was thought to be unreachable by the people who lived in the Heights.

Except for the Petrosian family. It was Mr. Petrosian's dream that one day, his extraordinary son would represent the Petrosian family in that unreachable realm. Mr. Petrosian started a Chevrolet dealership before the Second World War and made a considerable amount of money. When the United States converted its automobile industry to war production and discontinued the manufacture of new cars, Mr. Petrosian did not wring his hands in desperation. Instead, he seized what he saw as an opportunity to convert his business into an automobile service center and used car lot. He made money during the war, and, starting in 1946, his reborn Chevrolet dealership became a success. Americans lined up around the block to buy new cars, and the Petrosian dealership responded to that demand. He could afford to send his son to a "paying" college.

Aram's superb academic performance at George Washington High School, coupled with his varsity baseball achievements, virtually guaranteed his admission to a good college. During his senior year, he submitted applications to Yale, Harvard, Columbia, Cornell, NYU, Rutgers, and Swarthmore.

Dino asked him why he needed to send out so many applications. "You're a sure bet to get into any college you want."

"Dino, you never know whether the top colleges may be prejudiced against an Armenian kid from New York."

"I think you're paranoid. You think anybody cares about Armenians? It's not like you're colored."

"You can't be too careful when it comes to something as important as this."

"Explain to me," Dino said, "why it's so important to you. I sent an application to City College. If I'm accepted, great, I get to go to college. Why do you have to go to one of those highfalutin colleges?"

"I think I'm very smart . . ."

"You are. So what?"

"I think I'm very smart and can do well at a top school. I'll be really well educated and equipped to go out into the world and make a success of myself."

"What are you going to be? An engineer? A scientist? A doctor or a lawyer? What do you want to be?

"I have no idea. I hope my college education will point me in the right direction."

"Well, I really hope you're right about that. I really do. I've already made up my mind. I'm going to the business school at City College, and I'm going to get a job in management. I could change my mind if I find something that really interests me, but right now, I'm heading into the business world."

"You'll be good at that," Aram said. "Good luck to both of us."

Dino left that conversation with a nagging concern that Aram —as bright as he was—was just floating around aimlessly. He hoped that concern was unnecessary.

Every college Aram applied to accepted him. His father told him to go to Harvard, the best and most prestigious university in the United States, perhaps in the entire world. His mother—who had never heard of any of the schools that Aram applied to—told him in no uncertain terms that he was too young to live away from home among strangers and that if he had to continue in school, it had to be close enough so that he could live at home.

Annette, Aram's occasional girlfriend, told him she had applied to Radcliffe College, a girls' school affiliated with Harvard, and that it would be nice if he would go to Harvard so they could continue to see each other.

Aram didn't know what to do. He usually followed his father's advice, but he was troubled by his mother's admonition that he had to continue to live at home. The idea of causing any kind of distress to his mother was intolerable to Aram. He could easily go to Columbia or NYU and continue to live at home. Bernie and Dino were still going to live at home. Only Sean was likely to live away from home. But unlike Sean, whose home life was stressful and unpleasant, Aram was perfectly comfortable at home. He was a beloved only child. In his most private moments, he had no difficulty admitting to himself that he cared about his mother more than—much more than—he cared about Annette. His mother's love for him was unconditional, nurturing, reassuring, and constant. Everything he undertook to do in his young life—his diligent studying and academic achievements, even his baseball accomplishments—were built on the secure foundation that his mother provided by her assurances to him that he was the most perfect and precious person in the world. There was no possibility that he would do anything to cause her unhappiness. Columbia had to be his choice for that reason,

While Aram was wrestling with himself, Annette was playing a far more focused game. She told her father how much she would like Aram to go to Harvard so that the two of them could see each other frequently in Cambridge.

Dr. Nazarian was surprised to learn that Aram could even think about rejecting an acceptance from Harvard. "When I was his age," he told his daughter, "my application to Harvard was rejected. It was a blow from which I'm not sure to this day I've fully recovered."

"Oh, Daddy. You don't seem to be grieving that badly."

"Seriously, an acceptance from Harvard is not something to be treated lightly."

"Why don't you speak with Aram's parents about how important it will be for Aram to study at Harvard?"

It was almost as though Annette had intuited that Aram's reluctance to go to Harvard might stem from a childish separation anxiety from his parents. She knew how favorably Mr. and Mrs. Petrosian viewed their son's relationship with her. She knew, with certainty, that if they could—in this day and age—arrange a marriage for their son, she would be the bride. Even if Aram might not—in this day and age—be coerced into a marriage, he could almost certainly be coerced into going to the finest university in America.

Perpetually disinclined to refuse a request, or even a suggestion, from his beloved daughter, Dr. Nazarian proposed to his wife that they invite Mr. and Mrs. Petrosian to a dinner at which authentic Armenian food would be served. He passed on to his wife Annette's suggestion that they urge the Petrosians to prevail upon their son to go to Harvard. Mrs. Nazarian wondered aloud to her husband if that kind of intervention in Annette's relationship with Aram might not be the right thing to do.

"Why do you think that?" Dr. Nazarian asked.

"Because I'm not sure that Aram is ready to have a serious relationship with Annette. Or for that matter with any girl."

"Because he sometimes seems to be immature?"

"Exactly. He's a lovely boy, and he'll be a good match for Annette when he grows up. But he hasn't grown up yet."

"I understand exactly what you're saying," Dr. Nazarian replied. "But I think moving away from his comfortable nest on Laurel Hill Terrace into the real world of a great university might be the recipe that will cause him to grow from a boy to a man."

"Okay, I don't see any harm. You should phone Hagop and invite them for dinner a week from Saturday evening. You mentioned the word 'recipe.' I'll have to dig out my favorite recipes for Armenian food. I'm going to enjoy doing that."

"Is Hagop his name? I never knew that. What's his wife's name?"

"I'm not sure. We'll have to ask Annette."

Entrapment is a defense to criminal charges. It is perfectly legal otherwise.

Chapter 27

Aram, Annette, and Their Parents

And so, on a lovely Saturday evening in the spring of 1948, Hagop and Zada Petrosian drove from Laurel Hill Terrace to Payson Avenue in Inwood to have dinner at the home of Ralph and Elise Nazarian. Aram and Annette were having dinner that evening at the home of the Russo family, an invitation initiated by Theresa Russo in collaboration with Annette Nazarian.

There was some casual and slightly awkward conversation in Armenian following the arrival of the Petrosians. Zada Petrosian was unused to the customs of dinner invitations. Despite living in the United States for twenty-five years, she was still a survivor of the Turkish genocide, a shy, sheltered immigrant, unassimilated into American life. The Nazarians were fully aware of how strange the fully assimilated Nazarian home must have appeared to Zada, and, with grace and warmth, they welcomed her and tried to make her comfortable.

When Elise told Zada about the meal that awaited them that evening, Zada was moved by the effort that Elise had obviously made to turn the evening into something extraordinary. The dinner prepared by Elise Nazarian was a work of art, an extravaganza of Armenian cuisine. She had told her guests what was in store for them at the dinner table, and she could see Zada savoring both the thought of the food and the effort Elise had extended to make her feel welcome.

The dinner table was set with fine china and sterling silver cutlery. To Zada, the table was an image of luxury and elegance. And then came the food. The meal began with a soup made from dried beans, called *yahni* in Armenian, served chilled, that evoked for Zada memories long forgotten. Elise and Zada discussed the different ways in which this delicious dish could be prepared and served. The soup was followed by a remarkably delicious dish called *kalajosh*, a preparation of braised lamb, heated yogurt, and onions, garnished with fresh mint. Zada marveled at the flavor and complexity of the dish, remarking that it was the tastiest thing she had ever eaten, uniquely Armenian in character but one she had not previously eaten. She thanked Elise profusely for preparing and serving it.

Zada's initial awkwardness had been erased. She was among friends, lovely friends, people with whom she was entirely comfortable. And when a dessert resembling baklava but rolled with lemon syrup, walnuts, and cinnamon was brought to the table by Dr. Nazarian—Zada was still too shy to call a doctor by his first name—Zada was captivated by the Nazarians; she belonged to them.

Throughout the wondrous dinner, a lively conversation took place. Inevitably, a good part of it related to their children. Each father extolled the virtues of his son or daughter and, with equal fervor, the son or daughter of the other father. Each father described the long list of excellent colleges that accepted his son or daughter and the difficult choices that their respective children had to make in selecting a college from those lists. Elise Nazarian joined her husband in praising both Annette and Aram, remarking more than once how lovely it would be if the two of them became a couple. Because Elise's Armenian was not quite as fluent as that of the others at the table, she wasn't certain of the word to use for *couple,* and, consequently, the word that Zada heard was *engaged.* She responded to the first of Elise's comments by saying that she thought Aram and Annette were too young for marriage. Zada was plainly embarrassed when Hagop explained to her that Elise didn't say that. The tension on Zada's face gradually dissolved, and she agreed with Elise that their children were indeed a lovely couple.

Thus, it was easy for Ralph Nazarian to raise the subject of how good it would be for their children to be near each other while at college. Knowing that Zada's reluctance to have Aram live away from home was the issue that needed to be resolved, he said, "The first time I lived away from my parent's home in New Jersey was when I was a freshman at Johns Hopkins University in Baltimore. I'll never forget the day my father and mother drove me from Englewood to Baltimore. It was the longest trip I had ever taken, almost four hours."

"Were you nervous about being so far away from your parents?" Zada interrupted.

"I certainly was. Everyone was at least a little bit nervous if it was his first time living away from home. But I have to say I was more excited than I was nervous. I think that was also true about all the freshmen."

"Tell me," Zada asked, "what is 'freshmen'?"

Ralph had used the English word, *freshmen,* there being no real equivalent word in Armenian. "Sorry, Zada, it simply means a first-year student in a school."

"Thank you. So both of our children will be freshmens next year?"

Ralph chuckled. "The English plural of 'freshman' is *freshmen*. Our children will be *freshmen*."

"I'll never learn English. It's too complicated."

Elise jumped in. "That's no problem. We can always speak Armenian among ourselves, and that will give me an opportunity to practice the language before I lose it. Zada, I hope you and I will have many, many conversations, and you will make sure I speak Armenian correctly."

Zada was greatly pleased. She jettisoned all the timidity she brought with her to the Nazarian household and became an assertive and active participant in the ongoing conversation. When Elise made an offhand comment about the merits of the obsolete tradition of arranged marriages, Zada surprised the Nazarians when she disclosed that her marriage to Hagop had been arranged. "The first time I met Hagop was the day before we were married. After I was rescued from the massacre, I was taken to the home of a cousin of my mother in Aleppo, Syria. I lived with them for twelve years, and they were very kind to me. One day, my aunt— that's what I called her even though she wasn't really my aunt—my aunt told me that I was going to America to marry a very good man named Hagop Petrosian, who lived in New York City. You can imagine the effect this had on me. I was frightened, but I was also excited. I can say that I was thrilled. I was seventeen years old. I had never been alone with a boy, never been kissed, and now I was going to be married. Maybe you can't imagine how that felt."

Elise couldn't contain her excitement when she heard this news. "What a beautiful story. I must hear all the details. Zada, did you travel to America alone?"

"My aunt and uncle took me on a train to a seaport where I was placed on a ship. After that, I was alone. The voyage on the ship was very difficult. I slept in a little room with an old woman who didn't talk to me. I was vomiting the whole time. I'm sorry to say that at the dinner table. It seemed to be forever before we finally reached New York. Of course, I knew nobody there. Two people—who turned out to be Hagop's parents—looked for me and found me sitting on a bench, weeping and frightened. When I found out who they were, I was ashamed about how terrible I must have looked after the long voyage on the boat. But they embraced me and welcomed me to their family."

Hagop jumped in and said, "I wasn't allowed to see Zada until the day before the wedding, which was scheduled for the following Saturday, and Zada arrived on Monday. I had to move out and sleep in the apartment of a cousin in New Jersey."

"Hagop's mother," Zada continued, "took me to buy a wedding dress, and since I had no family in America, Hagop's mother made all the wedding arrangements."

"The first time I saw Zada was, as I said, the day before the wedding. She was in my parents' apartment and I am not ashamed to say I was stunned by how beautiful she was."

"Oh, Hagop, don't say things like that. The most important thing is that we have had a happy marriage for twenty-one years now, and we have a brilliant and wonderful son. That shows you what can happen in an arranged marriage. I wish we could do that with our children."

Ralph Nazarian had been waiting for an opening to return to the subject of Aram and Annette and the colleges they would attend. "Unfortunately, in America, in 1947, it's really not possible to arrange a marriage. But, as intelligent parents, we can do the next best thing. That is to make it possible for Annette and Aram to develop a close relationship that can lead to marriage. To do that, they have to be able to see each other frequently. I know they like each other, and if they have a chance to be together regularly, they may even begin to fall in love."

"That would be wonderful," Hagop said.

"I agree," Elise said.

"And I agree," Zada said.

"So, it's settled," Ralph said. "Aram will go to Harvard, Annette will be down the street at Radcliffe, and, with God's help and our encouragement, they will fall in love."

Zada promptly realized that she had agreed to permit Aram to go to Harvard. Her apprehension that Aram was not yet ready to live among strangers did not go away, but it was tempered by the force of Ralph Nazarian's comments and by the awakening of the blissful memory of her own experiences living among strangers.

Chapter 28

Aram, Annette, and the Russos

While their parents were discussing an arranged marriage between them, Aram and Annette were having dinner with the Russo family. The cuisine was assuredly not Armenian but Italian—in abundant quantities. What Aram didn't know was that Annette and Theresa had organized a concerted Russo family assault on him with the objective of persuading him to go to Harvard. Mr. and Mrs. Russo were enlisted in this campaign. Even Dino's younger brothers, Anthony and Marco, ages twelve and ten, and his baby sister, Isabella, age six, were part of the plot. Only Dino demurred. He didn't think it was fair—or appropriate—for his entire family to try to tell Aram what his choice of college should be. But that evening, Dino was vastly outnumbered.

Almost as soon as the seven Russos and Aram and Annette sat down at the dinner table, after Mr. Russo had kissed each of his children and both of his guests, Anthony Russo said, "You know my brother Dino is going to City College. Where are you two going?"

Annette replied promptly, "I'll be going to Radcliffe College in Cambridge, Massachusetts."

"I never heard of that college," Mr. Russo said.

"It's an outstanding women's college associated with Harvard. Harvard College is all men, and Radcliffe is the female version," Dino contributed.

"That's interesting," said Mr. Russo. "Aram, my friend, I heard you got accepted by Harvard. That's fantastic. Harvard. They don't get any better than that."

Marco Russo added, "I heard that Harvard is the best college in America. You must be really smart, Aram."

"And it's so nice that you will be near Annette while the two of you are in college," said Mrs. Russo. "I think that's lovely."

"Are you going to play baseball for Harvard?" Anthony asked Aram.

"Well, I haven't decided yet whether to go to Harvard or to Columbia here in New York," Aram finally replied after remaining silent until that point in the conversation.

"What are you saying, Aram? You thinking of turning down Harvard?" Mr. Russo asked, sounding skeptical. "I never heard of such a thing." Mr. Russo was being emphatic about a subject that theretofore he had not spent one minute of his life thinking about.

"Not everyone who's accepted at Harvard decides to go there," Dino pointed out.

"Well, that's hard to believe. Who do you know who turned down Harvard?" Mr. Russo asked Dino. "Name one person you know."

"I can't name anybody, but there have to be people who choose to go someplace other than Harvard," Dino replied.

"So you don't know what the hell you're talking about," Mr. Russo shouted at Dino.

"Well, neither do you. You don't know the first damn thing about Harvard," Dino shouted back at his father.

At this point, Aram raised his voice and said, "Please, please, don't have a fight about this. This is not really about Harvard. It's about me and my mother. I would prefer to go to Harvard. I agree with what you said, Mr. Russo, and I appreciate that. But my mother wants me to stay in the city and live with her and my father. If I go away to Harvard, that will be very upsetting to my mother. Most of you have never met my mother. She doesn't speak English. She rarely goes out except to church. My father and I, and the church, are all she has in her life. But I must tell you, I have a really great mother. She has encouraged me and helped me in my school studies. She has even encouraged me in my baseball playing, although she doesn't have the slightest idea what baseball is about." Aram smiled for an instant and continued, "It would be painful to me to do anything that would hurt my mom. I just don't know what to do."

Dino said, "Aram, only you can decide what the right thing is for you to do. No one in this room can decide that for you. Certainly not my father, not your friends, not Annette. Although we all want the best thing for you, and we may have opinions, they're of no use to you. This is your life and your decision. Whatever you decide, everyone—including your mother and father—everyone will respect your decision."

Tears appeared in Aram's eyes. "This is so hard," he said.

Annette embraced him and wiped the tears from his face with her handkerchief. For the very first time, he thought that he might be able to love her.

"Mrs. Russo," Aram said, "this is one of the best meals I have ever eaten. I hope you'll ask me to come back here for another one. But I now have to take Annette back home."

"If I had a car, I would drive you," Mr. Russo said. "It's a long walk from here to Inwood. At least take the subway to Dyckman Street."

"Thanks, Mr. Russo. We'll be okay. It's a beautiful evening for a walk."

"We all thank you for coming here tonight," Mr. Russo said. "You're a beautiful couple."

"Thanks for having us."

Aram and Annette walked up Audubon Avenue toward Fort George Hill, holding hands.

After at least five minutes in which not a word was spoken, Aram said, "Annette, I've decided to go to Harvard. I hope my mother will understand."

Annette grasped his hand harder and then put her arm around his waist as they walked down the steep and winding street that led from Washington Heights to Inwood. Aram felt as though he was walking from boyhood to manhood. *I think I may be moving into manhood too quickly*, Aram thought. *It's scary, but it really is exciting.*

Chapter 29

Tragedy and Its Consequences

"What a wonderful family I have," Dino said as soon as Aram and Annette left the Russo apartment.

"We didn't do anything special," his father said.

"Okay, you're right. I don't have a wonderful family."

"Smart-ass."

They hugged. Dino thought he had the most wonderful father in the world.

———

On the first day of their first semester at City College, Bernie and Dino agreed to meet at the 191st Street subway station and ride together to begin their next career as college students. They both had elected to enroll in the liberal arts school. Bernie was pretty sure that he wanted to become a lawyer, although the only thing he knew about what lawyers did he learned one evening when he and Dino went downtown to watch drunks being arraigned in night court. It was not a stimulating experience, but he thought he could perform better than any of the lawyers in court that night. Dino, on the other hand, was uncertain as to a career objective and really had no idea what college had to offer him. That was why he decided on the liberal arts program rather than the business school division of City College.

After much consideration and in spite of the urging of the baseball coach, Dino decided not to play college baseball. He knew he was not good enough to play professional baseball, and he thought that devoting time to the college team would detract from his studies. However, those were not the real reasons for his decision not to play college baseball. Deep inside his mind was another thought. He wanted to preserve the boundless joy he experienced as one of the Infielders, that intimate circle of friends who played for the George Washington High School city championship team. Nothing he could possibly do as a college baseball player would ever come close to that experience. Continuing to play at the college level, he believed, would only dilute the sense of achievement and comradeship he derived from the glorious 1947 championship season. He wanted to cherish and preserve that feeling for the rest of his life.

Dino's academic performance at City College was better than his high school record. He never thought of himself as a strong student, but he began to rethink that point after receiving his first semester grades: two As, a B-plus, and a B. Everything seemed to be going well for Dino. He almost effortlessly found himself at the center of an interesting group of fellow students, some of whom he regarded to be real friends.

In a single instant during the spring semester, everything changed.

———

This was the obituary in the *Bronx Home News, Washington Heights Edition*, March 21, 1948:

Frank Russo of Washington Heights died unexpectedly of a heart attack on March 15, 1948, at 2:30 p.m. while working on a road construction project. He was 42 years old. He was born in Naples, Italy, on January 10, 1906, and was brought to America by his parents when they emigrated to the United States in 1908. They settled briefly in New Haven, Connecticut, and moved to New York City when Mr. Russo was still a boy. He attended public schools in New York until he was 16 years old, when he began to work as a laborer in a road construction company. He was later promoted to foreman, a job that he held until his death. He never missed a day of work. Mr. Russo married Bianca Gallo in 1929. They are the parents of five children, Bernardino, Theresa, Anthony, Marco and Isabella. Mr. Russo was beloved by his family. A mass of Christian burial was celebrated at St. Elizabeth Roman Catholic Church in Washington Heights, attended by his family and numerous friends.

At his father's funeral, Dino tried to console his mother, who was inconsolable. He, in turn, was consoled by Sean, Bernie and Aram. They talked about the championship game attended by Dino's father, whose shouting and cheering could be heard above all the crowd noise. Sean got a small smile out of Dino when he said that. But there was no way to make this right.

A claim for workers' compensation was rejected by the construction company for which Mr. Russo worked for twenty-seven years. The reason given for the rejection was that the heart attack was not occasioned by the work Mr. Russo was doing because he was a foreman and was not doing physically taxing work. Aram thought that was preposterous and urged Dino to appeal. Bernie was doubtful that there was a real possibility that the rejection could be reversed. None of them knew what he was talking about, and the discussion simply added to Dino's confusion and distress.

The company did give Mrs. Russo a check for one thousand dollars in recognition of her husband's years of faithful service. That would help pay the rent and put food on the table for several months. Dino had to find a job. He was the oldest son, and it was now his responsibility to support his mother, his sisters, and his brothers. There was no choice. College was over.

He thought he had no qualifications for any kind of job. After all, the only work he had ever done for pay was grunt work, literally digging ditches for the construction company where his father worked. That was where he thought he would have to go to ask for a job. He made a mental list of his accomplishments:

He graduated from George Washington High School with an 85.4 average, which was almost in the top quarter of the class. He was captain of the city championship baseball team. He played shortstop and made only one error in eighteen games. He couldn't remember his exact batting average, but it was over.300. He was— he believed—the leader of a circle of very close friends who called themselves the Infielders. He made friends easily.

What a paltry list of qualifications for a real job in a real business in which people wore suits! He thought his mind wasn't working properly.

He had a good idea. He went to see his economics professor at City College, who had given Dino an A in the first semester basic course. Professor Rosen thought Dino would be good at sales and arranged an interview for him with a distributor of long-playing records. *Maybe this isn't a good time to have a job interview. I'm wearing sneakers, dungarees, and a ratty shirt. My mind is a mess, and my clothes are a mess. This can't turn out well. I should go home. My mother needs me. I miss my father. I slept late the morning he went to work for the last time. He didn't kiss me. Maybe he did while I was sleeping. I'll never get this job anyway, no matter what my economics professor thinks.*

He walked around the campus to see if he could find Bernie. It was almost lunchtime, and he knew Bernie usually brought his brown bag to the cafeteria. He dashed down the hall to the cafeteria and found Bernie seated with a bunch of students—mostly girls. Dino rushed to that table and said, "Sorry to break up your party, but I need Bernie to come with me."

Sensing that something important was going on with his friend Dino, something undoubtedly connected to the recent and tragic death of his father, Bernie immediately jumped to his feet, grabbed hold of Dino's arm, and said, "What do you need?"

"I need you to come with me to a job interview."

———

Sitting on the subway, speeding in a direction he wasn't sure was the right direction, perspiring, thinking negatively, frightened, grieving, Dino explained to Bernie what Professor Rosen had done for him. Bernie tried to get Dino to calm down, but Dino continued to be agitated. In a voice that was nearly a shout, confusing the people sitting around him, Dino declared, "I have to do this. I'm going to do this." He stood up and walked to the subway route map posted near one of the exit doors. He decided to get off this train at Times Square, take the shuttle to Grand Central Station, and walk from there down Lexington Avenue to 31st Street. The fresh air and the eleven-block walk would clear his head. "If you have half a brain, you don't have to get lost on the subway," he said to Bernie.

Bernie agreed. As the two young men walked south on Lexington Avenue, Bernie did everything he could to try to get Dino into a more natural and composed state of mind. "It's important that this guy see you as someone in control of himself . . . as a rational person. Which, of course, you are. More than I am, by far. You always make a good impression when you're your natural self. Remember that. Think about what the guy is talking about and tell him what he wants to hear. You're going in there carrying a strong recommendation from a professor who knows this guy and his business. You're not just some guy walking in off the street looking for a job."

"And," Bernie continued, "I ain't going in there with you. The last thing you need is a character witness. I'll wait outside for you. No matter how long it takes." They reached 31st Street and found the address of the record company.

Bernie waited outside the building for Dino to return from the interview. Only five minutes later, Dino was back on the street with Bernie.

"The guy asked me if we had a hi-fi at home. I had no idea what he meant. I asked him, and he said, 'If you don't know what that means, you can't possibly do this job.' He asked me to leave. So much for the professor's brilliant advice. I'm going to go to the construction company and see if I can get work."

"Before you do that, we should talk with Aram and Sean. They're both home."

"What good would that do? Neither of them has ever worked a day in his life."

Bernie insisted, "It can't do any harm. You never know. Let's go back to the Heights and try to find them, especially Aram."

They went to Aram's apartment and had a serious discussion

about Dino's problem. Almost immediately, Aram came to the rescue. "My father owns the Chevrolet dealership on Broadway. I'll bet he'll hire you as a salesman. That's something you'd be great at."

"The only problem," Dino responded, "is that I don't know how to drive, and I know nothing about cars. I've hardly ever been in one."

"That's a very small problem," Bernie interjected. "Aram's father can teach you everything you need to know, including how to drive."

"Why would he go to all that trouble?" Dino asked.

Aram and Bernie simultaneously responded, "Because you're an Infielder."

They were absolutely right. Mr. Petrosian was happy to give Dino a job and become his driving teacher and tutor for everything he had to know about automotive mechanics. He even bought Dino a suit to wear in the showroom.

It didn't take a very long time before Dino became the most productive salesman at Petrosian Chevrolet. He was a natural salesman. He had an intuitive understanding of what a prospective customer was looking for when he walked into the showroom. Mr. Petrosian was astounded by Dino's ability to transform a prospect into a customer, often at the sticker price of the vehicle.

All of this couldn't have come at a better time. Eleven months after Dino stepped onto the showroom floor of Petrosian Motors and sold his first car, Hagop Petrosian suffered what his doctors called a ministroke. Although the symptoms of a ministroke tend to resolve within minutes of the episode, the doctors advised Mr. Petrosian that he was at risk for the occurrence at some point in his life of a debilitating major stroke. The blurred vision, difficulty speaking, dizziness, and severe headache that were the symptoms of the ministroke were frightening enough to cause Mr. Petrosian to convene what he called a "family counsel."

Aram and Annette, Mrs. Petrosian—and Dino—were summoned to the Petrosian apartment. In both Armenian and English, Hagop Petrosian announced that he had decided to cut back substantially the number of hours he devoted to the business of selling Chevrolets. With great solemnity, he said, "God has given me a signal that I must no longer be a slave to my business, and, in his infinite mercy, he has given me the means to free myself from the burdens of making money. In his infinite wisdom, he called Dino's father to be with him in heaven, and as a result, Dino came to me and brought his great talents and skills with him. It would be a sin not to accept that gift. Dino, if you agree, I will appoint you as general manager of Petrosian Motors so that my beloved wife and I can enjoy our lives without worrying about the dealership. I know that in your hands, the business will thrive."

Mrs. Petrosian was elated to hear this news. Aram was privately surprised and embarrassed by his father's unexpected religiosity and the pomposity of his speech, but nevertheless, he thought his father's decision was a good thing for his parents and, of course, for Dino.

Annette was skeptical. She said to Mr. Petrosian, "I understand the motivation for your decision, but I wonder if you will be able to fully enjoy life without real involvement in the business that has occupied you for years. I'm sure Dino will do an excellent job managing the business. That's not what concerns me. I'm concerned about you. What will you do with all the time you used to fill up with your business responsibilities? Despite the ministroke, you're still young and vital. You won't be happy sitting by a swimming pool or learning to play golf."

"My dear Annette," he replied in Armenian so that his wife could understand, "you are brilliant and beautiful, but there is still much about life that you have yet to learn. You're right that I wouldn't be happy sitting by a swimming pool or—worse yet—playing golf, but I have Zada, my precious wife, with whom I have spent far too little time while building the business. Don't worry, my dear. I am looking forward to a wonderful life."

Zada Petrosian beamed.

Chapter 30

Bernie and Family

The Hellers were not a happy family. Bernie was their pride and joy, but the lives of his parents were permanently deformed by their abrupt flight from Nazi Germany one year after Hitler came to power. Mr. Heller had owned a small but prosperous business in Frankfurt that manufactured insoles for shoes. He had the foresight—that many of his fellow religiously observant Jews in Germany regrettably failed to grasp—that the Nazi regime posed a lethal threat to the lives of German Jews—even those who, like Mr. Heller, served honorably in the German army during World War I. He picked up his family and a few personal items that the Nazi regime allowed them to retain, left his business, his house, and the comfortable life that his family had enjoyed for generations in Germany, and sailed in steerage to New York. Mr. Heller's mother's brother—Uncle Erwin Ludwig—owned a kosher butcher store on St. Nicholas Avenue in Washington Heights. It was Ludwig's sponsorship and the offer of employment in the store that enabled the Heller family to enter the United States at a time when the gates to freedom and safety were closing.

The perpetual gloom that hung over the Heller household was intensified by the condition of Bernie's older brother, Werner. Werner had both physical and mental problems. He was deaf in one ear, a failure in school, and, worst of all, he was prone to psychotic eruptions of rage that were terrifying to Bernie when he was young and disgusting to him when he grew older. About the only thing that seemed to interest Werner was pictures of naked women. Bernie wondered where the supply of those pictures came from since Werner rarely left the apartment. Bernie suspected his father but was unable to understand his father's motive for providing those pictures and magazines to Werner. Perhaps it was the only thing he could give to his older son that would be appreciated.

Werner was rejected by the draft board, and consequently, he was virtually the only man of his age in the neighborhood who wasn't in the armed forces during the war. Werner hung around the house all day almost every day, and his unsettling presence added to the oppressive atmosphere of the Heller apartment. Bernie felt that living in the same apartment with his brother was an undeserved punishment, and he resented it bitterly. Bernie's bitterness added to the despair that his parents endured. He was aware of that and felt an occasional pang of guilt when he saw his mother weeping silently as she held Werner's hand. He could not help feeling the way he did.

Bernie's parents observed Jewish laws and customs as best they could in the United States, just as they did in Germany before Hitler. Mr. Heller regularly attended services at Congregation Gates of Israel on 185th Street between St. Nick and Audubon. He attended the daily early morning service in the synagogue except when the weather made it difficult to walk the four blocks from home to the shul. "Shul" was the only word he ever used to refer to the synagogue building. In bad weather, he prayed the morning service at home, wearing his prayer shawl called a tallis and binding his arm and forehead with soft black leather straps that held small black boxes in which certain verses from the Bible were inscribed on parchment. When Bernie was about five years old, he started watching his father say those morning prayers on rainy days and found the ritual—especially the leather straps—confusing and frightening. His father prayed only in Hebrew, which sounded like gibberish to Bernie. His father tried to instruct Bernie in the observance of the basic rules binding on all Jews: what to eat (and more importantly what not to eat) and what to do (and more importantly what not to do) on Saturday, a day his father called "Shabbos." An intelligent and sensitive man grieving over the murder of his parents by the Nazis and sorely troubled by the condition of his older son, Werner, Bernie's father placed his hopes for a fulfilled and worthy life in his bright younger son. Bernie's childhood indifference to his Judaism clouded those hopes. Although enrolled in the afternoon Hebrew school at Gates of Israel, Bernie frequently missed classes and paid little attention when he was present. He did manage to learn to read Hebrew, an accomplishment that gave his father a measure of joy.

When Bernie became a serious baseball player, he decided, with a certainty born of immaturity and ignorance, that he didn't want to be a Jew. His announcement of this decision to his parents was hurtful to them, and they said so. He considered his parents' expectations of him to be unreasonable, foolish, and hurtful. The schism in his relationship with his parents was never healed until years later, on the day that Bernie had raced home with the news that his father's indictment had been rescinded. Neither Bernie nor his parents would ever forget that Bernie joined his family that evening for Sabbath dinner. That was Bernie's first step on the road back to the traditions of his ancestors. But the dissonance within the Heller family was too deep to be cured with one joyous dinner.

It was inevitable that Bernie would seize every opportunity to get out of his house. Bernie's efforts to separate himself from his home life may well have led to his early precocity with girls. His youthful sex life was a highly effective distraction from the problems in his home. But girls also provided Bernie with venues where he could do his high school homework and study. He was a bright and engaging young man, and the girls welcomed the opportunity to have him in their homes as a study partner.

And then, of course, there was baseball and the circle of infielders. As much as Sean, Aram, and Dino valued the friendships that were formed among the Infielders, none of them cherished those relationships as much as Bernie did. It was not in Bernie's nature—demonstrative and outgoing as he was—to display his feelings to the Infielders about how precious their relationship was to him. To have done so—to Bernie's way of thinking—would have undermined his manly self-image. He was the least effusive of the four when it came to the group hugs that occurred frequently among them. They might not have realized it, but for Bernie, the Infielders gave him that sense of belonging that rightfully should have been the gift of his family.

Baseball and then college and law school were Bernie's places of refuge until he was able to establish a modest law practice somewhere—he hoped—other than Washington Heights. His sexual adventures were as much about escape from the melancholy of his family as the passion in his loins.

Chapter 31

Bernie in the Army

It was never clear to Bernie why it made sense for the United States of America to select him as the only one of the Infielders to be drafted while in college to serve in the nation's army. Bernie had heard that Sean Flaherty was determined to be physically unfit for military service because of a heart murmur detected during his physical exam. Bernie suspected that the heart murmur might have been a gratuitous favor to the Boston Braves organization. It was obvious that Dino would not be drafted; he was the sole support of his large family. Aram had received a student deferment. Okay, he was a student. But Bernie had just received notice from the local draft board to report for a physical exam.

He called Aram to discuss his exemption from the draft.

"What did you do to get deferred?" he asked.

"I applied," Aram replied.

"So did I," said Bernie, interrupting Aram.

"And I took and passed the test," Aram continued.

"What test?" asked Bernie.

"The test that you have to pass to show that you're a real higher education student. I could have passed that test in our first term in high school."

"I didn't know about any test. When was it given?"

"I think it was the day after we won the championship. No. It was the day after graduation. Maybe the next day."

"Shit, I forgot all about it. I was too busy celebrating. I'll call them. Thanks."

"I think it may be too late. Good luck," said Aram.

It was too late. Bernie was drafted into the US Army and assigned to Fort Dix, New Jersey, for basic infantry training. Two wasted years. *How could I be so stupid*, he thought.

Bernie turned out to be a pretty good soldier. His basic training platoon sergeant recognized Bernie's relative maturity among the new recruits and named him as one of the squad leaders. Bernie brought his baseball skills into the army. The eye that could hit a fastball could aim a rifle. He earned an expert medal for a very high marksmanship score with an M1 rifle. The sure-handedness that made him an excellent third baseman proved useful in advanced infantry training. He excelled in the use of a range of weapons, from machine guns to mortars to hand grenades.

He actually enjoyed playing soldier. It introduced a system of discipline that was missing from his personal profile. By the end of his tour of duty (entirely in the US), he was promoted to corporal and invited to go to Officers Candidate School. He declined that invitation and went back to New York and into law school.

Chapter 32

Bernie in Law School

Students at Brooklyn Law School either commuted to the school from their homes in various places in New York or lived in rented apartments within walking distance from the school. The school itself had no residence facilities.

Bernie Heller envied those students who lived near the school. The two hours a day that he spent on the subway were boring and burdensome. And, worse yet, living in his parents' apartment in Washington Heights, sleeping in the same bed, eating at the same kitchen table, studying at the same rickety desk, and surrounded by the same people he was surrounded by since his earliest childhood—all of this had grown beyond the limits of his tolerance by the time he completed his first year at Brooklyn Law School.

Together with two other law students, Bernie rented an apartment in a brownstone building near the law school. That solved the commuting problem and the problem of living with his parents and his brother. But it created the problem of having to find the money with which to pay his share of the rent and to buy food and other necessities that his parents provided for free. Never shy or retiring, Bernie went directly to the dean of the law school, Dean Herbert Farber, for help in finding part-time employment. He came away from that meeting with an opportunity to apply for a research assistant position with a professor who was writing a treatise on electric and gas company regulation throughout the United States.

When Bernie pointed out to the dean that he didn't know the first thing about electric and gas company regulation, the dean responded, "You're not alone. That's why she's writing the treatise."

"She?" Bernie asked.

"Yes, *she*. Professor Marshall is one of the first female law professors in the United States. She's absolutely brilliant. I think you'll enjoy working with her."

"Dean Farber, if she's so brilliant, do you really think I can keep up with her? Keep up with her needs, I mean?"

"I wouldn't recommend you to her if I didn't think you could. Go see her and talk it over. Her office is down the hall. Room 208. I'll phone her and tell her to expect you. It's the school policy to pay research assistants by the hour. Two dollars an hour." Bernie wasn't delighted with that rate. He'd need at least fifteen hours a week of work to cover his expenses.

The idea of a woman lawyer, no less a woman law professor, was perplexing to Bernie. Bernie's confident, almost cocky, approach to women was limited to young, naïve girls—girls with whom he was always the dominant party. The idea of working for —being an assistant to—a "brilliant" woman was disconcerting to him. He realized that he was actually afraid to knock on Professor Marshall's office door. But he had no choice. He needed the money, and he needed it badly. He would simply have to confront his anxiety and go to work for a female professor. He knocked on her door and heard her call from the other side of the door, inviting him into her office. The room was scarcely larger than a closet, awash with books on the floor, the windowsill, the desk, the spare wooden chair, and bookshelves reaching almost to the ceiling.

When he entered her office, Professor Lucille Marshall was standing on a chair reaching—stretching, actually—for a book on the top shelf of a bookcase above the window on the far wall of the room. Her back was toward him, and she was silhouetted against the sunshine coming through the window. *She has nice legs* was the first thought to form in Bernie's head, followed immediately by the question *How old is she?*

Professor Marshall found the book she was looking for, blew the dust off it, and extended a hand to Bernie for help in stepping down from the chair she was standing on. The touch of her hand set off two simultaneous jolts in Bernie's body—a stirring in his groin and an alarm signal in his brain. She smiled at Bernie, and her smile pleased him.

Bernie's sex life had been in a severe slump since he got out of the army and started law school. He literally didn't have the time to give the attention it deserved to that extremely important subject. Because the law school had no female students, there was no readily accessible population of prospective sex partners. Bernie had exhausted his inventory of girlfriends because no one he had met at City College came close to satisfying his exacting specifications for a long-term relationship. In law school, many of Bernie's fellow students had already established relationships with young women who were likely to become their wives, and a few, mostly war veterans, were already married. Barbara Gordon had been the only female in Bernie's life with whom he ever contemplated a "steady" relationship, and even with Barbara, the subject of marriage was never mentioned. Bernie rarely even thought about it. In any event, Barbara had married a guy whom she had met at a synagogue dance. Bernie elected not to attempt to win her back, thinking there were other opportunities awaiting him that were not as labor intensive as an assault on Barbara's marriage would be.

He later regretted that decision as he found himself in his second year at law school and leading an involuntarily celibate existence. Who would have thought that at this point in Bernie's life, Sean Flaherty would be seriously involved with that hot little Russo girl, and Aram—sweet, gentle little Aram—was probably spending five nights a week with Annette. He assumed Dino was still being adored by every girl in the Heights. And he, Bernie Heller, the Casanova of the Heights, would be alone in a room in Brooklyn? And, worse yet, he had been sexually stimulated by a middle-aged law teacher whose hand he had touched.

Professor Lucille Marshall was a plain-looking woman who appeared to be in her forties but might have been even older. She wore eyeglasses but no makeup. When Bernie first saw her, she was wearing a brown skirt, a white blouse, and a tan cardigan sweater. There was nothing in her appearance that could account for the stirring in Bernie's groin. Could it merely have been the touch of her hand that had aroused him? *No*, he concluded, *it was her smile. This is ridiculous*, Bernie thought. *An old woman with nothing to offer but a pleasing smile.* But then he thought, *Why is that nothing?* He was no longer a sexually precocious adolescent for whom women were nothing more than playthings. That was his rationalization in his search for an explanation of the attraction he felt for Professor Marshall. Why would a mature and intelligent woman not be precisely what he needed in a relationship at this point in his life?

"So, you're the Mr. Heller of whom Dean Farber spoke so highly. I've been waiting for you to show up. Welcome to the cave in which I am writing a legal masterpiece. Please see if you can find a flat surface on which to sit down amid this jungle of books and papers."

"You don't have to call me Mr. Heller. I'm just a second-year law student, and I wouldn't know a legal masterpiece if it fell on my head. My name is Bernie."

"In that case, my name is Lucille." She sat down on the chair from which Bernie had helped her climb down when she was standing on it. The only other chair in the tiny room was facing Professor Marshall's seat, so when Bernie sat on it, his knees and hers were just inches apart.

"I want to explain to you what we will be doing while we work together. I'm at the point in my writing where virtually all of my research has been done, and the results of that research have been summarized and are right at my elbow, so to speak, as I type my manuscript. That's where you come in. I'll tell you what the point is I'm trying to make, and I'll ask you to find a case or a ruling that supports that point. You won't have to start from scratch. My research notes are at your disposal. Well, I don't really mean that literally. I'll be very put out if you *dispose* of my notes."

She looked squarely at Bernie's blank face and said, "That was supposed to be a joke, Bernie, and you were supposed to laugh. Or, at the very least, smile at my witticism. People around here think I'm very funny."

"I'll try to remember to smile or even giggle the next time you say something funny."

"Good. I'm counting on that. Anyway, my research notes will be available to you, and you will dig through them to find the case or other authority that supports my point. Do you think you can manage to take on that responsibility?"

"I don't really know. I've never done anything like that. But I'd like to try, and I'll certainly do my best to be helpful to you."

Professor Marshall reached out and squeezed Bernie's leg just above his knee and exclaimed, "Wonderful! That's all I can ask of you—at least when it comes to our work together. How much time can you give me? I am falling behind the schedule I've made for completing this work, and I'm literally working night and day. I can use all the time that you can possibly spare to work closely with me."

"Well, except for my classes and reading cases for those classes, I don't have much else going on in my life right now," Bernie said.

"That describes my life, too. It seems as if we were made for each other, Bernie. Here are my phone numbers for this office and my home. Call me whenever you have time available to work with me, and I'll let you know if I'm here or when I expect to be here. I look forward to seeing a lot of you. And I hope you'll enjoy the time you spend with me. Really enjoy it, I mean."

"Me, too, Professor."

"Lucille, please."

"Okay, me too, Lucille."

Wait just a minute, Bernie said to himself as he listened to the alarm signal in his brain. *She's a teacher, and I'm a student at the same law school. Can anything bad happen to either of us if we start fucking each other? I must be growing up. I never used to worry about such things.*

A taste for adventure can be as dangerous as it is delicious.

Chapter 33

Bernie and Dino

Bernie called Dino to bounce the Professor Marshall situation off him. He thought that Dino might have some sage advice for him.

Dino seemed very pleased when Bernie called him. "I've got two tickets to the stadium for the game against the White Sox this Saturday night. Why don't we go to the game together? We can talk during and after."

"Wonderful idea," Bernie replied. "Remember when baseball was our whole life?"

"I miss those days. Life was so much simpler."

"Don't I know it! Where should we meet? I know you don't still live in your old house."

"Has it been that long since we've seen each other? I haven't lived there in three years. I moved into a nice apartment in Riverdale. Why don't you come to my place Saturday afternoon? We can have lunch together and schmooze and then go to the game. Hey, Bernie, I'm so glad you called. I can't wait to see you."

"Me too. Tell me, how's your mother?"

"She aged twenty years the day my father died. She's become like an old woman. She looks old and acts old. Bernie, you wouldn't recognize her today. That woman who used to be so full of life. No more. That all ended when my father died. It breaks my heart. How about your parents?"

"Ever since we managed to get that ridiculous indictment dismissed, my father's like a new man. My uncle made him a full partner in the butcher store. That convinces me my uncle was the real guilty party in that rationing scheme. Of course, Dad's getting old, and he's got aches and pains. He's still strictly Orthodox, but I'm happy to say that he's a more cheerful man than I ever remember him being. He takes good care of my mother. She's not aging as well as him. It's because of Werner, my brother. We had to put him in a home—really a psychiatric hospital. His behavior became more and more weird and dangerous over the last couple of years. It's costing my father a fortune. Every family has its own tragedy, Dino, as you well know."

"Yes, that's true. I'm sorry to hear about your mom. Look, write this down. My address is 625 West 247th Street in the Bronx, Apartment 6C. Come about twelve thirty, and we'll have a great day together."

"You've really come up in the world. From 186th to 247th. Sixty-one blocks. That's what I call an upward move. I'll see you on Saturday."

At lunch on Saturday at a pleasant little Italian restaurant with views out to the Hudson River and the Palisade Cliffs of New Jersey, the two young men reminisced about their high school baseball team. How sweet those memories were.

"That beautiful apartment you live in looks like you're as good at selling cars as playing shortstop," Bernie said.

"Yeah, I guess I'm a pretty good salesman. I make a living, which is more than I can say for some of Petrosian's other salesmen. It's a tough business. You know, I have to support my mother and my younger brothers."

"So, tell me, Dino, you got a girlfriend?"

"No, I'm still licking my Rachel wounds. Look, it's not because I want to change the subject, Bernie, but when you called me, you said you wanted my advice on a personal matter. Tell me about it."

Bernie lit a cigarette and said, "Do you remember the speech you gave our team before the championship game in '47? The speech in which you said my greatest challenge in life was keeping my pants on?"

"I sure do remember it. I hope you're not going to tell me you knocked up a girl."

"Quite the opposite, Dino. Quite the opposite. I haven't had sex with anyone since I started law school."

"If that's true, I'm going to call the *Daily News*. They'll put it on the front page. Big headline: *Heller Keeps Pants On!* That's hilarious. I've got to call Aram and Sean and tell them you've given up sex. Wait, here's ten bucks. Go find a streetwalker in Times Square."

"I'll bear that in mind, Dino. But listen, my problem is more complicated. Listen to this. My law school fixed me up with a job because I needed money after I moved out of my parents' house. You remember you used to think girls didn't become lawyers. And I said I thought the same thing."

"Bernie, can't you stay on one subject. I'm getting confused. Is this about sex or money or girl lawyers?"

"Please listen. The job I have is research assistant to a law professor who happens to be a woman who has the hots for me. She's about forty years old, maybe even older."

"Oh, now that's interesting. Have you done anything with her?"

"Not yet. That's my question. Do you think I should?

"No."

"Why not?"

"It's a terrible idea. It could ruin your life and definitely her life. Don't do it."

"Dino, you don't realize how horny I am."

"Oh yes I do, my friend—I remember you in high school! Nevertheless, screwing a professor is just too risky. For you and for her. For you, because she's likely to scream 'rape' after it's over."

"I knew it was a good idea to come to you with this problem. You've given me a lot to think about, and I thank you for that. I really mean it."

"You're more than welcome. Let's go to the stadium early so we can watch batting practice. It's a beautiful day."

There is hardly a more beautiful place on a sunny late afternoon in the early spring than Yankee Stadium. The meticulously mowed expanse of emerald grass, the elegance of the storied grandstands with their embroidered borders, the graceful athletes in their glistening white uniforms, and the soft buzz of excitement as the spectators file in to fill the seats—these were to Dino Russo and Bernie Heller like paradise. Although neither continued to play baseball, even casually, the sport still occupied a large space in their memories and in how they identified themselves. When Dino greeted Bernie at the door to his new apartment in Riverdale, his first words had been "Well, Bernie, at least half of the Infielders are here."

His visit with Dino was truly enjoyable. Dino paid for lunch at the nice restaurant and for the four hot dogs and four beers that they consumed at Yankee Stadium while Whitey Ford pitched a shutout for the Yankees. Bernie didn't envy Dino's apparent economic success, but he vowed to himself to try to emulate it.

Chapter 34

Bernie in Law School

Part 2

On the subway ride back to Brooklyn, Bernie began to wonder exactly what he had learned from Dino about his problem with Professor Marshall. Nothing, actually. *If I was turned on by a plain-looking forty-something woman*, he thought, *then my body was telling me that she could satisfy me.* "And I sure as hell can satisfy her. I'll bet she hasn't had a good lay in years."

An elderly man in a suit with a white shirt and tie and shined shoes sitting across from Bernie grinned and said, "Go for it, kid." Bernie realized he must have spoken his thoughts out loud. He grinned back at the man, only slightly embarrassed.

He resumed his thinking about the professor, making sure that he kept those thoughts to himself and didn't share them with his fellow passengers. By the time he arrived back at his room in the apartment near the law school, Bernie had pretty well convinced himself that he should accept Professor Marshall's invitation to become her lover. He actually had himself convinced that it was an act of courtesy—almost an act of kindness—to respond to that invitation. It would be a good deed, although he laughed out loud when he concluded that there probably was no Boy Scout merit badge for fucking a plain-looking middle-aged teacher. That evening he phoned the professor at her home to schedule time to work with her during the upcoming week. Tuesday, then Thursday and Friday, were the days that she wanted—"eagerly," she said—to see him in her office.

If she was eager, Bernie was breathless. In his entire career as the playboy of Washington Heights, he never approached an assignation with the excitement that he felt in the days leading to Tuesday. He phoned Dino to tell him what he had decided. Dino—with a notable lack of enthusiasm—wished him luck.

What's eating him, Bernie wondered. *I have no obligation to follow his advice. Sometimes I think Dino is too full of himself. Like he knows everything. When it comes to women, I've forgotten more than Dino will ever know. The hell with Dino! I'm going to do what I want to do.*

Now, the question is tactics. How do I do this so it works out perfectly, for both me and the professor? I mean Lucille. I'll let Tuesday just take its own course, be cool and calm, and see what she says and does. If she comes on to me, I just let it happen. But I think she is too mature to start taking her clothes off or something crazy like that. I'll play a bit hard to get. Make her hungry and thirsty, make her want me more and more. That always works. Tuesday's the day.

It turned out that Tuesday *was* the day, but not exactly the type of day Bernie had in mind. In the early afternoon, freshly shaved and doused with Old Spice aftershave, Bernie knocked on the door of Professor Marshall's office. He was surprised—and pleased—to see that the professor was more smartly dressed than she was the previous time he saw her. She was wearing a pleated skirt and a pink blouse, the top two buttons of which were unbuttoned, revealing a hint of cleavage. She was not wearing the cardigan sweater that she had on the last time, and he saw that she had an ampler bosom than he had imagined.

The professor greeted him with a warm and inviting smile. "Thank you for coming, Bernie. I really need you today. I hope you're prepared for some heavy-duty work."

"I'm at your disposal, Professor—I mean Lucille. Just tell me what to do, and I'll do it," he said as he lit a cigarette.

"I see you smoke Pall Malls. That was my brand the last time I gave up smoking. I give up smoking several times a month." They both chuckled. "Do you think I might have one of yours?"

"By all means." He shook a cigarette from the pack and handed it to Lucille. She put it between her lips. Bernie struck a match, and, as he lit the cigarette, she placed her hands on each side of his extended hand as if to shield the flame from a nonexistent breeze. Instantly, his sexual desire surged. As Lucille removed the cigarette from between her lips to exhale her first puff of smoke, Bernie placed his right hand behind her head, drew her toward him, and kissed her. Instantly, Professor Marshall pushed Bernie's chest with what must have been all her strength. She twisted her body away from him and slapped his face with the hand that held the cigarette, dropping the cigarette on the floor.

With a voice that was somewhere between a shriek and a groan, she exclaimed, "What on earth do you think you're doing, Mr. Heller? How dare you assault me that way? I should report this to the dean and have you expelled from the law school." She quivered with anger and indignation.

Bernie was stunned. He'd been turned down before but never as vehemently, as violently, as Professor Marshall's rejection. He was more than disappointed—far more. He was shocked, and he was angry. He absolutely believed that she had invited his advance. If she changed her mind, that didn't give her the right to make him feel like a rapist.

"You made me do it," Bernie shouted. "You made me think you wanted it."

"Oh my God. Is that what you think?"

"That's exactly what I think. All those little innuendos you've been throwing around. What did you expect me to think?" Bernie went on the offensive. "I should report *you* to the dean."

Lucille stared at him for a few moments, then turned, walked to the window, and stood there looking vacantly down to the street. "What a clumsy, inept woman I am," she said, more to herself than to Bernie. She sat down on the chair near her desk, the one she was standing on when Bernie first saw her. She then sighed and addressed Bernie directly. "I probably should just ask you to leave. I should tell the dean that I need a new research assistant . . . that it didn't work out with you. But I feel that I need to clear the air in here. Can we talk for a few minutes?"

"Sure, why not? I think we should."

"I've not had a lot of success with my research assistants. Without exception, they seemed to be indifferent to the work we were doing. When Dean Farber recommended you, he said you were a good student. But more than that, he said you had a lively personality and an engaging manner about you. I decided I would try to break with my normal stuffy personality and attempt to establish a friendly relationship with you. My hope was that it would help us to work collaboratively and, thus, more productively than was possible with my other research assistants. I hoped I could make you a partner in the work on my treatise. I hope you don't think this insulting, but a romantic relationship was the furthest thing from my mind. I find that I'm using the word 'hope' a lot. What happened a few minutes ago shattered those hopes."

She began to weep. "I am such a clumsy woman, such a helpless fool when it comes to dealing with people. That's why I spend my life in this horrid room writing about utilities regulation."

Professor Marshall's anguish seemed real. He was moved by it but was unable to formulate an appropriate response. Too much had happened too quickly. He was still standing on the spot where he stood when he kissed her. Before he could think of anything to say, he smelled smoke and looked down at the floor where some loose papers were smoldering, ignited by the dropped cigarette.

This was becoming a farce. He stomped on the smoldering papers and prevented a fire from breaking out. That task, easy as it was, seemed to clarify the chaotic thoughts racing through his mind.

"Professor Marshall, I feel worse about this than you do. And it's obvious that you are very upset. Let's start with what I did wrong. I totally misread your attempt to create a friendly atmosphere in this room. That's partially because I have been sexually inactive since starting law school, and to be perfectly honest, I was horny. That's a slang word for sexually needy."

"I know the word," Professor Marshall said in a soft voice with a hint of a smile on her face.

"So, it's not your fault that I misunderstood what you were doing. I had a need, and I shaped your words and actions to fit my needs. I am really sorry that I did what I did. I hope you can forgive me."

"I do."

"Thanks. But you sent out signals that could be misinterpreted. Like why did you have to hold my hand when I was lighting your cigarette? I don't think you know enough about men."

"Oh, Bernie, you're certainly right about that. I married my high school sweetheart when I was twenty-one. We were utterly incompatible. I was an intellectual, and he dropped out of college to become a professional bowler. Neither of us had the slightest understanding of what the other one was all about. He left me for a woman he met in a bar, and we were divorced after a year and a half of a pretty empty marriage. Since then, I've been consumed by the study of law. To be as candid as I can be, I purposely immersed myself in my studies. I found the law to be a challenge, but I could just as easily have buried myself in ancient history or Russian literature. I said I had been in an empty marriage. Bernie, I have an empty life. But I can't use you to fix my life. That would be an inexcusable abuse on my part. I must say, though, that I am rather pleased that a twenty-year-old boy found me sexually attractive."

"I'm twenty-four."

"Excuse me. A young man of twenty-four who is quite good-looking. Bernie, I appreciate what you've said. We've both made mistakes."

"That's bullshit. Whatever you did wrong was innocent. If forgiveness is necessary, you have to forgive yourself because there's no one else in this room who thinks you did anything bad."

"Bernie, do you think we can still work together?"

"I don't see why not. I'm adult enough to have a platonic working relationship with a truly interesting woman who told me more about herself than I had a right to know."

"Well, you told me you were horny. But I suppose I could have figured that out myself."

Bernie smiled and said, "We didn't get much work done today. How about we work tomorrow?"

Bernie and Professor Marshall worked together on her treatise for two years. They had an awkward personal relationship but a successful working one. When the treatise, *Marshall on Utilities Regulation,* was published, it contained an acknowledgement that read "I am particularly grateful for the assistance and invaluable insights of my research assistant, Bernie Heller, a student at Brooklyn Law School."

Notwithstanding the distractions, Bernie did well as a student at Brooklyn Law School. He graduated with honors and passed the New York bar exam on his first attempt.

Chapter 35

Aram and Annette

In Paradise . . . Almost

The decision Aram made to go to Harvard carried with it more benefits than he could have imagined. Aram thrived in his years at Harvard. He continued to display the academic brilliance that he demonstrated at George Washington High School. He graduated Magna Cum Laude with a double major in English and Philosophy. He was elected to Phi Beta Kappa. And to top all that, he tried out, albeit unsuccessfully, for Harvard's varsity baseball team. He did play second base for the junior varsity. Aram Petrosian flourished at Harvard.

He had no difficulty living away from home "among all those strangers," as his mother feared. Many of those strangers became his friends and companions. And then there was Annette. The tentative and uncertain relationship he had with Annette in high school grew in importance. First, he became—as he put it—"fond" of her. She became part of his circle of companions in Cambridge as he became part of hers. They saw each other with increasing frequency in their freshman years at Harvard and Radcliffe. Aram was not intuitively romantic; he needed instruction in the art of love. Annette provided that instruction with intelligence, tact, tenderness, and affection. They became a couple. All of their friends expected to find them together—even when he was playing baseball, she was in the stands.

It didn't happen in an instant. There was no sudden flash of inspiration. It just evolved, and ultimately, Aram realized that he was in love with Annette, and he told her so. The two sets of parents were pleased that their children would continue their education in Cambridge where they would be able to continue seeing each other on a regular basis. What they didn't know was just how regular that basis would be. Aram and Annette had agreed, secretly, to move into a furnished apartment off campus and live together during the next chapter of their lives. The couple debated whether to tell their parents about this, and they decided that doing so would complicate their lives and possibly dilute the joy that their parents were feeling. That joy was so tangible, so intense that Aram and Annette could feel it washing over them, and they took delight in it.

Eventually, they made love. It seemed to both of them that sex was an integral and inevitable part of what was happening between them. Their lovemaking techniques were clumsy, and that made them laugh at themselves. Aram suggested that they get an authoritative instruction book, a suggestion that made Annette laugh even more. "I think we might be better off calling Bernie Heller," she said with a straight face.

"I couldn't possibly do that," Aram replied, making Annette laugh again.

"You are so impossibly literal. Did you ever hear the words *irony* or *sarcasm* in any of those courses you took at Harvard?"

"You're mocking me again. You must enjoy that."

"Oh, I do. And you are so mockable. That's one of the things I love about you."

"Well," Aram said, "do you have any suggestions other than calling Bernie?"

"Absolutely," she replied. "Practice makes perfect. Do you want me to say that in Armenian?"

"Not necessary. I take your point. By the way, we have a problem. Our parents will be coming to the graduation."

"Of course, they'll be coming," Annette said. "Why is that a problem?"

"I'll tell you. It will be impossible to hide the fact from our parents that we're living together. I'm not sure how any of them will deal with that fact. Remember that I had to pass a test given by your father before I could even take you to the movies. How about sleeping in the same bed? What will he think about that? My mother will be dumbfounded. She'll probably think she somehow missed the wedding."

"Why don't we get married before we graduate?" Aram asked spontaneously at breakfast on a particularly lovely morning in the early spring of 1952.

"What—other than your boundless love for me—caused you to bring up that subject this morning? Aram, I think you just proposed marriage. You can't imagine how many times I have wished for this moment—how many times I have prayed for it. Aram, my dear Aram, I have wanted you to be my husband ever since we were introduced by Theresa Russo while we were in high school. Aram, my darling, my love, I accept your proposal."

"I was hoping you would. I was on pins and needles for the past fifteen seconds while I waited for your response. Let's call them now so they can arrange a wedding at the Holy Cross Church on 187th Street. I'll tell them we want a small wedding."

"That's fine with me, but I can assure you that my mother will want to be with me to pick out my wedding dress. I'll tell her I'll come to New York for that purpose," Annette remarked.

"Good idea. By the way, the real reason I brought up this subject is not my fear of our parents discovering our sinful relationship. It was because I love you and want you to be my wife and bear my children. I understand that sex without a condom is a blast."

"Bernie must have told you that."

"No. I read about it in a book."

They hugged and kissed and dashed into the bedroom to celebrate.

They were married in the Holy Cross Armenian Apostolic Church on 187th Street in November 1952. Their wedding was attended by the Infielders, including Theresa Flaherty, whom Aram had named the Ladies Auxiliary of the Infielders. It was not the small wedding that Annette had initially suggested. Virtually the entire Armenian community of Washington Heights—to whom Aram and Annette were a source of pride—flocked to the celebration. The couple had scheduled the wedding in November when the baseball season was over so Sean and Terry could attend. The wedding was festive and jubilant. At the dinner following the wedding, Annette's father, Dr. Nazarian, delivered a stirring speech—in Armenian and then in English—expressing the happiness that the parents of the couple felt and the special significance of the event to the Armenian people. "If we could have searched the world for a husband for our daughter and arranged her marriage, today's wedding would have been the outcome of that search." Those words, of course, had a special resonance with Hagop and Zada Petrosian.

Chapter 36

Sean

The Ballplayer and in Real Life

The two and a half seasons in which Sean played minor league baseball in Hartford proved to be a difficult and stormy time in the relationship between Sean and Terry. Notwithstanding the relative proximity of Hartford to New York City, the couple rarely saw each other during the seven-month baseball season. In the autumn of 1948, following the end of his first season as a professional baseball player, Sean returned to his family's home in Washington Heights and was visited almost immediately by Terry. She was in a confrontational mood.

"Either we get married before the next season or we're finished," Terry proclaimed before even saying hello. "I'm not going to spend another year of my life waiting around like a nun without a man in my life. You have a great time playing ball like a teenage boy, and I sit around in my mother's dreary apartment like a girl who can't get a date. No more. That's over or we're done, and I'll go back into circulation. I'll fuck every guy in the neighborhood while you're playing ball. I'll get laid more times than you get hits!"

By this time, Terry was shouting so loudly that Mr. Flaherty came into the hallway where Sean and Terry were standing and sharply told her to keep quiet. He turned to his son and said, "Is this the girl who's been running after you all these years? I'm no expert, but I'm sure you can do better. You should send her on her way and tell her to take her filthy mouth with her."

Terry exploded with rage at both the father and the son. "Fuck you, both of you," she shouted as she turned and left the apartment, slamming the door behind her.

Sean was stunned. He stood mutely, trying to process what had just happened. His father simply returned to his desk and resumed whatever he'd been doing before the brief and dreadful encounter with his son's girlfriend. Sean decided to go see Dino at the Chevy dealership.

Dino was busy trying to sell a car. Sean found a place to sit down and waited anxiously for Dino to be available to talk with him. Dino noticed that Sean appeared deeply troubled and asked the prospective customer to excuse him for a few moments. He welcomed Sean back to the neighborhood and asked if he had a good season with the Hartford Chiefs.

Sean shrugged and said, "I have to talk to you about Terry. I think we just broke up."

"I'm not surprised. She mentioned to me several times in the past few months that she was tired of waiting around for you to—as she put it—take her seriously."

"She said 'fuck you' to my father."

"That doesn't mean anything. She's got a terrible temper and a filthy mouth. She thinks it makes her sophisticated to use bad language."

"What should I do?"

"What do you want to do? You two have been circling around

each other for so many years you both must be dizzy by now. Why don't you just back off and see what happens?"

Sean then told Dino that he had a chance to play winter baseball in Cuba. "My manager recommended it because it could be good for my career."

"That's not a bad idea. If she's really the right girl for you, she'll come running back when you return. If not, you'll know how you feel and how she feels. It'll also get you out of your father's house, where I know you're miserable."

Sean followed Dino's advice, and his long-running romance with Dino's sister was put on ice.

Chapter 37

Sean and His Da

By the end of the 1950 season, Sean's decision to play professional baseball looked like a wise one. Over the course of three and a half seasons as the first baseman of the Hartford Chiefs, he succeeded in reducing the frequency of his strikeouts without compromising his ability to hit powerful home runs. In the 1950 season, he hit 52 home runs. His batting average was an outstanding .327, and he produced 122 runs batted in. It was a spectacular season.

Following the final game of the season, the manager of the Chiefs called Sean into his office and told him that he had been traded to the Chicago Cubs and that it was likely that he would be the Cubs' first baseman when their aging star, Phil Cavarretta, wound down his career. In March 1951, Sean would be on a major league roster.

Five years after the end of World War II, most of the families in Washington Heights had a telephone in their apartments. Not so, however, with the Flaherty family. A combination of limited means and Mr. Flaherty's insistence that he not be disturbed by a ringing bell while composing his poetry resulted in the absence of a telephone in their apartment. Consequently, Sean Flaherty was unable to contact his family directly to tell them that he was returning home from Hartford and that he was heading to the big leagues. That was just as well as far as Sean was concerned. His relationship with his immediate family, never especially warm, had cooled during his absence from home during the long baseball seasons. Although Hartford was merely two hours away from New York by train, Sean never visited his family during the baseball season, and no one in his family ever came to Hartford to watch him play.

Using the telephone in the manager's office, Sean called Dino's home number, hoping to reach Terry or Dino. There was no answer at Dino's home. Sean then phoned Aram's number. Again, there was no answer, and Sean realized that Aram was away at college and his mother probably didn't answer the phone because she couldn't speak English. At that point, Sean was reluctant to continue to use the office phone to call Bernie, so he said goodbye to the manager and began to make his way back to Washington Heights without anyone there knowing that he was coming.

During the years that Sean was diligently trying to hit fast-moving baseballs thrown by professional pitchers, his father was diligently trying to find exactly the right words to express in poetry the rage of the Irish people at the misfortunes thrust upon them by history and the rage in his own heart at the tragedies of his own life. During that time, Patrick Flaherty actually attained success as a poet—to the extent that anyone who devotes his life to writing poetry can ever be said to have been successful. In June 1950, he mailed a set of three poems to *Modern Poetry Magazine*, risking once again the disappointment of rejection that he had experienced time and again. On a rainy day the following August, he received a letter that was not a rejection but an expression of praise and an indication that the poems would be published in a forthcoming issue of *Modern Poetry Magazine* as the featured poems in that edition. The letter also indicated that it was the policy of the magazine to pay one dollar and fifty cents per line for poems that it accepted for publication. The three poems contained a total of seventy-eight lines. That would yield a payment of one hundred seventeen dollars to be remitted as soon as the magazine received from him an indication of his agreement to those arrangements.

But far more important to Mr. Flaherty was an accompanying inquiry as to his interest in publishing a collection of his poetry in book form. "Am I interested in publishing a collection of my poetry in book form?" Patrick Flaherty asked himself, speaking aloud. "What a question that is. They might as well ask if I am interested in breathing, or in the uniting of all the counties of Ireland, or perhaps if I am interested in spending eternity in the arms of my Savior. What a question!"

In August 1950, the publisher announced the publication of *A Book of Tears: The Collected Poems of Patrick T. Flaherty*. A highly favorable review of the book appeared in *The New York Times* the following month. And on a day in September 1950, it was announced that Patrick T. Flaherty of New York City was selected to win the Hannigan Prize for the most meaningful contribution to the art and traditions of Irish poetry to appear in many years. A telegram to that effect was sent to Mr. Flaherty. The prize was accompanied by a five-hundred-dollar grant "to encourage continued creative work in the field of Irish poetry" and an all-expenses-paid trip to Dublin for the poet and a companion to attend the award ceremony.

Sean was on his way to New York when the announcement of his father's prize was made. Since the award was anything but front-page news in any of the New York newspapers, it is not at all surprising that, when Sean rang the doorbell of his family's apartment, he was utterly ignorant of that event. It was not without some reluctance, even trepidation, that Sean waited at the door for someone—most likely his father—to open the door. Although he felt that his relationship with his father had improved somewhat as a result of the heartfelt conversation that they had several years back about whether Sean should go to college or play professional baseball, neither he nor his father had done a solitary thing to continue or strengthen the quality of that relationship. If anything, they had never been as remote from each other as they were during the three baseball seasons that Sean lived away from Washington Heights. They would go six months or more without exchanging a word and, in all likelihood, also with rarely a thought of each other.

Mr. Flaherty opened the door and peered into the dimly lit hallway. He stared at Sean for a moment and then roared, "I knew in my heart that you'd come to celebrate with me the instant you heard the news. What a good and thoughtful son you are to be with your Da at a moment like this."

Sean wondered how his father had heard about his assignment to a major league team. And the words his father was using didn't quite seem to fit the occasion. Thinking he might not have correctly heard what his father had said, he asked, "How did you learn about it, Da?"

"They sent me a telegram. What a strange thing this life is. I've received two telegrams in my life. The one about the death of your sainted brother brought the worst news ever. And now this one brings the best news of my life. And you knew enough to come and share my joy." After pausing a moment, he continued, "Sean, how about you come to Dublin with me. You'd enjoy it more than your Ma, and if the truth be told, I'd enjoy your company more than hers. What do you say? Will you come to Dublin with your Da?"

By this point, it was clear to Sean that his father wasn't talking about major league baseball. "Da, excuse me, but I'm not sure I understand what you're talking about. Why will we be going to Dublin?"

"Because of the poetry prize that I won. What did you think?"

"I didn't know that you'd won a poetry prize. That's very nice."

"Nice, he says. It's the best thing that ever happened to me. It proves that I haven't been wasting my time all these years. But wait, if you didn't know about the prize, why are you home?"

"I'm home because the season's over and because I have some very good news to share with you."

"I wish you had come home to share my good news with me."

"Well, I'm very happy that we have good news to share with each other. It hasn't always been like that, you may remember."

"So, what's your good news?"

"I've been traded to the Chicago Cubs. I'll be playing in the major leagues next season, and I'll probably be earning at least double my salary."

"Now, Sean, you're talking about something your Da doesn't know a thing about. I do understand about double your salary. That sounds like a good thing, but what the hell does 'major league' mean?"

"It's like this, Da. Professional baseball has the major leagues at the top and Class D at the bottom. For the past three years I've been stuck at Class Double A. That's higher than A, B, C, and D, but lower than Triple A. The Chicago Cubs organization thinks I showed enough promise to be ready to jump to the major leagues. So, they bought my contract from the Braves and promoted me from Double A directly to the National League, one of the two major leagues."

"They bought your contract? What are you, an indentured servant?"

"What's a dentured servant?"

"You understand all that gibberish about Double A and Triple A, but you still don't know the English language."

"Please, Da, don't start insulting me again. And tell me what a dentured servant is."

Laughing, Mr. Flaherty said, "I'm tempted to tell you that it's a servant with teeth, but you probably wouldn't understand that."

"No, I wouldn't. Now please answer my question so I can know what you're talking about."

"Son, an indentured servant is a worker who is little more than a slave."

"Well, Da, that's not your son, Sean J. Flaherty. I'm anything but a slave. They pay me real money to play a game that I played for free until the age of nineteen. How many men do you know who are paid to play a boy's game?"

"Tell me this, Sean. This salary of yours, which has now doubled, can you live on it?"

"Easily, Da. Comfortably."

"Can you support a family on it?"

"What family do you have in mind?"

"I'm not asking you to support your Ma and me. What about your own wife and children?"

"How did you know that I had a wife and children? I must have forgotten about that. Seriously, Da, the money they're going to pay me next season would be enough to support a wife if I had a wife. By the time I have a child, I'm pretty sure I can swing that, too. But I don't really know how much it costs to support a child. I don't think they eat very much for the first few years."

"Well, it looks like you're making a success of yourself in this baseball business."

"And, you know, I might never have done it but for your advice to me four years ago. Do you remember that?"

"Of course, I remember that. I told you not to waste your time going to college."

"And I thank you for that."

"What a strange picture the Flaherty family presents to the world—a great Irish poet and his son who makes money playing a child's game. Come, sit down. We've been standing this whole time that you're home. Sit down with your Da and have a glass of Jameson. We've both got much to celebrate."

In his entire life, Sean had never had so much as a glass of beer with his father. He was not even aware that there was a bottle of Irish whiskey in the house. He had no recollection of seeing his father have a drink, but he did remember his father railing against what he called the "slanderous" portrayal of the Irish as drunkards by the "fookin English." For all Sean knew, his father was a teetotaler.

The two men were sitting at the table in the tiny kitchen of the Flaherty apartment, a green bottle of Jameson Irish whiskey standing on the table between them. Mr. Flaherty wiped the dust off the bottle with a paper napkin and poured a couple of inches of whiskey into two unmatched tumblers, handing one to Sean. It occurred to Sean that he had never sat at the kitchen table with his father. Never, not once. The Flaherty kitchen was too small to accommodate the entire family at one time for a meal. The children were always fed first, and then their mother and father would sit at the small enamel-topped table and have their meal together. This was assuredly a special occasion, and it gave Sean a warm and joyful feeling. He sipped his whiskey and quickly emptied his glass. His father promptly refilled it. As the alcohol began to take its pleasurable effect on Sean, some unexpected, unplanned thoughts began to form in his head. Looking calmly at his father sitting, sipping, and smiling across the table, Sean heard himself say to his father, "I wanted to ask your opinion about something. Something that might be important."

"And what might that be, son?"

"Do you think I'm too young to get married?"

"Who might the lucky lady be?"

"Why don't you ever answer my questions? If I'm too young, there won't be a lucky lady."

"Now you're beginning to think like a poet. Poets don't just answer questions. They force you to think, to seek, to find answers yourself rather than having them fed to you. So, if I ask, 'Who might the lucky lady be?' there is hidden in that question the path to your answer. It will lead to a discussion between us about that lucky lady and whether a match between you and her at this time looks like one for which you are either ready or too young."

"You never knew my friend Dino's father, Mr. Russo. He died a few years ago. If Dino ever asked him a question, he got a straight answer."

"Ah, but now his Da is dead and can't answer Dino's questions. Dino hasn't been taught how to look for answers himself. The paths to those answers are all in shadows, and Dino may one day take the wrong one because his father, bless his soul, never taught him how to look for the right path."

"Da, there's no need to worry about Dino. He's doing fine. Can we now have that discussion about whether I'm too young to get married?"

"I'm sure Dino's doing fine, and I'm sure he's a fine young man. But do you think for a moment that in the life that spreads out before him, he will never encounter a question that he doesn't know how to answer? That's not possible. So, we need to hope that somehow, he will have the wisdom or the good luck to choose the right path to the answers that he needs."

"Da, my question about getting married."

After a silent pause, during which Sean felt as if he was holding his breath, Mr. Flaherty said, "Son, there is no answer today. The answer is hidden in the future. In order to find that answer, you will have to be married, which is obviously what you want to do. You see, what you want from me is not an answer but a blessing. So, who is the lucky lady?"

"Dino's sister, Theresa."

"The Italian girl with an Irish temper and a foul mouth. A perfect match for you. Maybe some of her spirited temperament will rub off on you. Now answer my question about Dublin."

"That's easy. You must take Ma with you. No question about it."

There was noise at the front door. Sean's mother was returning from her day job at a house and office cleaning service in which she now had a part ownership interest.

She rushed into Sean's arms the instant she saw him, overjoyed at the sight of him. That was the end of Sean's conversation with his father.

Sean understood his father's circumlocutions as constituting an endorsement of the idea of marriage with Terry. The fact that it was an idea that originated with her and that she pursued him incessantly since high school was no guarantee that Terry would still be willing to marry him. Terry was not someone to be taken for granted, not with her temper and her overpowering personality. As Sean thought about all this, he realized that Terry's temper and her overpowering personality were exactly the things that he found to be exciting and attractive about her.

Sean reflected on the things that had happened in the past few days. He received an unexpected promotion to a major league team. His salary would be doubled, or maybe even more. He saw his father reveling in joy and exhilaration that he had never before seen. He sat and had a drink and a good conversation with his father. He thought he might marry Terry.

Sean had a good feeling he'd not experienced previously except on the baseball field. He felt empowered. He called Dino and told him that he intended to marry his sister. He was dumbfounded by Dino's response.

"It hurts me to tell you this, but the last thing in the world you should do is marry my sister. She's not the same girl you think she is. Since you and her broke up, she's become a disgusting person. She's an alley cat. The neighborhood slut. I can't warn you strongly enough. Stay far away from her."

"But, Dino, I love her."

"It's your life," Dino said, and he hung up the phone.

Sean was distraught. Just when things were finally coming together for him—his baseball career, his relationship with his father, his financial circumstances that enabled him to decide that he was in a position to marry Terry—everything had just unraveled. He needed help. Whenever he needed help in his life, he turned to Aram. In desperation, he called Aram's home in Boston. Annette answered the phone. The first thing he said was, "I need to talk to Aram."

Annette understood immediately that Sean was in some sort of crisis. She called Aram to the phone and explained that Sean had asked to speak with him and that it sounded serious.

Aram picked up the phone and said, "What's up, Sean? Did the Braves release you?"

"No, they traded me to the Cubs, and I'm going to play in the majors next year. That's not my problem. I need your help with Terry."

After listening intently to Sean's description of his conversation with Dino, Aram said, "Are you sure you want to marry Terry after all this? It doesn't sound to me like a very good idea."

"I know it sounds crazy, but the answer is yes. I want her. I just know we can be happy together."

"Okay, Sean, as Dino said, it's your life. I'll get Bernie to go to work on it. This is a situation that requires his involvement. He's the Infielders' expert on the subject of women."

"I'm grateful to you. And I'm sorry to dump my problem on your lap."

"That's what we Infielders do, Sean. I hope it turns out right. I'll contact Bernie and put him to work."

Chapter 38

Bernie the Matchmaker

Bernie was busy studying for final exams. Law school was harder than he expected. He hadn't studied as diligently as he should have. He was apprehensive about those exams. One exam per course at the end of the school year, and his grade for each of those courses depended on how he did on those exams. The pressure was disturbing. He wondered if this business with Sean and Terry was a responsibility that was worth the effort he would have to put into it. After all, was it really a good idea for Sean to reclaim Terry from the trash heap of his past? *With Sean's good looks and with the cachet of now being in the major leagues . . . if I were in his place, I'd get laid every night.*

And then Bernie's thoughts wandered off into a territory that was deeply troubling to him. *What, exactly, has Sean ever done for me that I now have to break my ass to help him put back together his broken relationship with Terry? Compared to Dino and Aram, he's done nothing for me. When we were just boys, Dino and Aram helped me with my father's case. But Sean, what did he ever do for me? Nothing but negative things. He has constantly made all of us feel sorry for him, feel obligated to help him—even, sometimes, he made us feel pity for him. Yes, he's a sweet and nice guy. That's what we always say about him. Yes, he hit a couple of home runs that won us the city championship. But what exactly do we owe him for* sweet, nice, *and a couple of home runs?*

Wait a minute, Bernie said to himself, *what am I thinking? Aram asked me to do something—something I already agreed to do. There is no way that I will let him down. But it's not only for Aram. It is for Sean. Sean needs my help. That's enough of a reason to do it. But I don't know how to do this.*

Early that evening, he walked the few blocks separating his apartment from the building in which the Russo family had been living for as long as Bernie was aware of their existence. He walked up three flights of stairs to Apartment 4B, which still bore the name of Frank Russo under the doorbell. He hesitated before pushing the doorbell button, a hesitation reflecting his uncertainty regarding the wisdom of this mission.

He was deeply troubled about the likely outcome of his effort to persuade Terry to consider reuniting with Sean. There were two possibilities as he thought about the outcome. *One, she could tell me to get lost or—more likely, given Terry's vocabulary—to go fuck myself. The other possible outcome is she actually agrees to marry Sean. Which was the more desirable outcome? If I were Sean, I'd find myself a new partner and not settle for damaged goods. But that's one of the many things in life that's so interesting—I'm not Sean. I wasn't made like him, I wasn't raised like him, and yet I want so much for him to be happy—happy on his own terms, not on my terms.*

He rang the doorbell. The indistinct sound of voices filtered through the closed door. No one came to open the door, although it was obvious that there were people in the apartment. Bernie rang the doorbell again, twice in succession. He heard a woman's voice shout, "Get the damned door." Approaching footsteps, then silence. Then the sound of unlocking multiple locks followed by someone opening the door barely more than an inch.

"Who is it?" an unseen woman asked.

"It's me, Bernie Heller. Dino's friend. From the baseball team."

Suddenly, the door opened, and Bernie saw a small elderly woman in a black dress, her gray hair disheveled, with a look of panic on her wrinkled face. It took several seconds before Bernie realized that this was Mrs. Russo, the most accessible, the most pleasant, the most exuberant of the mothers of the four Infielders. This was Mrs. Russo who prepared the most delicious lasagna he had ever eaten, the woman who welcomed Dino's friends into her house as if each visit was an occasion for a celebration. Bernie realized he had not been in this apartment since Mr. Russo's funeral. The place looked shabby and uncared for. Mrs. Russo obviously recognized him, but she stared at him with fear in her face. He hadn't prepared what he was going to say, and he stood mute and confused.

She spoke first. "Is anything wrong with Dino?"

That question immediately explained the terror in Mrs. Russo's face and gave him the opportunity to break his awkward silence. "Oh no, Mrs. Russo, there's nothing wrong with Dino. He's doing great. I haven't seen him very often since I started law school. But he's fine."

"He don't come to see us very much, and I worry about him. He sends us money by mail. That's what we live on."

"Honestly, you have nothing to worry about. He's very busy in his business, but he's healthy and happy."

"I bless you for telling me that. You need something to eat? It's almost seven o'clock. Have you had your supper? I could make a pot of spaghetti."

He started to laugh. "I'll never forget how well you fed me and the other guys when we came up to your house when we were boys. I've been to lots of fine restaurants, and not one of them serves anything as delicious as your lasagna."

Realizing that they were still standing in the hallway of the apartment, Mrs. Russo took Bernie's hand, led him into the familiar kitchen, and asked him to sit down. "Tell me all about yourself. I don't remember the last time I saw you. I heard you're going to be a lawyer. I have to say that I'm a little surprised by that. Of all of Dino's friends," she paused, and a faint smile appeared on her face, "you were the one I thought was a brat. You always had a big mouth, and you said dirty words. I hope you don't hate me for saying that. You want some spaghetti?"

"Thanks for the offer, but I'll take a pass on the spaghetti, Mrs. Russo. Don't worry. Nothing you say could ever make me hate you. In fact, I really was a brat in those days, but I think I've outgrown that. At least I hope so. I remember those days as happy days. I hope you still have happy days." He didn't bother to explain to Mrs. Russo that he was still waiting for his final grades from law school.

She leaned over the table and kissed his forehead. "Bernie, not me. Not after Frank. Not with my Theresa. Not with my Marco." Her eyes swelled with tears.

Bernie didn't know what she meant by "with my Marco," but he decided not to pursue that subject. He reverted to the speechless person he was when he entered the apartment. He had no idea what to say. He leaned over the table and kissed Mrs. Russo's forehead.

She smiled and said, "I'm glad things are good for you."

It was time to get down to business. "I'd like to see Theresa. Is she home?"

"Now she's home all day and out all night. She lost her job in the diner because she was missing too many days of work. I'll see if she's dressed and tell her you're here."

Bernie waited nervously, pacing around the kitchen and trying to decide on his opening remarks to Terry. This was more stressful than waiting for a jury to return a verdict. *What on earth am I doing here?* Bernie asked himself. *Doing my duty, that's what,* he answered his own question.

Terry walked casually into the kitchen as if the presence there of an old acquaintance whom she had seen only once or twice in several years was entirely unremarkable. Bernie was shocked by her appearance. She was wearing a bathrobe. Her face was puffy as if she had just awakened from a deep sleep. Her long hair was unkempt and tangled.

Bernie's opening remarks flew from his mouth without forethought. "Terry, you look like shit. Are you all right?"

Terry laughed. "I wasn't exactly expecting a distinguished visitor today. To answer your question, no, I'm not all right. I feel the way I look. How are you?"

"I'm fine. I'm terribly sorry to hear that you're not okay. I hope you're not sick. Please tell me you're not sick."

"No, I'm not sick. I don't have a disease. But look how I live. I have a miserable life. I can't hold a job. I screw around like a whore. I drink too much. Anything else you want to know? Why are you here?"

Bernie was appalled by Terry's appearance and astonished by the candor of the disclosures she had just made. He composed himself as quickly as he could and responded to her question by saying, "Terry, I suspected things were not going well with you, and I'm truly sorry to learn that my suspicions were correct. My reason for wanting to see you was to talk with you about Sean."

"Sean? What about Sean?"

"Terry, I have a lot to tell you. Have you eaten supper yet? I'd like to take you out to eat somewhere where we can have a good conversation."

"You want to take me out? Like on a date? I thought you were married."

"No, Terry, not like on a date. Like a friend who cares about you and about Sean. Go, get yourself dressed and ready to appear in public. I'll wait for you here and chat with your mother. And no, I'm not married. I just got out of the army."

"You're serious about this. It'll take me a while to get myself ready."

"I've got time. You like Chinese?"

"I love it. I'm up to my ears in Italian food."

"Great. I know a good place. I'll get my car while you're getting ready."

It was late in the evening, and Bernie and Terry were the only diners at the Peking Palace on Broadway near 182nd Street. Bernie asked the pretty Asian woman who greeted them whether it was too late for them to have dinner, and she said they stayed open until eleven.

"Don't rush," she said. "Enjoy your meal."

Bernie was highly skeptical that this would be an enjoyable meal. In fact, he dreaded having to talk to his dinner companion, who was dressed like a streetwalker in a short, tight-fitting dress with half of her breasts exposed as the front of the dress plunged toward her waist. The two of them looked at the menus without comment until Bernie said he was going to order shrimp chow mein. Terry said she would have the same thing, plus an egg roll. After placing their orders with a polite waiter, they sat silently in the empty restaurant as Bernie tried to decide how to broach the subject of Sean.

Terry didn't make this any easier when she broke the silence, saying, in a manner that Bernie felt was aggressive and challenging, "So, what do you want to tell me about Sean that's so important that we have to eat Chinese while you tell me?"

"Terry, I didn't bring you here to have an argument or a fight with you. I would like to have a calm and friendly conversation about an important subject—a subject that I frankly think is more important to you than it is to me."

"Okay, so talk. I'm listening."

"Sean is going to be playing for the Chicago Cubs in the major leagues."

"I know. I heard that from someone in the neighborhood. I don't remember who. I didn't think he was that good."

"Apparently he stopped striking out so much, and the Cubs need a power-hitting first baseman."

"I suppose I should be glad for him."

"Terry, Sean still loves you and wants to work things out with you. He wants to build a life with you."

The waiter brought the egg roll for Terry. While chewing, she said, "That's a fine how-do-you-do! The last time I saw him, he threw me out of his apartment. Now he wants to build a life with me. You know about that? I know you know about it, and you got a fucking nerve telling me to go and build a life with him."

"Listen, Terry, I'm trying to talk with you as a friend and as a friend of Sean's."

"I'll bet he told you that I cursed out his father when I came to ask him to marry me."

Terry suddenly started to cry. Not just a little whimpering, but a full-blown convulsive wailing that built up in intensity the longer it lasted. At first, Bernie just sat staring at Terry, but after a couple of minutes of waiting for the weeping to subside, he reached across the table and took hold of Terry's hands. At precisely that moment, the waiter arrived with their food. He quickly turned around and went back to the kitchen, having judiciously decided that the diners were not ready for shrimp chow mein.

Holding both of Terry's hands, Bernie exclaimed, "Terry, Terry, talk to me. Tell me why you're crying. All I said was that Sean wants to build a life with you. Why'd that cause you to break down like this?"

Terry continued to weep and said nothing in reply to Bernie.

He said, "Terry, let me take you home. This was a mistake. I knew I shouldn't have started this. I'm sorry, let's go."

She resumed weeping. Bernie rose from his seat, walked over to Terry, and put his arm around her shoulder. She looked up at him and said, "Do you remember how I loved him, how I chased after him? You remember that, don't you?"

"Of course I do. Everyone in the Heights knew about that."

"I ruined my life, and I ruined his life. And I ruined Dino's life, too. Bernie, I'm a really bad person."

"Terry, you were too young when you fell in love with Sean. You were too young when your father died. And now, you're too young to give up on your life. Your friends—who are also Sean's and Dino's friends—we're all going to try to make things better. Now let me take you home. I want you to get a good night's sleep. I'll pick you up at eleven o'clock tomorrow morning, and we'll take a walk. Is that okay with you?"

"I guess so."

"Good. We've got work to do."

With her face still puffy and wet with tears, Terry kissed Bernie—the first time that ever happened.

"That was nice," Bernie said, "but next time you do that, Terry, please blow your nose first."

He left a ten-dollar bill on the table and drove Terry home.

———

Bernie went up to Sean's house for the first time in his life. He urged Sean to reach out to Terry and "see if the old chemistry is still there." There was no way for them to talk privately in Sean's apartment, so they walked to Bernie's apartment.

It didn't take long for Bernie to get to the point. While they were sitting in his bedroom, Bernie phoned Terry and said, "Sean's in my house, and he'd like you to come up here and see him. You know where I live?" He hung up the phone and told Sean that Terry was on her way.

Bernie tried to prepare Sean for what Terry looked like. He also briefed Sean as to how he should gently approach Terry. "Remember," he said, "the last time you saw Terry, there was a really bad argument, and she said 'fuck you' to your father. You need to try to repair the damage."

All of Bernie's efforts at preparing Sean for the confrontation with Terry proved to be unnecessary. The instant Terry walked into Bernie's room and saw Sean, she ran toward him, jumped so she could wrap her legs around him, and kissed him passionately. When she had caught her breath, she screamed, "Sean, I'm so sorry. I love you so much!"

Bernie decided to leave the room.

From the *Bronx Home News, Washington Heights Edition*, March 3, 1951:

The wedding of Theresa Anna Russo and Sean James Flaherty, both of Washington Heights, was celebrated at a mass at St. Elizabeth Roman Catholic Church on Wadsworth Avenue and 187th Street on Saturday, March 1, 1951. Father Thomas Garrity officiated. The bride was escorted in the entrance processional by her mother, Bianca Russo, and her brother, Bernardino Russo, who also served as

best man and as the lector of the reading from the Old Testa-
ment. The bridegroom was escorted by his parents, Patrick
and Margaret Flaherty. Patrick Flaherty served as the lector
of the New Testament reading and also read a poem that he
composed for the occasion of his son's wedding. The maid of
honor was the bride's friend, Annette Petrosian. The bride-
groom's sisters, Maureen, Joanna, and Mary Flaherty, were
the bridesmaids. The bride's brothers, Anthony and Marco
Russo, and friends of the couple, Bernd Heller and Aram
Petrosian, served as ushers.

After the reception, the newly married couple left on a
honeymoon trip to the Berkshires in Massachusetts. They
will reside in Chicago, Illinois, the home of the Chicago
Cubs, the National League baseball team for which the
bridegroom is a player.

Sean was keenly aware that a new chapter in his life was about to begin, and he was full of joy and optimism. Terry had never before looked as beautiful in his eyes as she did on the day of their wedding.

Life doesn't follow a smooth parabolic trajectory. It zigs and zags, up and down peaks and valleys.

Chapter 39

Champions • Ten Years

Sean and Terry

Despite its inauspicious beginning, Sean and Terry had a good marriage. Terry understood, but never said out loud, that it took a man with Sean's gentle manner and even disposition to remain happily married to her despite her volatility and cheekiness. She was grateful that she had snared him and retained him. It still gave her joy that he was her husband and, as things turned out, the father of their two daughters.

Sean's career as a major league baseball player entailed seven or eight months each year, from spring training in Arizona to seventy-seven games in Chicago and another seventy-seven games on the road. The season didn't end until September. The Cubs never won a championship. Until Terry was pregnant with the first of their two children, she went everywhere that Sean's career took him. After living in a hotel in Chicago during his first season with the Cubs, Sean and Terry bought a small house in the Chicago suburb of Brookfield. They returned to Washington Heights at the end of each season and spent a great deal of time with Mrs. Russo, to whom being with her grandchildren brought moments of joy into her perpetual sorrow.

Sean was perfectly aware of the fact that he was not a star ballplayer. One of the coaches once called him a "journeyman." He thought that sounded important, even flattering, until he looked in a dictionary and saw that it meant "a sports player who is reliable but not outstanding." He agreed that the definition fit him. He did have one outstanding season in which he made the National League all-star team. He hit forty-four home runs that season, the most in the league. He was convinced that he would not have been even a journeyman student at NYU. Sean was certain that, in following Bernie's and his father's advice and becoming a pro ballplayer, he had made the right choice. His father was right; he would earn his livelihood with his hands, not his brains. But he knew that he was approaching the point in his life where he would have to make another choice. He would not choose to stop playing ball, but ultimately, that would not be his choice. His splendid body would gradually begin to lose the strength and agility required to play in the major leagues, the setting that all professional players called "the big show." That happened to every player. He didn't know what his choices would be when that happened to him. He was now a husband and a father in addition to just being a journeyman first baseman.

Chapter 40

Champions • Ten Years

Bernie and His Parents

After spending two years in the army, Bernie graduated from City College in 1953 and from Brooklyn Law School in 1956. He was admitted to the New York Bar that same year and opened an office for the practice of law on St. Nicholas Avenue one flight up over a hardware store. It took him both time and a major sustained effort to build a successful law practice. He tried court cases—mostly personal injury claims—and handled divorces, wrote contracts, drafted wills, and generally was diligent in the service of his clients. He worked very hard, spending ten to twelve hours a day, six days a week, tending to the legal needs of his clients and prospecting for more clients. All this, of course, had a somewhat chilling effect on his social life.

He met and dated an attractive woman named Catherine, who was working her way through Iona College in New Rochelle when he met her. She was a fine young woman, intelligent, ambitious, and a religious Roman Catholic. He was introduced to her by a client whose motivation for the introduction was to reward Bernie for obtaining an especially good result in the client's difficult case. Bernie was fully aware of that motivation, but when he met Catherine, it instantly became irrelevant. Catherine was beautiful and charming. Knowing that seduction was going to be a wasted effort because of her devotion to her faith, Bernie was able to relax when he was with Catherine. Even when he was just thinking about her.

There was no doubt in Bernie's mind that his parents would object strenuously to a marriage with a Catholic woman. When they learned that Bernie might be serious about a Catholic woman, all hell broke loose in the Heller household.

"We didn't escape from the Nazis to have Catholic grandchildren," Mr. Heller screamed at Bernie.

"You marry that shiksa and you're not my son anymore," Mrs. Heller wailed.

Bernie was not allowed to say anything. He was actually afraid that his father would physically attack him. Realizing that there was no possibility of a productive discussion with his parents, Bernie simply left their apartment and walked down St. Nicholas Avenue to his office.

It was late in the evening. Shops on the avenue were closed, and no one could be seen walking on the streets. Bernie sat in the darkness in his office, trying to understand what the dreadful treatment his parents received in Germany meant to them. His thoughts ranged over a wide variety of related questions. The questions he asked himself had waited a long time to be asked, but he shied from the subject every time it intruded into his consciousness. He could evade it no longer.

Okay, I'm Jewish. All that has ever meant to me is that I have Jewish parents. My parents are good people. They both lost their parents in the Holocaust. I'm not sure I understand why I've never discussed that with them. Was I afraid of that subject?

Have I been afraid of being a Jew? My closest friends are not Jewish.

I'm thinking about Aram. Being an Armenian has been a defining element in his life. Is that something he appreciates or something he resents? It certainly put boundaries around his social life. Imagine if I had to be interviewed by the father of a girl I wanted to date. No way—no way— would I have agreed to such an indignity.

My father believes in God, I suppose, but that seems crazy to me. His parents were murdered by the Nazis in the worst crime in human history. How can he believe in—how can he worship—a God who allowed that to happen? What is such a God worth? Shit, it happened to God's chosen people. Who needs to be chosen? What do you get out of it? I have to sit down with my father and ask him those questions. How can he pray to a God who gave him Werner as a son?

I wonder if I should try to learn something about Judaism. The only thing my parents ever taught me was I can't date a woman like Catherine. There's got to be more to it than that. Something inside my parents that they may not even know is there. Things are out of proportion here. Something that never was important suddenly became the biggest deal of all time between me and my parents. I've got to figure this out.

Bernie realized that he was never going to understand Judaism the way his parents wanted him to if he was dating a Catholic. Though it pained him to do so, he resolved to end things with Catherine.

I don't know if I should tell her the real reason. How could she understand it if I don't? I have to try not to hurt her.

He walked to Laurel Hill Terrace, to the same building where Aram used to live. He had decided to move out of his parents' apartment while in law school, and Laurel Hill Terrace was the

best address in Washington Heights. While walking, he remembered that Aram once told him about being lectured by Annette's
father about having Armenian children.

*Why was it more important to Armenians to have Armenian
kids than having Jewish kids is to me? I have big questions to deal
with, and I really should do that before I grow old.*

Chapter 41

Champions • Ten Years
Aram: Triumph and Tragedy

On a bright, hot day in June 1952, Aram graduated from Harvard with multiple honors. In the audience, shielded from the sun by two colorful parasols, were his proud parents, Hagop and Zada Petrosian, and Annette's parents, Ralph and Elise Nazarian, who seemed equally proud. The next day, in the same place, under the same relentless sun, the Petrosians and the Nazarians watched Annette graduate from Radcliffe with highest honors.

"Do you see what we have produced?" asked Dr. Nazarian in Armenian.

Answering in Armenian, in what may have been the first ironic quip ever uttered in her life, Zada said, "No. I wasn't watching. What have we produced?" The parents embraced, laughing heartily, feeling blessed.

At the celebratory dinner in the restaurant of the hotel where the elder Petrosians and Nazarians were staying in Boston, the conversation—conducted primarily in Armenian as a courtesy to Zada Petrosian—centered on the future of Aram and Annette.

Aram had been accepted by Harvard Graduate School, where he decided to study English literature and comparative literature and work toward an MA and PhD degree in both subjects. The combined program would take four or five years. Meanwhile, Annette would be at the Harvard Graduate School working toward a doctorate in microbiology with a concentration in research on the possible connection between microorganisms and certain types of cancer. Even in Armenian, this discussion was virtually incomprehensible to Zada Petrosian. All she knew was that her son was extraordinary, and that was sufficient for her.

————

No one gets a pass in this life was the thought that burst into Bernie's mind when he heard the devastating news that Aram and Annette had lost a child. The baby was ten weeks old, the couple's second child. Her name was Anush, the Armenian word for sweetness. The cause would, in future years, come to be known as sudden infant death syndrome.

Aram phoned each of the Infielders on the morning that Anush was found lying peaceful, sweet, and dead in her crib. Annette was the last to see her alive when she nursed Anush at about two in the morning.

Until that morning, Aram and Annette had been living in an idyll.

Aram was a tenure-track professor at Boston University. He taught comparative literature, a subject he loved, and was the author of an acclaimed book on the work of the Armenian American author, William Saroyan. Annette was a research biologist at Massachusetts General Hospital and the mother of Berj, a healthy, lively, and much-loved two-year-old boy with a good Armenian name.

The funeral of their infant daughter was so poignant, so heartrending, that there wasn't a person in attendance at the interment at the cemetery who didn't weep openly as the tiny casket, not much larger than a violin case, was gently lowered into the earth.

After he received Aram's harrowing phone call, Sean rushed to Wrigley Field to beg the manager of the Cubs for permission to miss a few games because he couldn't play baseball knowing how his dear friend was suffering. The manager, seeing Sean's face wet with tears, said, "Son, there are many things in life more important than baseball. One of them is friendship."

Sean would remember and cherish those words. He and Terry flew to Boston on the first flight they could catch. Sean comforted and consoled Aram.

Annette and Aram coped with their grief as well as anyone possibly could. They showered each other with affection. They framed an enlarged photograph of Annette holding Anush on the day of her birth and hung it in a prominent place in their living room. Aram came up with the idea of saving money so they could endow the Anush Petrosian Chair in Armenian Studies at Boston University. Annette was thrilled with that idea. They were deeply grateful for the solicitude of friends, especially the Infielders for whom the death of the infant was treated as a communal tragedy.

They eventually put their great loss in a compartment in their minds that they visited from time to time, each time with diminished pain, but pain that never disappeared for the rest of their lives. A couple of years following the death of Anush, they had another child, a boy, whom they named Mark. Berj adored his little brother.

The elder Petrosians were devastated and never really reconciled themselves to the death of their granddaughter. The Nazarians were stoic and processed the loss quietly and privately.

Chapter 42

Champions • Ten Years

Dino Alone

Dino's life since the day his team won the New York City baseball championship was profoundly influenced by two events: the tragic death of his father and the humiliating experience of being caught by her parents in the act of having sexual intercourse with Rachel Schechter. His father's death would have been a deeply felt loss even if it did not result in his dropping out of college and being thrust into the role of sole support of his family. He loved his Papa and would always miss his uplifting spirit.

The Rachel incident was as much farce as tragedy, but its consequences were severe. Dino's self-confidence was impaired. His once graceful ability to attract young women was lost. And his desire for relations with the opposite sex was degraded. In his own eyes, he wasn't the man he used to be.

He was successful as manager of Petrosian Motors, but with each passing day, that success diminished as a source of self-esteem.

Chapter 43

Champions • Ten Years

Four Grown Men

Thus, the Infielders were no longer boys; they were no longer just growing; they had become grown men. The likely trajectories of their lives became dimly visible to each of them and to one another.

Part Four

Champions • Fifteen Years

1962

Chapter 44

Reunion

The Infielders were never completely out of touch with one another in the years in which they set the direction of their adult lives. Inevitably, the frequency of their contacts diminished over time, as did the intimacy of their communications. In the year of the championship and for several years after that, there was hardly a scrap of information about any of the Infielders that wasn't known by all of the Infielders, except those very few scraps subject to pledges of secrecy.

Things began to change in a totally unforeseen way, beginning a few days after New Year's Day 1962, when Sean Flaherty realized that 1962 was fifteen years after the city championship. Although, at age thirty-three, he was still quite young by the standards applied to most human beings, Sean was on the edge of the inevitable decline toward obsolescence that eventually overtakes every professional athlete. He realized that, and, as many people do when they cross a border that may be closer to the end than the beginning, Sean found himself thinking more about the past than the future.

It occurred to Sean that it would be wonderful if the Infielders could have a fifteenth anniversary party to celebrate the championship. As with most things, Sean consulted with Terry, and she concurred. He then phoned Bernie to get the ball rolling. Bernie promptly phoned Aram in Boston and Dino at the Chevrolet dealership, and both promptly agreed to attend the party. Aram said that Annette would come with him. Dino said he would probably come alone. Bernie didn't say whether he would come alone or with a companion. Two weeks later, on a freezing cold Monday night, the Infielders gathered in a private room at Dominic's Italian Restaurant on Broadway near 175th Street.

First to arrive were Sean and Terry, who unilaterally assumed the role of hosts for the occasion. Sean was nattily dressed in a banker's gray suit, white shirt and striped tie, and well-shined black shoes. Terry—who by this time was the mother of two children—was no longer a skinny kid. She wore a red, blue, and gray dress with a flared skirt and a wide red belt that emphasized her thin waistline.

Bernie and his latest serious girlfriend, Betsy Weinstein, arrived shortly after Sean and Terry. They were dressed much more casually than the Flahertys. Bernie was in corduroy slacks and a plaid wool shirt, and Betsy—notably disturbed about being improperly dressed—wore a simple sweater and skirt.

Terry immediately perceived Betsy's concern. She greeted her warmly and said, "I told Sean we were overdressed for a friendly get-together like this."

Bernie formally introduced Betsy—an attractive young woman with long dark hair worn in a ponytail—saying, "Believe it or not, I met Betsy in court where she was sitting on the jury in a case I was trying."

"Is that proper?" Terry asked.

Bernie laughed and said, "We weren't dating until after the

trial was over. In fact, I lost that case. Betsy and the other jurors voted against my client."

"That sounds like the start of a great story that you should tell when everyone's here. I'd love to hear the rest of it," Sean said. Then, turning his attention to Betsy, he asked, "Are you two serious?"

"About what," Bernie replied with a wry smile lighting up his face.

Terry jumped in and said, "You know how Sean is. Whatever is in his mind immediately comes out of his mouth."

Addressing Betsy, Bernie asked, "Are we serious?"

"Very," was Betsy's response.

Sean and Terry embraced Bernie and Betsy. "Will we be invited to the wedding?" Sean asked.

"There he goes again," Terry said. "Sean, who taught you proper manners?"

"I thought you did."

At that point, the room was brimming with happiness. Bernie wondered if things weren't happening a bit too fast.

Minutes later, Aram and Annette arrived. If anything, they were dressed even more elegantly than Terry and Sean. But it is unlikely that anyone other than Betsy noticed their attire. Like a sudden rain shower on a sunny day, they abruptly changed the mood in the room without saying a single word. Their faces were grim. Aram, the mildest of men, looked angry. Neither Sean nor Bernie had ever seen the look on his face that Aram brought into the private room at Dominic's Italian Restaurant. After a perfunctory hello and a moment of bemusement upon spotting Betsy, Aram quietly said to Sean and Bernie, "I need to have a private word with the two of you."

Terry called across the room, "Has there been an accident?"

Annette responded cryptically, "Everyone we know is

healthy." Then she added, "Why don't we three women go to the powder room? I'd like to get to know Bernie's friend."

"Stay here," Aram said to the women. "We'll go outside behind the building in case Dino arrives."

What did that mean? Terry wondered.

Chapter 45

Embezzlement

As soon as the men had left the room, Bernie asked Aram, "What the hell is going on?"

Aram replied, "I'm glad Dino isn't here yet. We have a very serious problem. It's very likely that Dino has been embezzling money from my father's business—lots of money."

"How do you know?" Bernie asked.

"I know because my father told me. The real question is how he knows. He told me that 1960 and '61 were great years in the new car business. It was the first year that he pushed for the sale of Chevy trucks, Silverados, and they sold like hotcakes. But he sensed something was wrong. The cash position was always less than he expected it would be, given how many vehicles were sold. My father had completely turned the day-to-day management of the dealership over to Dino several years ago. He thought Dino was doing a great job. He brought in better salesmen than my father had when Dino arrived. He said Dino straightened out the service department from a losing operation to a profitable one. He said the showroom looked better than any dealership he'd ever seen. Morale was terrific. Everything was great. Except it wasn't. My father did some random checking of the monthly financial statements, and they didn't make sense to him. There was always less gross revenue and higher overhead expense than there should have been."

"Wait a minute," Sean said. "I don't see how that proves Dino did anything wrong. Did your father discuss the problem with Dino?"

"Not yet. You're absolutely right," Aram responded. "There's no solid proof of anything. My father hasn't really been running the business, and all he has at this point is a feeling that something's wrong. That's why he told me about it. Do you guys think we should talk to Dino about it?"

"Well, that's a great way to ruin a friendship," Sean said. "We go up to our old friend Dino, our shortstop—our captain—and we say, 'We hear you've been stealing from Aram's father. What've you got to say about that?'"

"He's right," Bernie said. "But that doesn't mean we shouldn't be involved in this situation. Whether he's guilty or not, we can't just ignore the fact that Dino is our friend, and Aram's father believes he's a crook. I think we should take some time—as much time as necessary—to think this thing through. Now we have to go back into the party—shit, that's a fine thing to call it, isn't it? Some party. We may remember it as the night we broke up our friendship with Dino."

"We can't let that happen," Sean implored.

"Maybe Dino has arrived," Bernie said. "He did say he was coming. We might learn something just by watching him and listening to him."

"Okay," Aram said. "That makes sense. Let's go see if Dino has arrived. If he has, I suggest we act as if nothing has happened. Try to act normal, as if we're having fun."

Sean and Bernie agreed and went back into the other room. Dino was there.

Chapter 46

Life Stories

Dino was dressed in fashionable casual clothes—a gray tweed sports jacket, neat black slacks, and a pink open-collared shirt. When the three men came into the room, he greeted them with slightly less warmth than they expected. "I wish I had known you were taking a leak. I would've joined you. I just got here a couple of minutes ago. Which way's the bathroom?"

Sean pointed the way, and Dino left the room. Aram quietly asked Annette what she had said to the women, and she indicated they now knew about the problem. Bernie then said to everyone, "Let's pretend all is well, and let's try to have fun. That includes you, Terry. We're going to try to work everything out. Don't forget, Dino is still an Infielder, and we love him at least as much as you do."

"More," said Terry.

When Dino returned moments later, Terry said, "Let's have a great party. We've been separated from one another too long. Living in Chicago has been okay, but it ain't the Heights, and it ain't George Washington High School. In addition to eating good

Italian food and drinking 'til we drop, Sean and I thought it would be nice if we shared memories of fifteen years ago. Betsy, that will probably bore you. You should have gone to George Washington High School."

"I wanted to, but I failed the entrance exam," Betsy responded, and everyone laughed.

When the laughter died down, Terry resumed talking about her and Sean's ideas for the reunion. "Sean and I also thought we must have missed things about one another over all these years that we'd be interested in knowing about. Especially Sean and me. Because of his baseball, we've lived away from here for so much of the time, we really want to be caught up on stuff we've missed. For example, a little while ago Bernie told us that he didn't know I had two children. I don't know how that happened. He should try having a baby. He'd tell the whole world about it. So, those are some of our ideas about what we should talk about tonight."

"I think those are great ideas," said Bernie, "and I'd be happy to tell everyone about me—and about Betsy." He turned toward Betsy and said, "Terry thinks I should have a baby. What do you think?"

"Not while everyone's watching, Bernie. Maybe later."

Everyone laughed.

The group gathered around the bar that Dominic's Italian Restaurant had set up in the private room for them. It took about fifteen minutes of small talk and drink mixing before everyone had a drink and some hors d'oeuvres.

Then Bernie signaled for quiet and began to speak. "Hello, everyone. I'd like to introduce myself. My name is Bernie Heller. I used to play third base."

Amid a room full of chuckles and smiles, Sean called out, "Great speech, Mr. Heller. Who's next?"

"You know, we lawyers, we talk good. One day, about eight or nine months ago, I was trying a personal injury case in the city court on Centre Street downtown. It was a case in which my client drove his car into the rear end of a delivery van and banged his face into his steering wheel, breaking his nose. Our claim was that the truck should have had its emergency lights flashing because the driver was delivering a package to a store next to where the truck was stopped. The case sort of fell apart when my client was asked, on cross-examination, whether he had any difficulty seeing the van that he drove into. He answered that it was broad daylight, so of course he could see the van. The insurance company lawyer then asked my client why, if he could see the van, didn't he stop or drive around it. I swear this was his answer: 'Because I thought if I hit it and got hurt, I'd have a case.' If there was some dignified way I could have run out of the courtroom, that's what I would have done. After two minutes of deliberation, the jury returned a verdict against my client."

Dino interrupted and asked, "Are you telling us this story to prove that you're an idiot and an incompetent lawyer?"

"No, I told you this story—which is absolutely true—because sitting on the jury was one of the loveliest women I had ever seen. She is Betsy Weinstein, and I think we're going to get married, right Betsy? And after that, maybe a baby."

"Damned right," she answered.

Applause broke out and continued while everyone hugged and kissed and congratulated the happy couple.

"I made a point of meeting Betsy as she left the courthouse. I asked if she'd join me for a drink. I knew immediately she was my kind of girl when she said, 'I'll bet you really need one.'"

More laughter. The tension that was in the room when Dino arrived seemed to have dissipated. Aram understood that that was Bernie's objective and felt grateful to him.

Bernie continued, "But wait, I'm not done with my report on

my life after baseball. I was drafted into the army just before I was expecting to start law school. I spent two years learning how to kill people. Turns out, I was quite good at it."

"No surprise," said Dino.

Bernie ignored what might have been an insult. He continued his remarks. "I was promoted to corporal before my discharge, which, you may be surprised to learn, was honorable. I did okay in law school and opened an office on St. Nicholas Avenue. I actually have some clients, and I earn enough to live on. That and Betsy are the most important things in my life since the last time we were all together."

Sean said, "The story of how you and Betsy got together is hilarious. It's a story you got to tell your children."

"That's what I was going to say," Annette said. "I also want to say I'm not sure Aram and I have properly thanked all of you for your kindness when our baby died. You all helped us deal with that loss. I hope you know that we have a son, Berj, who, I'm happy to say, enjoys robust health and has an interest in baseball."

Terry then said, "If it's any help, when the baby died, every one of us felt like we lost a member of our family."

Annette smiled warmly at her. "Aram and I felt that closeness and it gave us comfort. It still does. We'll always be grateful for your kindness."

"Now here's something I don't think any of you know," Bernie said. "For the last couple of years, I have been taking adult education courses on the Jewish religion and Jewish history. Those of you who have known me since PS 189 can't possibly recall a single moment in which the fact that I was a Jew seemed important to me. I had a bar mitzvah at my synagogue when I was thirteen, but I don't even think any of you were there. That's because it wasn't important to me until I had a ferocious confrontation with my religious parents, who told me that they would disown me if I married a Catholic girl."

Dino, looking dumbfounded, said, "That sounds to me like more of a reason to stop being Jewish than to begin taking it seriously."

"For a while, I thought exactly the same thing, but then I thought if this was such a hugely important thing to my parents, maybe I should try to find out what it was all about. I'm very happy that I'm doing that. My greatest regret, Dino, about returning to the faith of my ancestors is that I'll no longer be able to eat any of your mom's magnificent food."

"Why is that?" Dino asked.

"Because I'm commanded not to eat certain foods, including the delicious things that your mother cooks so wonderfully."

"Commanded? By who?" Dino asked.

"God" was Bernie's answer.

"This is getting a little too heavy for me," Dino said in an unfriendly tone.

Aram, ignoring Dino's comment, remarked about a conversation that he recalled having with Bernie many years ago. "We were sitting on the sofa in my parents' apartment, sort of getting to know each other better because of the baseball team. I don't remember why, but you told me that your grandparents were killed by the Germans because they were Jewish. And then you started tearing up."

"Oh my, you remember that? Now I do, too. That was the conversation in which you told me about the Turks killing Armenians. We were just boys when we had that conversation." Bernie paused for a few seconds and then said, "Dino's right. We should go on to another topic and another Infielder."

Terry pushed Sean forward, but he had an attack of shyness and refused to move over to where Bernie had been standing when he spoke. She solved that problem by announcing, "Sean would like to tell you about the game this past season when he hit three home runs against the Cincinnati Reds."

"You all know that I'm not the most articulate of the Infielders," Sean began, but he was interrupted by Dino.

"*Articulate?* Where'd you learn that word?"

Sean continued, irked by Dino's question. "I must've picked it up somewhere, traveling around playing baseball for the past fifteen years. Dino, you should know I'm more of a grown man now than the dumb kid who played first base when you were our shortstop and our captain. That's really what I want to say about my life for the past fifteen years. I married Terry. We have two beautiful children. Two sons, Patrick and Frank. I've been a major league ballplayer for eleven years. Not a star. A journeyman. Although I did make the all-star team one year. *Journeyman*, Dino, that's another fancy word that I learned in my travels. I probably have one or two decent years left in me to play big league ball. Terry and me have started to think about what I should do when my big league career comes to an end. We've saved up enough money so I can take my time to find the right place for me. I might like to stay in baseball as a coach, but I might want to try something completely different. Terry will be a great help. I don't know if any of you know that Terry's gone back to school—actually college. When I think about the past fifteen years, all I can say is that I feel blessed."

Aram and Bernie rushed to shake Sean's hand. Aram said, "Sean, we are all so happy for you and Terry. And thanks for putting this party together."

"Now we'd like to hear from you," Sean said to Aram.

"Okay," Aram said, "I'll be brief. Annette and I keep reminding ourselves that we have been living our dream. Professionally, we are right where we want to be. We both have reason to expect that we'll be going further in our chosen fields. Annette is going to be a world-famous scientist. I know that with a degree of certainty that Annette thinks is overly optimistic. She is too modest. I will not be world famous, but I have found a niche in the world of literature that gives me pleasure, stimulates my mind, and illuminates the human condition . . . I better stop talking like that. That's not how a second baseman who couldn't hit should be talking. Let me just say that Annette and I are happy with our lives and with each other. We are grateful to the Infielders for making that possible."

There was another round of handshakes among the Infielders, and then Bernie said, "Hey, Dino, I'll never forget that day we went to Yankee Stadium, and you gave me good advice about my sex life."

"I want to hear about that," Betsy said.

"No way," Bernie said. "Dino's sworn to secrecy."

Chapter 47

Dino's Rant

Dino remained seated, sipping a pink drink from a martini glass. He seemed hesitant, uncertain as to what he needed or wanted to do. Terry wished she could run from the room as the silence moved from seconds to minutes.

Eventually, Sean said to Dino, "Are you all right? Need help?"

Dino finally broke his silence. "I'm okay, Sean. It's just that I've been wrestling with myself as to what to say to this group."

Aram trembled as he thought Dino was about to confess. He was utterly uncertain as to what he would do or say if Dino did confess. He knew everyone would look to him for guidance, for an appropriate reaction. He was unprepared to provide guidance; he needed it himself.

"You people are not going to like what I'm going to say," Dino began. "But you asked for it, so here it comes. For me, sitting here listening to my three friends talk about their lives—that's been torture for me. I'm sure none of you gave any thought to what effect your little speeches would have on poor Dino, the unmarried car salesman with no future that's going to be any better than where he is right now. Well, now I'll tell you what effect your words had. I've been jealous of all of you for years. I was the captain. The leader. And now I'm a failure. And you rubbed that in my face."

"What do you mean, 'rubbed it in your face'? How can you say that?" Sean exclaimed.

Dino continued as if Sean had not said anything. "I never expected to envy any of you, especially you, Sean. I expected you to flop as a ballplayer. I thought you'd strike out in life the same as in baseball. Instead, you stand here bragging about being a major leaguer, a fucking all-star! Looking across the room at me, thinking how far ahead of me you've gotten. And you married my sister, my skinny, stupid, sex-crazed sister, and she sits there like a queen because her moron of a husband hit three home runs in a game. And she looks across the room at me and thinks, 'I'm the winner in the Russo family, and you're the loser. The *principe* of the family has been replaced by the *indigenta*.' For those of you who don't know Italian, that's the pauper replacing the prince. I heard Terry reads books now that she's a major leaguer and goes to college. Well, you're right. You and Sean are winners. And I'm not. I hope that makes you happy. It makes me feel like shit."

The room had been silent for a minute or two when Bernie said, "There's no need for you to go on like this, Dino. I'm absolutely stunned. You just said some awful things. You've ruined our party. I don't want to hear any more from you. I wish you'd leave."

Dino continued his rant. "Bernie, you've never gotten past being that smug wise guy that you were in the fourth grade. Now I hear you're studying to be a good Jew. Does that mean you're no longer fucking every girl in the neighborhood? What do you want, a medal? You want me to call you Rabbi? I'll leave this room when I choose to leave, and you can go to hell."

Sean was afraid a fight might break out between Bernie and Dino. He placed his large, athletic body between them and said, "I can't believe this is happening between us. Stop it, both of you. Dino, you shouldn't have said what you did about Terry. For God's sake, she's my wife, and she's your sister. Why did you come here if you intended to say such ugly things about us? We were your closest friends. If something terrible is bothering you—and that's the only explanation I can think of—you should have come to us— at least one of us—to talk it over, the way we used to . . ." Tears began to roll down his cheeks. "The way we used to when we were friends."

Terry pushed past Sean, took Dino's arm, and led him out of the room.

The five people remaining in the private room sat silently, stunned and deeply troubled. Even Betsy Weinstein—a virtual stranger to the main players in this looming tragedy—felt deeply engaged in the fear, guilt, and anguish that seemed to paralyze everyone around her. She observed, "He must be suffering terribly if he could say such things."

"I think he is suffering," Aram said, "and we all know why. Practically every waking moment since yesterday when my father told me about the missing cash, I've been wondering what reason Dino could have for stealing money from the business, for betraying my father. Dino wasn't short of money. He made a decent income from the dealership."

"He was getting ready to announce all his grievances against me," Bernie said. "Betsy, I'm glad you didn't get to hear all the stuff that Dino was going to say about me. There's plenty of stuff that I'm not proud of, but I want to tell you myself. In private."

"I'm sure he was going to attack all of us," Aram said. "The question is why? Bernie, do you think we should go to the police?"

"Absolutely not," Bernie said emphatically. "Why should we

put this in the hands of the police? We know everybody involved in this, from Mr. Petrosian to you to all of the Infielders, including Dino. I don't think we should put this in the hands of strangers, at least until we know more about the underlying facts."

"Okay, I think what you're saying makes sense," Aram replied, "but how are we going to learn the underlying facts? That is, if there are underlying facts. All the facts might be right on the surface."

Bernie replied, "In the first place, we need to hire a forensic accountant to do a complete analysis of the dealership's financial records. It's not enough that your father has a feeling that cash is missing. I'm not accusing him of making anything up. God forbid! But I'm not comfortable working on this case without being absolutely certain about what happened."

Sean, who had been listening attentively, asked, "Bernie, I have two questions. What does 'forensic' mean, and what do you mean by 'working on this case'?"

"I don't know what the word means exactly, but it's a term lawyers use when accountants look for crimes or other irregularities in financial records. As to your other question, aren't we all working on this case? Don't you feel a responsibility to try to help Mr. Petrosian, and to help Dino, if that's possible? To save the Infielders, if that's possible? I do."

"I would do anything—anything—to make this all go away," Sean said.

Terry returned to the room alone. She said, "Dino's gone. I don't know where he went. I told him what Aram was told by his father. He became enraged. He denied the accusation. He made some incoherent remarks about Aram's father. Then he began weeping uncontrollably, almost hysterically. He was out of breath. I thought he might have a heart attack. I was about to come in here to call for help when he suddenly screamed something that sounded like 'My life is over, I've lost everything,' and he ran out of the restaurant and disappeared into the darkness. It was awful to see what he was like. He was someone I didn't know . . . didn't recognize." And then she began to sob. "What have we done to him? He was your friend, and I think we destroyed him."

Chapter 48

The Infielders Unraveling

Dino had disappeared. Two days later, Bernie, Aram. Sean, Terry, and Annette spent nearly twelve hours contacting everyone they knew who might have knowledge of Dino's whereabouts. No one, not one person in the dozens of people they spoke with, had even seen a passing glance of Dino in the past two days. Bernie and Aram went to Dino's apartment in Riverdale. The door was locked, and no one answered repeated knocks and doorbell rings.

A neighbor spotted them in the hallway and said, "That guy hasn't lived here for a long time. He works at the Chevy dealership on Broadway." Neither Aram nor Bernie was aware that Dino had moved. The employees at the dealership were worried. Dino hadn't shown up or phoned anyone for three days.

It was as though Dino had evaporated when he bolted and ran while Terry had been talking with him. When it became apparent that the search had come to a dead end, the group gathered in Bernie's office. Each of them was exhausted and frustrated. It seemed that no one had anything to say.

"He'll be back when it suits him," Terry said. She could no longer bear the silence in Bernie's waiting room. "Even when I was a kid, he would sometimes just disappear for a full day. It drove my mother crazy, but my father always said he was just a boy spreading his wings. And he was right. He always came home . . . without an explanation."

"Well, this time," Aram said, "he better come back with a full explanation, not only about his appalling behavior the other night but also about what's going on at the dealership."

"He desperately needs help," Terry said, "and we should all get together to give him the help he needs. We're all that he's got."

"He's also got a lot of my father's money," Aram said. "He won't get any help from me or Annette unless we solve that problem."

Sean put his hand on Aram's shoulder. "The Infielders," he said. "Please don't forget the Infielders, Aram."

"What about the Infielders?" Aram asked. "What does that mean in this context?"

"*Context*? What does that mean?" Sean asked, in all innocence.

Aram, with obvious annoyance, responded, "Sean, it's a word in the English language which means, in this case, something like the word *situation*. Do you need a definition of that?"

Bernie intervened. "Please, Aram, don't be childish, and don't be picking a fight with Sean. That won't do anyone any good. Sean raised a point that we should not lose sight of during this difficult time. Being one of the Infielders has been one of the most important, most valuable things in my life. No doubt that's true in Sean's case and, I sincerely hope, in yours as well. In doing whatever we need to do to untangle this mess, if it is humanly possible to do so, we should try to preserve the thing we called the Infielders. I want you to know that at the lowest points in my life, I've drawn strength from the thought that I am a member of the Infielders."

"That's what I was trying to say," Sean said, addressing Aram and Annette.

Aram ignored Sean's remark and addressed Bernie. "First of all, don't ever call me childish again. It brings back irritating memories of when we played ball together, and I was the smallest and, I suppose, the least manly player on the team. You guys made fun of my size and my high marks in high school. I resent that, bitterly."

"Stop it, Aram! Just stop it," Bernie shouted. "I don't know what you're hoping to accomplish by dredging up a grievance from years ago that I, for one, never knew you had. If what you're trying to do is destroy what Sean and I have been trying to preserve—the notion that there is something that we all created years ago called the Infielders that is precious to us—then all I can say is fuck you, fuck your father's money, fuck your high and mighty intellectual achievements, just fuck you! Please leave my office and never come back."

"Don't say that," Sean pleaded. "Aram, please say that's not what you're trying to do. I understand that it hurts you that a member of the Infielders may have stolen money from your father. But you're still an Infielder, aren't you?"

Annette spoke up. "Aram, listen, Bernie and Sean are right. We're dealing with a matter that has far-reaching implications for all of us, as well as for Dino. Think for a moment about how you will feel if Dino goes to jail. Sean and Bernie, think for a moment about how you'd feel if Aram's father's business goes bankrupt because of the theft. It's a pity if either of those tragedies causes another tragedy: the destruction of the friendships of innocent people. I mean all of us. We're all innocent, and we're struggling to do the right thing. Please, let's all forget the harsh words of the past few minutes. We won't be able to forgive ourselves when this is over if our friendships have died as a result."

Her remarks had a sobering effect.

Aram said, "I'm sorry for how I spoke. You all know I am terribly conflicted."

"Me too," Bernie said. "Annette mentioned the possibility of bankruptcy as a result of the embezzlement. Right now, none of us knows if that's a real possibility. I am going to hire a forensic accountant. Aram, please ask your father for permission to have a guy named Sheldon Applebaum review the dealership's financial records. He is a whiz at uncovering irregularities. It won't take him long to determine how much is missing, how it got to be missing, and who is likely to have done it. Okay, Aram?"

"Absolutely," Aram replied. "I'll do that right now."

Part Five

Dino's Story

Chapter 49

MoMA

It all began on a rainy Sunday in April 1960. The previous day, Dino had closed the sale of the most expensive car he had ever sold at Petrosian Motors. It was a Corvette Stingray convertible with every option in the portfolio. He sold it for $6,950, a price that was higher than the list price. He should have been in a celebratory mood, but he was not. Selling cars was no longer a rousing experience for him. He had been selling cars for twelve years and had nothing to show for it.

Sure, I'm the general manager of Petrosian Motors. Sure, the business is immensely successful. Money flows to Mr. Petrosian, a man like my papa. Big deal, he thought. *Sean plays baseball in the major leagues. Bernie is a successful lawyer, probably making buckets of money, getting laid every weekend. Aram's a college professor. And I am just a glorified car salesman.*

He had just about given up trying to find a woman with whom he could be happy. He had dates with various women, but none of them compared favorably to Rachel—Rachel who still occupied his dreams and against whom every woman fell short. But on that day, he was home alone, bored, and feeling sorry for himself. His life felt empty and directionless. He had begun to read extensively. The great books. He started with *Crime and Punishment*. He was moved by it, so he turned to the other Russian classics, *War and Peace, Anna Karenina,* and *The Brothers Karamazov.* He read Turgenev, Gorky, and others. Then he moved on to other classics. Dickens, Austen, even Orwell. He was reading Thomas Mann's *The Magic Mountain. That's what you do to fill up your life when it is empty and meaningless and you are alone,* he thought.

He sat on the sofa in his living room, staring out the window, looking at the rain, feeling sullen and morose. The Yankee baseball game that he had intended to watch on television had been rained out. He had to do something to break out of this despondency.

The guy who bought the Stingray had mentioned something about the Museum of Modern Art. That was just a part of the typical blather that accompanied every car sale experience, and Dino had paid little attention to it at the time. However, one of Dino's innate talents was an ability to draw, a skill he never seriously exploited but one that gave him occasional satisfaction. He decided to visit the museum, a place of which he was vaguely aware until yesterday's conversation with the car customer. He knew absolutely nothing about modern art, but he was curious to see what it looked like. *That might bring some brightness into this gray day,* he thought.

The museum was housed in an architecturally interesting building, a fact that Dino noticed as he approached it on 53rd Street, and that raised his level of anticipation as he entered and paid the modest entrance fee. The names of the most prominent artists were unknown to him. He asked the woman at the reception desk if there was any kind of guide to the museum and explanation of the exhibits. There was indeed such a thing, and he purchased a pamphlet that would serve his purpose.

Dino's walk through the rooms of MoMA—as he was given to understand was the nickname of the museum—was an uplifting experience for him. Just what he needed. Viewing the works of such artists as Kandinsky, Miro, Chagall, Klee, and Picasso—especially Picasso—gave him more satisfaction and enjoyment than almost anything that had happened in his life since the baseball championship. After several hours of walking and looking at paintings and sculptures, Dino felt overwhelmed by what he had seen. But he was sated. He had to stop and digest what he had seen. He stepped into the museum store and gazed at the souvenirs of this wondrous day that he might purchase—posters, books, reproductions. After he had been browsing for several minutes, Dino was approached by a young woman clerk who asked him if she could help him.

Dino looked at the young woman and thought, *What a miraculous day this is. This girl is the most beautiful person I have ever seen.* After realizing with embarrassment that he had been staring at her, he mumbled, "I might like to buy a poster of something by Picasso."

"*Guernica*," she said.

"No, Picasso is what I'm interested in."

She laughed. Her laughter was almost musical, at least in Dino's ears. "*Guernica* is the title of an amazing painting by Picasso. It's huge, as large as a wall. You should definitely go see it. On the second floor."

"I must have walked right past it when I was walking around. I was walking for so long I thought I would drop."

"Well, don't drop. Let's go look at the *Guernica*. I'll go with you. The shop will be closing in a few minutes. I can't look at it too many times. Every time I see it, I learn something new about it."

Dino was thrilled at the prospect of walking through the

museum in the company of this beautiful woman. "Thanks, thanks a lot. I'd appreciate that. What's your name, by the way?"

"Désirée, but everyone calls me Desi. What's your name?"

"Dino. It's Italian. Actually, it's short for Bernardino, which nobody except my mother ever calls me. I think Desi and Dino make a good combination." The ice was not only broken, it was shattered. He was comfortable talking with her.

A voice suddenly declared over the public address system that the museum would be closing in fifteen minutes. "That's too bad," Dino said. "We won't have time to look at that painting."

"Not a problem. You're with me, and I'm an employee. We don't have to leave until six o'clock. We have plenty of time. It takes time to look at *Guernica* and understand what it's telling you. I'll try to help."

"I feel lucky to have stumbled onto you. A happy accident. I know almost nothing about art, modern or otherwise. I need all the help I can get."

"That's what I'm here for. I love this place. Let's go."

Without realizing what he was saying, he heard the words coming out of his mouth. "After *Guernica*, will you have dinner with me?"

"Delighted to," Desi immediately responded.

Desi led Dino to the room where the giant *Guernica* painting covered one of the walls. At first, Dino didn't understand what the painting was depicting. Desi carefully and fluently explained how the painting was created by Picasso as a protest against the bombing of the village of Guernica in the Basque region of Spain by German and Italian warplanes in support of the fascists in the Spanish Civil War. Dino didn't admit that he didn't know what *Basque* meant. He decided to save that and other questions until dinner.

He did ask one question that Desi thought revealed him to be a deep and thoughtful person. After listening for about ten minutes to Desi's discourse on the symbolism in the picture, he asked, "Can you tell me why this is considered a *beautiful* work of art?"

Desi nearly quivered with excitement at the aesthetic acumen that she thought Dino's question revealed. After a few moments in which she gathered her thoughts to prepare a response worthy of the question, she launched a five-minute discourse on art, aesthetics, and the varieties of individual appreciation of works of art.

This woman is extraordinary, Dino concluded. *Beautiful, brainy, and also sexy. I want her. I could love her, even though she's a Negro.* Desi was a Black woman, although *black* was simply one of the words used to identify her race. Dino was thinking about that word. *Why,* he wondered, *do we describe Negroes as* black *and people like me as* white? *Those words are meaningless. I'm certainly not white. And Desi's not black. She's more like the color of my walnut desk . . . better than that . . . smooth deep brown with a glow that's almost golden. She is absolutely beautiful.*

Chapter 50

Desi

The only restaurant in Midtown Manhattan that Dino knew the name of was Sardi's, so that's where he took Desi after MoMA closed for the night. The rain had stopped, and it had turned into a pleasant spring evening. Dino suggested that they walk the ten blocks to the restaurant, and Desi enthusiastically agreed. She took Dino's arm and cuddled next to him as they walked.

"Where are you taking me?" she asked.

"Have you ever heard of Sardi's?"

"Isn't that where all the celebrities go for dinner?"

"After tonight, everyone will be talking about that elegant couple whose presence at Sardi's dressed up the joint on Sunday night. We'll probably be interviewed and see our name in the *Daily News* tomorrow."

"You're joking, aren't you?"

"Would I lead you on?"

"I think you might."

"Get used to it, Desi. I'm a playful guy. But I must tell you that

I have never in my life been to Sardi's. I've been saving it for an extraordinary event. You'll have to tell me which hand to hold the fork in."

"How would I know? I've never been to a fancy restaurant."

"To tell you the truth, neither have I."

"Well then, this will be a new experience for both of us."

They walked briskly down Broadway to 44th Street to Sardi's Restaurant. Dino was relieved to learn that there was a table available for them. He was worried about that.

Neither Dino nor Desi could think of a way to start a conversation after they were seated. Both kept their noses in the menus that had been handed to them for several awkward minutes. Noting that there was sort of an Italian cuisine described on the menu, Dino asked if Desi needed any help with the Italian items on the menu. She said no, and the silence resumed.

Finally, Desi opened with, "I didn't really come here just to eat. I thought we might resume the great conversation we were having at the museum."

"Thanks, Desi. I can eat Italian food any day of the week just by walking into my mother's kitchen. I really want to continue discussing modern art. I'd also be interested to learn how you became an expert in the subject."

"Oh, Dino. I am far from being an expert. I learned whatever I know about the pictures at MoMA by asking questions of the real experts at the museum and by reading books that they recommended to me. I also learned quite a bit about art in general in high school."

"In high school? I don't think they even had art as a subject at George Washington High School."

"I went to the High School of Music and Art. My mom recommended I apply there when she saw that I had some artistic ability. You need to pass a test to get into Music and Art."

"The only thing you needed to get into George Washington was to live in Upper Manhattan. Let's get back to your explanation of why *Guernica* is a beautiful painting."

"I could talk all day about that, but I'd like to talk about other things as well. *Guernica* is obviously not beautiful in the conventional sense. I believe it's beautiful because of the stimuli that it sets off in your brain. In the power of its condemnation of fascism and the violence of war. Hardly what happens when you look at a lovely landscape or the Mona Lisa. But great art, like great literature, is an impetus for thought, reflection, and learning. But I'm talking far too much, Dino. I must sound like such a kook."

"Absolutely not, Desi. You amaze me."

"That's nice for you to say. Why don't you try to amaze me?"

Dino mulled over that invitation to talk about himself. *Baseball, not cars. Certainly not an intellectual match, but I might throw in* The Magic Mountain. *Taking too much time.*

"Well, Desi, I can't match the depth of your understanding of art. Or anything else, for that matter. I'm going to try to impress you with what I feel is my greatest accomplishment."

"I'm all ears."

"In 1947, George Washington High School's baseball team won the high school championship of New York City. I was one of the stars of that team. I played shortstop, and I was the captain of that team. As I said, it may not mean as much as your knowledge of art, but it's the best I can offer."

"On the contrary, that's an amazing accomplishment. I became a baseball fan in 1947. Not because of your championship, I'm sorry to say, but because that was the year Jackie Robinson joined the Brooklyn Dodgers as the first Negro player in the major leagues."

"It looks like we have at least two things in common. Are you still a Dodgers fan?"

"I'm conflicted. The team left Brooklyn. I feel betrayed."

"I fully understand. They just packed up and left Brooklyn without even a polite goodbye."

Their waiter asked if they wanted drinks before dinner.

"Let's order drinks," Dino said.

Without first asking Desi, Dino ordered a bottle of champagne. The only time in his life he had ever drunk champagne was on the night of the championship game when Aram ordered it at the Tropical Gardens Pizzeria and Bar on St. Nicholas Avenue. He much preferred the chianti that his father sometimes opened at the family dinner table when he was feeling happy. The champagne was intended to impress Desi, and it did.

Dino raised his champagne glass and proposed a toast "to a newborn friendship."

Desi said, "I'll join that toast!"

After a discussion about the food, Desi ended up ordering a pork chop while Dino opted for the somewhat more exotic crab cakes with an array of side dishes. Desi was clearly shocked at the prices, while Dino casually remarked that they were probably typical of high-quality restaurants in New York.

After the couple had concluded the business of ordering and before anything other than rolls and water had arrived at the table, Dino said, "I'd like it if you told me more about yourself."

"I wanted to be an artist and thought I had a real chance to be a painter of modern art. I produced a lot of paintings and carried those that I thought were the best around to every gallery I could find. But none of them wanted to display any of my work. I got the job at MoMA about a year ago. And then you showed up."

Conversation became increasingly easy. They talked about baseball, Picasso, the Dodgers, MoMA, where each of them lived and with whom they lived (her mother, in the case of Desi, and no one, in the case of Dino), and whether they could have a less fancy dinner next Sunday.

At this point in the conversation, the bottle of champagne was empty, and both Desi and Dino were a bit tipsy. They were giggling when the waiter arrived with the dishes they had ordered. The conversation continued while they were eating. There was more talk than eating, and the waiter asked if there was anything wrong with their food.

"I don't think either of us has ever had a better meal," Dino said. "We haven't seen each other in a long time, so we have a lot of talking to do to catch up." The waiter seemed pleased with that response but looked at the mixed-race couple with a fleeting expression of bemusement as he walked away.

"You are so amusing," Desi said to Dino.

"I'm glad you appreciate me."

Desi remarked, "You said you were the shortstop and the captain of the George Washington High School baseball team that won the New York City high school championship in 1947."

"That's what I said."

"You didn't say if you were a really good player. Were you?"

"Yes, I was. Not the best on the team, but very good. Are we done with this cross-examination? My crab cakes are getting cold."

It was now past ten thirty, and although Sardi's was still full of diners and lively chatter, the waiter had put the bill on their table at least half an hour before Dino noticed it. Dino gave the waiter a credit card that had been given to him by Mr. Petrosian to cover expenses Dino might incur in going to meetings sponsored by General Motors. He had no other means of paying a seventy-five-dollar dinner bill. That was the first time he used that credit card for a personal expense.

They emerged from the restaurant into a balmy spring night. The air was fresh, cleaned by the day's earlier rain. They were holding hands as Dino hailed a taxi. Desi gave the driver her address on 122nd Street, and Dino wrote the address and Desi's telephone number into an address book that he kept in his pocket. "How about dinner next Sunday at a less fancy place in your neighborhood?" Dino asked.

"With pleasure," Desi responded. "Will you pick me up at my home? I'd like you to meet my mother."

"Perfect. Six o'clock?"

"Great. I'll pick the restaurant."

Best date, by far, I have ever had, and no kiss at the end. I think I'm in love with that girl. I could have been in love with her because of her beauty alone. But she is the smartest, sharpest girl—no, woman—I've ever met. What a prize. Her eyes—so enchanted by the beauty of great art—are themselves things of beauty. They are like the "Kyrgyz eyes" that captivated Thomas Mann's protagonist in The Magic Mountain, *delicately slanted, subtle, and seductive. Who knows what remote ancestor contributed the gene that produced the startling blue-green color of her eyes? Her frizzy jet-black hair framed her brown face like a halo in a Renaissance painting. I'm so excited I think I'm going to burst. I can't wait until next Sunday. I am in love with her. And I'm frightened. Why am I frightened? I don't even want to think about it.*

On Monday evening, Dino called Desi to try to schedule a date before the next Sunday. Desi didn't hesitate and said she had the day off from work at MoMA every Wednesday. She also said her mother worked in the evenings, and therefore, it might be best for Dino to come in the afternoon and for them to have lunch. Dino instantly agreed. To Dino, the time between Monday evening and Wednesday at noon seemed as long as a month. On Tuesday, he got a haircut and had his best suit pressed. He sat in his office reading Thomas Mann. The only thing he did on Tuesday relating to the car business was to have the service crew make sure that a Stingray convertible was washed and ready for his use the next day.

He awoke early, showered, shaved meticulously, dressed in a white shirt, his favorite tie, his best suit, and made sure that his hair looked exactly right and was locked into place with Brylcreem. He drove from his home in Riverdale to the dealership. He told his assistant manager that he would be away all day.

He parked on 122nd Street near the corner of Manhattan Avenue and looked for Desi's building. He found it and walked up to the second floor to apartment 2A. He noted the name Bradley under the doorbell, rang the bell, and waited anxiously. The door was opened, not by Desi, but by the woman who must be her mother.

Before Dino could say anything, the woman said, "Ah, you must be Dino, the man Désirée has been talking about."

"Right."

"Welcome. I've been looking forward to meeting you."

"Likewise."

"Do you ever speak in complete sentences?"

I can play that game. "No."

"She said you were funny. I assume you're here to pick up my daughter for lunch."

"Correct."

She laughed. "She'll be ready in a few minutes. She's trying to make herself beautiful. Please come in."

She led him into the living room, which was nicely furnished with comfortable-looking upholstered chairs and two sofas, color coordinated with the drapes and carpet. Dino made himself comfortable in one of the upholstered chairs, and Mrs. Bradley sat opposite him on a sofa.

"It's a waste of time for Desi to make herself beautiful because she's already the most beautiful woman I have ever met."

Mrs. Bradley smiled. "Thank you, Dino, for saying that. I agree that my daughter is beautiful."

A moment later, Desi walked into the room. She said, "I've been eavesdropping on your conversation. I'm very glad that the two of you agreed that I'm beautiful. That's good for my ego. Mom, do you see what I meant when I described him?"

"I already figured that out," Mrs. Bradley responded. "By the way, there's nothing wrong with your ego. Go have a nice lunch. Where are you going?"

"Someplace in the neighborhood," said Desi.

"I had an idea," Dino said. "I've never been to Tavern on the Green in Central Park. It's a gorgeous day, and we can sit outside to eat our lunches."

"I thought we were going to go somewhere less fancy," said Desi.

"We'll do that next time," Dino answered, taking note of the fact that neither Desi nor her mom balked at the suggestion that there would be a next time.

"That sounds lovely," Mrs. Bradley remarked.

"Well, that settles it," Dino said. "It's been a real pleasure meeting you, Mrs. Bradley."

She responded, "I'd prefer if you called me Rose."

"Okay, it's been a pleasure meeting you, Rose."

Desi kissed her mother goodbye, and the couple departed.

Chapter 51

Dino and Desi

Second Date and More

Comfortably seated at an outdoor table in the shade of a huge oak tree, the couple chatted casually. Desi said, "You know much more about me than I do about you. Tell me what your greatest achievement has been so far in your young life."

"Without doubt, as I told you at Sardi's, it was being captain of the high school baseball team that won the New York City championship in 1947."

"Why does that mean so much to you?"

"Because it was a once-in-a-lifetime experience and because it cemented the friendship of the four guys who played the infield."

"Tell me about the other three guys. Are they still your best friends?"

Dino sketched the key elements of the biographies of Sean, Aram, and Bernie and ended by saying, "They remain my dearest friends and will for the rest of my life."

Desi smiled. "I knew there had to be more to your life story. It is a blessing to have such friendships."

The couple saw each other several times a week. Beginning

with the kiss that ended the day of the lunch in Central Park, Desi and Dino became more and more intimate. Each of them realized that they were in a serious relationship, and they were glad about that.

About two months after Tavern on the Green, the couple were having a thoughtful conversation about their relationship. They were seated at a table at a bistro on the Upper West Side. In the course of the conversation, Desi asked, "I have one extremely serious question. Have you ever had any kind of relationship—male or female—with a colored person?"

He paused to think about the question, closing his eyes as he pretended to scan his memory. He knew the correct answer to the question was simply no. But he wasn't confident that that answer would dodge the bullet.

He finally came up with the answer. "On our baseball team, we had a pitcher and two outfielders who were Negroes. I was friendly with them, but we weren't close. They didn't live in Washington Heights, so I was never in their homes. For that matter, they were never in my home. As for women, I never gave a moment's thought to having a date with a colored girl until I met you."

"How do you feel about that?"

"Desi, you're not a colored girl in my eyes. You are the woman I love."

Desi left that piece of the conversation dangling, not fully comfortable with Dino's answer, but she thought she could work around the issue of color. At least she hoped she could.

A few months after Desi moved in with Dino in his bachelor apartment in Riverdale, Dino decided that they needed to live in what he called "more appropriate quarters." Without letting Desi know what he was doing, he quietly shopped for a house in an upscale New York suburb. He came home from the dealership one day in early 1961 and waited for Desi to return home from MoMA. As soon as she walked into the apartment, Dino said, "We have to pack. We're moving out of here."

"But it's so nice here. Why do we have to move?"

"The short answer is I heard the people who live upstairs talking about you living with me, and they used a filthy, bigoted word to describe you."

"I'll bet I can guess the word."

"I know you can. The longer answer is . . . we both deserve to live in more appropriate quarters. By that I mean a house with no one upstairs and no one downstairs. A house with no one in it but us. I grew up on the fourth floor of a grubby building on Amsterdam Avenue. I've got a good job, and you're a person of good taste. The time has come for us to be good to ourselves. I found us a house in New Rochelle."

"Where exactly is that?"

"It's in Westchester County, about twenty miles from the city. It's a quiet town, full of trees, and the house I found for us is a six-room split-level, with a garage, two bathrooms, and a paneled den. Desi, you're going to love it."

"Can you afford it? I know I can't."

"Sweetheart, leave all that to me. You deserve as much beauty around you as the beauty you bring wherever you go."

"You say the nicest things, Dino. But I don't want you to go into debt. I'm very happy living here with you. This is by far the nicest place I've ever lived in."

"No debt, I've saved up enough money to pay cash for the house. No mortgage. We own the house free and clear. Just wait until you see our new home in New Rochelle. We're going to fill it with paintings and other beautiful things. I want so very much for you to be happy there."

Two weeks later, Dino and Desi moved into their new home in

the suburbs. They settled in quickly and comfortably. Their next-door neighbors greeted them cordially, but the people across the street said something about property values. "The hell with them," Dino said.

"White trash," Desi pronounced.

Dino taught Desi how to drive. She didn't need a car to get to MoMA. It was much more convenient to take a train to Grand Central than to drive into the city and try to find a place to park. It was just something that seemed right to Dino that Desi should be able to drive. It was part of the suburban image, and it mattered to Dino.

Chapter 52

The Question of Color

One Sunday in late October 1962, the couple slept late, and Dino decided he would cook brunch. He whipped up a pile of pancakes, fried rashers of bacon, and brewed coffee. The kitchen smelled like a diner, a point that Desi made with a sparkling grin on her face.

"Are you really happy here," he asked.

"Dino, I'm happy just hearing you snore at night."

"I don't snore."

"So, who's the guy sleeping next to me when I wake up in the morning?"

"What does he look like?"

"Like an ordinary handsome white man."

"Does Italian count as white? Can you love an Italian man?"

"The Italian man who snores in my bed? Him I could and do love with all my heart. I love him enough to marry him. How about it?"

The happy, bantering conversation had taken a serious turn. The eighteen months that Desi and Dino had lived together were

—for each of them—a dance through the Elysian Fields. Neither of them had ever felt the happiness that they had felt during those months. Dino lavished gifts on Desi, who invariably insisted there was no need for him to spend so much money on gifts for her. Dino said to Desi, "Petrosian Motors, thanks to me, is an immensely profitable business. I have access to all the money I need to care for you in the manner I think you deserve. Don't worry about how much I spend."

"Does your boss know that his company is spending money on paintings for the woman you're living with?"

"Mr. Petrosian loves me like a son. He has put me in total charge of the dealership. I decide how much each employee is paid."

"Yes, but does he know how much you are paid?"

"Believe me, he doesn't care."

"Well, I must tell you that's hard to believe."

"Okay, next time I see him, I'll tell him exactly how much I have allocated to myself. One problem is I hardly ever see him. He has health issues, and he hardly ever comes into the dealership."

"Promise me you'll do that."

"I promise."

Dino had various techniques for skimming money out of Petrosian Motors. He felt like a wealthy man, and it was a good feeling. He purchased abstract expressionist paintings by unknown artists who later became famous, like Gerhard Richter and Anselm Kiefer, together with numerous works by painters whose names remained unknown outside a very limited audience. He had a remarkably sharp eye for good art, and Desi was thrilled by the passion for visual art that they grew to share with each other. He bought lithographs, etchings, prints, posters, oils, and watercolors until there was no longer any room on the walls of the house in New Rochelle.

But each of them was aware that in a distant corner of their paradise, there lurked an uncertainty that threatened their happiness, a threat that neither of them had the confidence to acknowledge and confront openly. The words *marry* and *marriage* had never been uttered by either of them since that moment at breakfast when Desi casually said she loved the man who snored enough to marry him. And suddenly, there it was. With no context or prelude, out of the blue, Desi said, "How about it? Let's get married."

Dino's thoughts immediately flashed to his family and then to his friends, the Infielders. *I can't*, he thought. *The neighborhood. How could I bring her to the neighborhood? She'd be jeered at. I'd be jeered at. Wait a minute, this is the 1960s, not the 1940s. The country has changed. Maybe the neighborhood has changed. Except for the time I spend in the dealership, I haven't spent any real time there in years. Why do I worry about how this looks to others? To me, it looks beautiful. To others, she'll just look colored. I wish I could discuss this with Bernie. Will Mr. Petrosian ever find out about the money I've taken out of the business? Will it matter to him? There's just too much to think about here.*

"You know I love you, Desi. But this is complicated. I need some time to think about it."

"I've thought about it ever since that first night in your Riverdale apartment. Do you mean to tell me that getting married never crossed your mind in the past year and a half?"

"Of course it's been in my mind. It's just more complicated for me than for you."

"What the hell does that mean? Does it mean that it's more complicated for a white guy to marry a colored girl than vice versa?"

When Dino didn't immediately answer that question, Desi got up from the table and walked out of the house, slamming the screen door. About fifteen minutes later, she returned. Dino was still sitting at the kitchen table. The remains of the brunch were still waiting to be cleared. It seemed to Desi that Dino hadn't moved since she stormed out of the house. In fact, he hadn't so much as changed the position he was in. He was inanimate.

"We have to talk. Right now," Desi said.

Dino just stared at her vacantly.

"Are you all right?" Desi asked.

"No, I'm not all right," he mumbled. Then he stood up and walked to the kitchen window. He remained there, not looking at Desi. He took a deep breath and, turning toward Desi, he said, "I can't marry you. Why can't we just stay as we are? We love each other. Everything is perfect as it is. It's the same as married, isn't it?"

"Sit down," she ordered. They sat facing each other across the kitchen table, a table laden with unwashed dishes. "Dino, the way we are now, the way we've been for a year and a half, that way is not nearly the same as married. Maybe it is for you, but not for me. Let me tell you how it's not the same as being married. Here's a small example. If one of us gets sick and is in a hospital, the other won't be allowed to visit because we're not a family. We can't be covered by each other's health insurance, that's another small example. Neither of us has the rights we would have as a married couple. If we have a child, it'll be . . . like me . . . a bastard."

"Your parents weren't married?"

"No, he was a white man. He was a bus driver, and he was killed in an accident. He died when I was an infant. But to me, it's much more than those legal things. You've made it clear we can't visit your family or your friends. In fact, we have no friends. Or, rather, you have your friends, and I have mine. We have none together. That's because of color, Dino. Do you hear me, Dino? Color. Say that word and be honest, Dino Russo. You can't marry me because of my color. You know what that's called? It's called bigotry. It's called race prejudice.

"Every day of my life, I am reminded that my color is a problem. I've heard people say, 'Isn't she beautiful for a nigger.' I thought when I met you, when we embraced each other, when we had wonderful sex together . . . when you bought this house because we had a bigoted neighbor in Riverdale . . . when we lived together and were happy together, I thought . . . Dino, I thought I'd reached a point in my life where my color didn't matter. But it does matter, doesn't it, Dino? It matters a whole lot. It's the most important fact in our relationship, isn't it? Well, I can't ignore it. And I can't live with the constant reminder that when you look at me, you see a colored woman, a woman you can't marry, a woman you can't show to your family or your friends. Well, I can't live with a fence around me. You'll never know how much it hurts me to leave you, but it's your decision, not mine."

By the time Desi finished these remarks, tears were streaming down Dino's face.

"Don't leave," he muttered. "I'll move out. This house and everything in it are yours. I'm so sorry . . . so very sorry. I'll grab some clothes and say goodbye. You don't have to say anything more."

They said nothing more to each other.

Dino moved into a hotel, and when he went to work at Petrosian Motors the next day, he received a call from his sister Terry inviting him to a reunion of the Infielders.

Part Six

The Infielders in Crisis

Chapter 53

How Much?

Bernie phoned Aram in Boston as soon as he received the report from the forensic accountant. "Aram, I wish this wasn't true. With all my heart, I wish this wasn't true. But there's no question. Dino did it."

"How did he do it? How much did he steal? When did he start? Is he still doing it?"

"Hey, Aram, one question at a time. I've just read the report. I'll send it to you. And Sean, although I don't think he'll get much out of it. But he's on the team."

"Absolutely, he should see the report. Is it very detailed?"

"Part of it is meticulously detailed, and part consists of estimates that the auditor thinks are accurate as far as they go, but he concluded it wouldn't be efficient to look for every nickel and dime."

"So, what's the bottom line?"

"The auditor is certain about how much he stole by faking the selling price of cars and pocketing the difference between the amount paid by the customer—usually through GMAC—and the amount Dino entered in the books."

"What's GMAC?" Aram asked.

"General Motors Acceptance Corporation. They provide customer financing. Applebaum found that starting about two years ago, Dino reported sales of 239 cars at an average of $607 under the actual price. That means that Dino took home $145,073 that belonged to the company. In addition to that, during the same period, he charged hundreds of personal expenses to the company using a company credit card. Applebaum estimates the total amount of that scam at about $50,000, plus or minus. A lot of that went to buying paintings. We're looking at a total amount of nearly $200,000."

"Oh my God! What are we going to do?"

"I think we should all get together as soon as possible and discuss what to do. We shouldn't be hasty, but we also shouldn't sit on this too long. When can you and Annette come back to the city?"

"How about this weekend? I assume there's still no word about Dino's whereabouts, right?"

"That's right, Aram. This weekend will be fine. Call me when you get here. I'll call Sean and Terry. I have a sneaking suspicion she knows where he is."

"Why do you think that?"

"She went to his apartment in Riverdale, and there was someone else living there. He had moved out about two years ago. I think she may have an idea where he went."

"That's incredible. This whole damn thing is incredible. It's also heartbreaking."

Bernie said, "It is heartbreaking. For Dino to do that to your father after what he did for Dino."

"What about what Dino did to us? A knife in the back of his three best friends. I'll see you on Saturday. I don't want to talk about this anymore right now."

Sorrow and anger swirled around each of them, mixed with disbelief. Anger and sorrow.

Chapter 54

The Infielders Falling Apart

Terry was adamant. In a voice shrill with emotion, she said, "We can't! We simply can't call the police until we've found Dino and heard his side of the story. He's my brother, for Christ's sake!"

The three Infielders, Terry, and Annette were gathered in the waiting room of Bernie's office. They had been discussing the accountant's report and what they should do about it. There was tension in the room.

Annette spoke up for about the third or fourth time, always making the same point. "I don't understand why you all think it's our responsibility to do something, to do anything, about the accountant's report other than to give it to Aram's father so he can decide what to do about Dino and the money he stole from the business. Will somebody explain that to me?"

Bernie responded, "Annette, for the umpteenth time, try to understand. Dino's problem is our problem. That's what we meant when we swore to one another that there would always be a bond between us, that we would always be ready to step up and help any one of us when he needed help. We've been doing that for years. Turning Dino over to the cops will take the whole thing out of our hands. Then we'll never be able to help Dino. And that will be the most egregious violation of a basic principle around which we became the Infielders."

"Don't you think you're being a bit silly, invoking a decades-old oath made by a group of boys who played baseball together?" Annette asked with a sharp, almost mocking, intonation.

For the first time in all the years he had known and respected Annette, Bernie yelled at her. "Damn it, Annette! I once thought you were smart. Now I'm beginning to doubt that. How many times do you have to hear about the Infielders and what we mean to one another, how important our relationship is to all of us? How many times, I ask you, before it isn't 'silly' to you?"

"Don't you dare shout at my wife," Aram snapped. "Perhaps if Dino valued our relationship as much as he should have, he wouldn't have stolen money from my family."

Annette shot back at Bernie, "The very idea that there is such a thing as the Infielders with a capital *I* is a myth. A childish myth."

Aram looked at Annette quizzically, almost incredulously.

Sean entered the fray for the first time. With a grief-stricken look, he said, "That's not true. How could it be? We were supposed to be the Infielders for life."

"Thank you, Sean," Bernie said. "I think we all ought to try to lower the temperature in this room."

Annette would not be appeased. "Your so-called friend for life —the distinguished captain and shortstop of a boys' baseball team —is a thief and a coward. If anyone is responsible for breaking up the Infielders, it's Dino Russo. Aram's father placed his faith in Dino, and Dino stole his money. End of story. End of Infielders, as far as I'm concerned."

Terry stared angrily at Annette. She looked as if she might physically assault her, so much so that Aram edged closer to Annette as if to shield her. Terry, pointing her finger at Annette, shrieked, "You bitch. You're all bent out of shape because of money. Is the Petrosian family suddenly in the poorhouse? You're all about money. How about family? Dino is my brother. If he is arrested, it will kill my mother. You know my mother. She fed you. She fed your husband, time and again. Now you want to kill her. Because of you, I'll lose my mother, and I'll lose my brother. Is that what you want? Bitch."

Pushing his way past Bernie and Annette, Sean grabbed hold of Terry's elbow and pulled her toward him—probably somewhat more forcefully than he realized. "Friends," he said, "Terry and I are leaving now. I think the meeting's over." He retrieved their coats and quickly left the room, Terry trailing immediately behind him.

"You hurt me," Terry complained.

"I'm sorry. I didn't mean to hurt you," Sean said. "I just had to get you out of there. I agree with everything you said to Annette except calling her a bitch. I wish you hadn't said that."

"She'll get over it."

"Probably. But I don't know if Aram will get over it. He's the one I care about."

Chapter 55

Dino Emerges

S itting on the edge of the bed in a dingy motel room where he had spent the past three days, after finishing nearly a full bottle of Four Roses whiskey, Dino tried to think through and beyond the worst headache he ever experienced.

Two mistakes—catastrophic worst stupidest mistakes ever made. Broke up with Desi ran away—coward—she pleaded with me to marry her—could have her with me now not feeling sorry for myself—threw a stink bomb at my closest friends—my Infielders— my team—threw away friendships supposed to last a lifetime, threw them away along with Desi, why, why, why, why must have lost my mind must be crazy—be honest try to be honest don't lie to yourself be honest with yourself—did it because Mama—beloved Mama— she's to blame for my stupidity—that's crazy, crazy—not her fault my fault never want to hurt Mama—marry Desi marry a colored girl hurt Mama—that's it that's why I did what I did—excuse!—no, no, no, Mama not prejudiced not a bone in her body—I am—deep inside me—might hate Negroes—never shook hands with the colored players' team captain—part of my team—couldn't bring myself to touch them. Mama never talked about colored people no way to know how she feels—who does Mama hate—no one —she hates no one, when she learned Marco was homo after the priest told her it was a sin in the eyes of our Church, she said to all of us all— all of her children, "God made him that way, and it would be a sin to call him a sinner." Why didn't I connect that to colored people? My fault. The whole fucking thing is my fault. Is it a sin to love Desi? Is it a sin to love Desi and hate her color, the color that God made her? I have to fix this if I can. Please, God, let me fix this.

Dino ran from the room that was his purgatory, jumped into his Corvette, and headed toward New Rochelle. He rang the doorbell.

The door was opened, but not by Desi. It was Rose, her mother. She said, "You made a bad mistake, Dino. I hope you're here to fix it."

"That's why I'm here. I came here to say I'm sorry."

"Not going to be that easy. She don't trust you. I don't either."

"Please, Mrs. Bradley—"

"My name is Rose. I told you that the first time we met."

"I can't call you Rose. You're Desi's mother. And I deserted Desi."

"I don't care if you call me anything. Call me whatever you want."

"I'd like to call you Mother."

Instantly, Rose started to laugh. Her laughter grew louder and more uproarious the longer it went on. Dino was utterly confused by what had happened. He just stood there, vacantly looking at the woman. After a minute, possibly two or three, Rose took a deep breath and sputtered, "Mother! Mother! Funniest thing ever. Good-looking white man says he wants to call me Mother. Mother! I can't stop laughing."

"I didn't intend to be funny. As far as I am concerned, you are the mother of a beautiful, brilliant, thoughtful young woman. And if she still wants to marry me, I will call you Mother."

"I'll go tell Desi that you're here. Go wait in the living room."

Dino made himself comfortable in an easy chair while waiting for Desi. He realized he was too comfortable in that chair. He stood up and walked to the window. He looked out and remembered the guy whom Desi had referred to as "white trash" when they moved into this house. *God, don't let her think I am white trash, even though the label fits me.* His hangover headache had nearly subsided. After about ten or fifteen minutes, he began to wonder what was happening. Five minutes later, he began to feel some anxiety. After waiting for Desi to appear for half an hour, he began to panic. He paced the floor of the living room from one corner to the next. He looked out all the windows. *How happy I was in this house.*

A moment before Dino decided to go look for them, Desi and her mother arrived. Desi, neither smiling nor frowning, had a piece of paper in her hand. She gave it to Dino. It was a letter addressed to Dino, written by Desi in her neat and legible artist's handwriting.

Dear Dino,

I would be lying if I didn't say I am happy that you've come back. I am extremely happy because I love you, and I want you in my life. But, as you certainly know, I want to be your wife, not your girlfriend.

I will marry you if you do the following things. If you do not do these things, I will be forced to leave you and, with a broken heart, try to get on with my life. Here are my demands.

1. Not later than tomorrow, introduce me and my mother to your mother.

2. Not later than one week from today, introduce me and my mother to each of the Infielders.

3. Buy me a diamond engagement ring.

4. Buy me a white wedding dress with a train and a veil.

5. Buy my mother a dress of her choice to wear at our wedding.

6. Select one of the Infielders to be your best man.

7. Ask your sister Terry to be maid of honor.

8. Arrange to have the wedding ceremony at St. Elizabeth Church in Washington Heights.

9. As soon as you finish reading this letter, swear on the head of your mother and the grave of your father that you will never leave me again.

10. If I think of something else, do it!

With all my love and hope,

Desi

Dino read the letter, read it again, and then a third time just for the joy of reading it. Desi and Rose watched him as he read, and they both grew increasingly anxious as they wondered about his reaction to it.

He placed the letter on the sofa and, speaking softly, with what appeared to be some difficulty, he said, "Desi, I swear upon the head of my mother and the grave of my sainted father that I will never leave you."

Desi rushed forward and leaped up onto Dino, her arms around his neck. Rose applauded, literally clapping hands as if she were a spectator at a show.

With her feet back on the floor, Desi said, "Don't be afraid, Dino."

"Afraid of what?"

"Introducing us to your mother. She will get used to us."

"Better than that," Dino said. "This morning, that was all I could think about. I think she'll love you." He paused to let that sink in. "Ladies, we have to go to Washington Heights to fulfill the first requirement in Desi's Bill of Rights. But we have a problem. I drove here in my Corvette. It only holds two people. Isn't that crazy? I have a business with more than a hundred cars, and I picked a two-seater. Stupid."

Rose, looking perplexed, asked, "What do you want to do with a hundred cars?"

"Sell them, I hope. You didn't know your daughter was going to marry a simple car salesman?"

"Mom," Desi said, "Dino manages a Chevrolet dealership. He makes a lot of money."

"We have to get to my mother's apartment before she goes to bed, and I don't have a car that can get all of us there. I'm going to call Gus at the dealership."

"Don't just say it. Do it," Desi quipped.

Into the phone he said, "This is Dino. Connect me to Gus right away. I don't care what he's doing." After a brief pause, "Hey, Gus. You always wanted to drive the Corvette. Here's your chance. Get a shiny Impala sedan and drive it to New Rochelle. That's where I am. I'll give you the address. The Corvette is here. I want you to drive it to the dealership. I need the Impala to drive myself and two others back to the Heights. Yes, thanks." He handed the phone to Desi. "Desi, give Gus the address."

After Desi hung up the phone, Dino said, "This is good. It'll take Gus thirty or forty minutes to get here. We need to do some planning. Let's sit down. Rose, my mother—whom I call Mama—is much older than you. She came to America when she was about twenty. She had an older sister who lived with her family in Washington Heights. Mama moved in with them. Soon after, she met Frank Russo in church one Sunday, and they got married. They had five children. I'm the oldest. My father died very young. My baby sister, Isabella, was an infant when he died. Mama still mourns him.

"Mama is a caring, loving person. To her kids and almost everyone. She speaks good English with a lovely Italian accent. Two of the kids—Tony and Isabella—still live with her on Amsterdam Avenue, where I grew up. My sister Terry is married to my friend—I hope he's still my friend—Sean Flaherty, a major league baseball player. They live in Chicago, but I think they're in New York right now. My brother Marco is a homosexual, and he lives with his boyfriend in New Jersey. We see him on Christmas and a few random days during the year. Whenever we see him, his boyfriend is with him."

Dino stood up at that point and paced around in the living room, gathering his thoughts. After a few moments, he said, "Rose, Mama has no connection I know of with any colored person. Washington Heights is almost a one hundred percent white neighborhood. The people Mama hangs out with are almost all Italian women of her generation. I don't think she has ever spoken with a colored person. She is a religious Catholic. I can't promise that you and Desi will be welcomed. I can't promise that Mama will bless my marriage with Desi. That will break my heart. Hers too. I pray to God that she accepts us. I love your daughter enough to break my mother's heart." Dino walked out of the living room and opened the front door of the house. He stared at the driveway, waiting for Gus and the sedan. He stared intently as if that would bring Gus sooner.

Finally, Dino raced into the living room and shouted, "Looks like Gus is here with a car the three of us can fit in."

Chapter 56

Meeting Mama

There was hardly any conversation among the three of them during the half-hour drive from New Rochelle to Amsterdam Avenue. The stakes were too high for small talk, and they had already talked enough about tactics for this vitally important confrontation.

They walked up three flights of dimly lit stairs to the door to the Russo apartment. The name in the slot over the doorbell still read "Frank Russo." Dino rang the bell, standing in front of the women to obscure them from being seen when the door opened.

When Anthony Russo saw Dino standing on the doorstep, he turned and shouted, "Mama, Dino's here!"

From deep in the recesses of the apartment, a voice could be heard, "*Grazie a Dio, il mio primo figlio.*" Mama was awake. She came rushing to the door wearing a bathrobe over a nightgown. She embraced Dino's head, filling his face with many kisses. After the kissing, she said, "*Mi rendi così felice.*"

Dino responded, "Mama, I'm about to make you even happier." He paused for effect. "Mama, I am getting married."

Instantly, Mrs. Russo's expression changed from exultant to serious. "Is the girl Catholic?"

"She is Catholic, Mama. She wants to be married in St. Elizabeth's."

"*Grazie a Dio.*"

This was the moment. Dino beckoned to Desi to step into the apartment. "Mama, this is the girl I love with all my heart. Her name is Desi."

"What kind of a name is Desi?"

"It's short for Désirée. That's French for *Desiderata*."

"That's a beautiful name for a beautiful girl." Mrs. Russo hugged Desi. "Welcome to my family."

Dino looked up to the ceiling and quietly whispered, "Thank you, Jesus." He then said, "I also want you to meet Desi's mother, Mrs. Bradley. She is a widow like you."

Rose stepped forward, and the two women shook hands. "I wish you would call me Rose."

"Ah, good, and you call me Bianca."

Dino briefly introduced Desi and Rose to his brother and sister, Anthony and Isabella. Then they returned to their rooms. On the way, Isabella said, "They're colored," and Anthony replied, "Not very."

Dino said, "I met Desi at the Museum of Modern Art, where she works. She is an expert on modern art."

Desi jumped in and said, "Now that I'm going to be part of an Italian family, I'm sorry that I didn't study Raffaello or da Vinci or Caravaggio or the other great artists of the Renaissance *Italiano*. Sorry, I don't know how to say Renaissance in Italian."

Bianca Russo tilted her head back as if she was looking toward heaven. Her eyes rolled back and then closed for an instant before she took a deep breath and said, "My child, I am so happy Dino chose you for his bride. Now, if you don't mind, I would like to go into my kitchen with Rose and spend a couple of minutes alone with her. Dino, show Desi your old room."

The two women, holding hands, walked into the kitchen.

"Tell me about your husband, Desi's father," Mrs. Russo said to Rose.

"He was a bus driver for the Fifth Avenue Coach Company. He died in an accident when a drunk driver crashed into his bus when Desi was only eight months old. She never knew her father. He was a white man, very kind, very soft—I mean gentle. Treated me with love and respect. Ralph was his name. His death was the worst thing ever happened to me. The insurance company paid me a lot of money for what they called 'damages.' How do they put a value on a man's life? I had a beautiful little baby, and the insurance money made it possible for me to stay home with my baby. I moved to a better apartment.

"As Desi was growing up, I knew she was a special person. Smart. Sassy sometimes, but I liked that she could think for herself. She started to draw when she was nine or ten years old. With a crayon or a pencil, she could draw pictures. People's faces, animals, houses. I could see she had talent. When she was in junior high school, a teacher told me Desi should go to the high school named 'Music and Art.' I never heard of that school, even though it was on 135th Street, walking distance from where we lived. She had to take a test to get into that school. She passed it easily, she said. That's where she learned how to paint pictures and how to understand art and love it. She got a job in the modern art museum, and that's where she met your boy. Best thing ever happened to them and to me. I'm talking too long. You look like you're going to cry. Did I make you sad with all my talking?"

"Your story, Rose, is so close to mine that I can feel your pain and also your joy."

Rose had introduced the subject of race in such an offhand

way that the subject, the one Dino was so afraid to confront, no longer had any relevance to Dino and Desi.

Mrs. Russo called out to Dino and Desi to join her and Rose in the kitchen. When they all sat around the kitchen table, Mrs. Russo took charge. She was in her headquarters. "Dino, you will sleep in your old room. Desi, you will sleep in the empty bed in Isabella's room. And you, Rose, will sleep in the empty bed in my room. I apologize to all of you. You must be hungry, and I've not offered you anything."

Dino said, "None of us have eaten anything since breakfast. I hope you have some leftover lasagna. Mama's lasagna is the tastiest food in the world."

"I'm so sorry. No lasagna tonight. Tomorrow, I will teach Desi how to make lasagna. That way, her husband will never leave her. Tonight, I'll just prepare spaghetti, and Desi and Rose can watch how I make my sauce."

The meal was a celebratory feast.

Chapter 57

Dino and Bernie

Early the next morning, Dino phoned Bernie at his office. This was the telephone conversation between Dino and Bernie.

Dino began, "I'm going to marry Désirée Bradley. My mother loves her."

Bernie shouted into his phone, "Where the hell have you been? We wanted to help you, but you've been gone since you ran away from the reunion, and it looks to us like you've stolen a ton of money from the Petrosians! You committed a serious crime. And then you disappear like a common criminal. And now you call me, and the first thing you say is a fucking wedding announcement. What do you expect from me at this point?"

"Please calm down, Bernie. Everything will get worked out. Believe me. Please be happy for me."

"Give me a reason to be happy for you."

"I'll start again. I'm going to marry Désirée Bradley. My mother loves her."

"I'm happy to hear that. But I think I'm missing something.

Who is Désirée Bradley? How long have you known her? Why haven't I met her? How did all this happen?"

"I was hiding in a motel. I got drunk on a bottle of Four Roses. I thought about why I was afraid to introduce Desi to my mother. I realized I had underestimated my mother. So I picked up Desi. Her mother was with her, and we went straight to my old house on Amsterdam, and I introduced them to my mother. That's where I am now. We all slept over in my old apartment."

"I'm not following this story. What does getting drunk in a motel have to do with getting married? That just doesn't make sense. There's got to be more to the story. I don't understand why you were afraid to introduce this girl to your mother. Wait a minute. I just got a brain flash. The girl's a Jew, ain't she? Your mother is a mensch, always was."

"You have no idea."

"Dino, I'm happy for you. I'm sure I'll like Desi. But there is an ogre in this fairy tale—the subject that Terry told you about when you ran away from the Infielders reunion party."

"Yeah, I know."

"I hope to hell you realize what deep shit you're in. Right now, as we speak, I have no legal strategy for keeping you out of jail. Did you hear that word? Jail! What you did carries a multiyear prison sentence. Your first priority has to be staying out of jail. We have to try to keep the whole ugly subject of the money you swiped from Petrosian Motors as an Infielders' problem. Otherwise, we may have to attend your wedding in Sing Sing, where you'll be serving five years for embezzlement."

Dino replied, "I'll tell you all about the money, and then you'll tell me what to do. Can I come to your office?"

"You know I can't be your lawyer."

"Yeah, I know, but you can be my friend."

"That's okay. I have a client coming in at noon, so we have a couple of hours."

"I'll walk right over. Give me fifteen minutes."

That was the end of the conversation. Bernie was annoyed and confused. For the first time ever, he had no idea what was in Dino's mind.

Dino explained to Desi and the two mothers that he had to go talk with Bernie Heller about the car business. He put on his warm jacket and walked three blocks to Bernie's law office, which was one flight of stairs above a hardware store on St. Nicholas Avenue.

The two men sat facing each other, Bernie behind his desk and Dino in the visitor's chair.

"I want you to talk to me about the money that seems to be missing from the car dealership. Go ahead. I'm listening," Bernie said.

"I've been the manager of the dealership for more than fourteen years. Until about two years ago, when I met Desi, I never took a dime more than the salary and commissions that Mr. Petrosian knew all about. He paid me enough to take decent care of my own needs and to support my mama and the kids living with her."

"So, all the extra money you took from the business . . . it looks like around two hundred thousand dollars . . . all came out in less than two years? Since Desi?"

"That's right. Desi was living with her mother in an apartment in Harlem. Eventually, she moved in with me in Riverdale, but I soon had to take her away from there. Neighbors were complaining about a Negro in the building, but they didn't have the decency to use the word Negro."

"Holy shit! Desi's colored?"

"I never told you that? I thought I did."

"Well, that explains a few things."

"I bought a house in New Rochelle, and we've been living there."

"I assume that's where most of the money went."

"Yes, of course. But I want to give you some background on the money that I think is important. When I became manager of the dealership, it was in terrible shape. Mr. Petrosian is a wonderful man, and I'll always respect him and feel grateful to him. But he's a lousy businessman. His general manager was an idiot, and the salesmen couldn't sell water in a desert. General Motors was threatening to pull the franchise. The accountant for the business was some Armenian guy who couldn't pass the CPA exam. I tell you, the place was a mess. The books were indecipherable. Mr. Petrosian was paying himself with borrowed money. The dealership was one inch away from bankruptcy.

"Bernie, I worked day and night to turn that place around. I replaced everyone in the sales room. I hired competent mechanics for the service functions. I studied the market and changed the mix of new models in our inventory. I upgraded our used car operations and turned them profitable. I did all of that and more, and now the business is booming. And I did all that with only two nominal raises in salary in all those years. I must say that I felt entitled to the extra money I paid myself. Not legally, but morally. I don't feel guilty about it."

Bernie, who had been scribbling notes vigorously as Dino spoke, said, "This story needs to be told to the Petrosians and the other Infielders. I'm going to call Aram and arrange a meeting with him and his father."

"Please don't, Bernie, I need to handle this myself. I appreciate your offer, but the problem is my problem, and I need to deal with it personally. I'll be back to you. By the way, will you be the best man at my wedding?"

"I won't agree until you introduce me to Desi."

"How about tonight at my old house?"

"Perfect. But tell your mama that I can't eat there. Remember when you called me a rabbi? I think I'll ask Betsy to come with me. I must say I am absolutely astonished that you're going to marry a Negro. I can't wait to meet her."

"Nice idea, to bring Betsy," Dino said before leaving Bernie alone to digest all that he had told him.

Later that evening, Mrs. Russo, holding Dino's hand, welcomed Bernie to her home. She vividly recalled Bernie's role in bringing about Theresa's marriage to Sean, and she called upon God to bless Bernie for that lifesaving deed. She took it upon herself to invite Theresa, Sean, and their children. In addition to Anthony and Isabella, her son Marco and his boyfriend Julian visited from New Jersey at Mrs. Russo's invitation.

The small kitchen was never intended to hold twelve people. Everyone was standing, pressed on all sides by other people. Marco and Julian pulled a couple of kitchen chairs into the living room to create a bit more space in the kitchen.

Mrs. Russo's keen understanding of people informed her decision to transform the evening into a memorable occasion. Dino's closest friends will be meeting the woman he will marry. Mrs. Russo was happier than at any time since the death of her husband. She embraced Bernie when he arrived, and she signaled to Anthony to bring them in.

When Desi and Rose appeared at the kitchen door, Mrs. Russo said, "Theresa, Sean, boys, Marco, Julian, Bernie, Betsy, this young woman is going to marry my son Dino. That's her mother, Rose Bradley, standing next to her." Sounds of "welcome" and "hurrah" resounded in the tiny kitchen.

"I have lasagna for everyone and pastrami sandwiches for Bernie and Betsy. From Dave's kosher deli."

Dino clinked a wine glass with a spoon to quiet the crowd. "I have an important announcement to make. Bernie Heller will be the best man at our wedding."

That makes a lot of sense was the thought that flashed through Sean's brain. *I wish he had been my best man. I wish Dino hadn't stolen that money.*

Bernie whispered to Dino, "She is beautiful."

Chapter 58

Bernie and Betsy

After what turned out to be a grand party in the Russo apartment, Bernie and Betsy walked to Bernie's office. They had enjoyed their pastrami sandwiches and enjoyed even more the thoughtfulness of Dino and Mrs. Russo in providing them with kosher food.

Betsy remarked, "Dino and his family seem to be such quality people, but I don't understand how Dino could be in such a celebratory mood after stealing that money. Mrs. Russo has embraced Dino's Negro fiancée. I doubt that many Jewish mothers would have been as welcoming. And Dino, the poor guy has got his hands full, the embezzlement problem on top of introducing Desi to his family and friends. And yet he arranges kosher food for us. Remarkable. By the way, where is there a kosher deli in this neighborhood?"

"Dave's Delicatessen, corner of 189th and St. Nick."

"The sandwich was good even though the pastrami wasn't hot."

"If we were to get married, do you think we should serve hot pastrami sandwiches at the wedding?" Bernie quipped.

"What do you mean by 'if'?"

"All right, all right, you win. Seriously, do you think I should ask Dino to be my best man?"

"That's your choice. But I would veto selecting Dino unless the missing money problem is resolved. We don't want that hanging over our wedding," Betsy stated with emphasis.

"Agreed. I'd like to discuss that with you. I know the whole story, at least Dino's version.

"Tell me about it."

Bernie told Betsy everything he had heard from Dino, including the fact that Dino didn't feel guilty about taking the money.

"What's the legal picture?" Betsy asked.

"According to Dino—and I'm inclined to believe this—but for his skill and diligence, there wouldn't have been any money in the cookie jar for him to swipe. If the Petrosians go crazy and demand that Dino be arrested, I think it's unlikely that a jury would convict him. The fact that he saved a failing business and made it thrive would make him far more sympathetic than your average embezzler. And a jury of working people would surely be influenced by the fact that he had only two modest raises in fourteen years. No, he may have committed a crime, but I don't think the DA would bring him to trial, especially if he repays the money.

"Will you represent him?"

"I can't. I told him that, and he understands. I think he has a plan to try to work things out."

After several minutes in which neither of them said a word, Betsy broke the silence, saying, "I think it would be great if Dino could be your best man. I really like him."

"So do I. Very much."

Chapter 59

Dino and Aram

A Confrontation

A great weight had been lifted from Dino's chest. His mother's embrace of Desi was more genuine, more loving than he had dared to hope it would be. Bernie and Sean confirmed their commitment to their friendship with him by their unquestioning acceptance of Desi. But he had much more to accomplish before he could truly begin to live the life he desired.

He awoke the morning after the celebration in the kitchen in his old room on the bed he slept on throughout his boyhood. He slid into the trousers he had worn the night before and walked into the kitchen where Desi and Mama were engaged in an animated conversation about, it seemed, art. Words like *perspective* and *harmony* were being added to Mama's vocabulary. He asked if Theresa was up yet and was told that she doesn't live here anymore.

"Oh, I forgot. I don't live here anymore, either," he said, laughing. "I need her to do some shopping for me."

"I can do the shopping," said Mama. "I always do."

"Not this shopping," Dino said. "First of all, good morning to both of you. Desi, I need Terry's help in shopping to comply with three items of your Bill of Rights. Will you coordinate with her? I'll give her my personal, not my dealership, credit card. I don't want to do any more embezzling." He raised his fingers to make quotation marks in the air with that last word. "Tell Terry to spend lavishly but in good taste. She'll need to have Rose with her for the dress. A dress for Mama also. Desi, I'll explain *embezzling* tonight. I have to find Aram now."

The two women sitting at the table looked to be totally dumb-founded.

Dino went back into his room and finished dressing. Then he phoned Bernie to get Aram's phone number in Cambridge. He called that number, and Annette answered. He identified himself and asked if Aram was available. When Aram came to the phone, Dino said, "I need to speak with you and your father. Can you come to New York? As soon as possible."

Aram said that he and Annette and the children were intending to visit their parents that afternoon at Laurel Hill Terrace.

"Can you and your dad break away for a while for an important conversation with me?"

"Where are you?"

"At Mama's house."

"We can't meet there. I'll phone you when we're on Laurel Hill Terrace. We'll work something out."

"I hope so."

"Do you have a lawyer, Dino? We do, but I don't want her to come to New York today."

Dino said, "I don't have a lawyer, and I don't need one." The conversation almost ended there.

But Aram said, "That depends." Then he hung up.

Chapter 60

The Trial

The Petrosian apartment on Laurel Hill Terrace had more people in it than Dino expected when he arrived there in response to a telephone invitation from Mr. Petrosian. In addition to the senior Petrosians and Aram, Annette was there with her parents, Dr. and Mrs. Nazarian, and even five-year-old Berj.

They were arranged in a semicircle. Aram and his father were seated together on a sofa in the middle of the large living room. Mrs. Nazarian and Mrs. Petrosian were seated together on a small sofa at the left end of the main sofa, angled toward the center of the room where a plain wooden chair stood empty. Opposite them on upholstered armchairs at the other end of the main sofa were Annette and Dr. Nazarian, with Berj on his lap. They, too, were facing the empty chair.

Aram opened the door when Dino rang the doorbell. He thanked Dino for coming and led him into the living room. He pointed to the empty chair, and Dino sat there—the prisoner in the dock.

As soon as Dino was seated, he was surprised to hear Dr.

Nazarian's voice. "I understand you want to talk to Aram and his father. They regard this to be a family matter. That accounts for all of us being here." After a momentary pause he said, "You wanted to talk, so talk."

Dino struggled to repress the anger welling up within him. There were no arms to the chair. Dino squeezed the wooden edges of his seat with all his strength. He was outraged that these people would treat him this way. An idea came to him. He turned to his left, where Mrs. Petrosian was sitting with Annette's mother. "Mrs. Nazarian, I presume you speak Armenian. I wish you would tell Aram's mother that I am still grateful for all the delicious fruit she served me the numerous times I came to this apartment to visit with my friend, her son."

Mrs. Nazarian leaned toward Aram's mother and spoke quietly to her. Mrs. Petrosian smiled, looked at Dino, and nodded.

Dino spoke, looking toward the two mothers. "Thank you." Then, looking straight ahead at Aram and his father, he said, "I asked to meet with the two of you because I wanted to tell you I made a mistake. I did something wrong. I want to apologize and tell you I regret what I did. I intend to repay the money I took improperly from the dealership. Obviously, I won't be able to pay it all back immediately, but I'll do the best I can. Mr. Petrosian trusted me, and I should have asked him for the funds I took. What hurts me so much about what I did is that I know Mr. Petrosian would have given me permission to take that money if I had asked for it."

"Wouldn't that depend upon the reason you wanted the money?" This question came from Dr. Nazarian, who was seated to Dino's right.

Dino looked to his right and saw Dr. Nazarian staring at him with his jaw jutted out as if he had just scored a point.

Dino paused for about twenty seconds, waiting for some

acknowledgement from Mr. Petrosian or Aram of what he had just said about permission from Mr. Petrosian. There was no such acknowledgement. There was a small up-and-down movement of Mr. Petrosian's head that might have been the universal indication of an affirmative response, but it was too subtle for Dino to rely on. The room was utterly silent, with not even a cough or the clearing of a throat. It was apparent that everyone was waiting for Dino's response to Dr. Nazarian's question.

I'll make them wait, just as we make a potential customer wait for a discount from the list price of a car. The longer we wait, the smaller the discount. I'm going to just sit here for a minute or two, staring at Mr. Petrosian.

Finally, Dino addressed Dr. Nazarian. "Sir," he said. "in all the years I have worked for Mr. Petrosian, he never once asked me what I did with the money the dealership paid me. Not once. Never. Your question indicates an ignorance of the relationship I had with my friend Aram's father."

The atmosphere in the room became icy.

Then Dino resumed his remarks. "Mr. Petrosian and Aram, I want to tell you what I did with the money. Not because of Dr. Nazarian's question but because I came here today prepared to tell you how I spent the money. First, I'd like to give you some background. In more than a dozen years of working for the dealership—from day one until about two years ago, every dollar that was paid to me was a dollar authorized by Mr. Petrosian. Under my management, the dealership went from the edge of bankruptcy to a dealership in the top five percent of Chevrolet dealerships in this country. I know Mr. Petrosian looks at every General Motors report of dealership performance. I have to ask you, Mr. Petrosian, in front of all these people, is what I just said about the performance of Petrosian Motors correct?"

Mr. Petrosian immediately said, "That's correct." And then he added, "You did a good job, Dino. But why didn't you tell me you needed more money? Why?"

"Because I fell in love." Dino stopped talking for at least a minute, and everyone in the room waited to hear the love story that had changed Dino into an embezzler.

It was Aram who broke the silence in the room. "Dino," he almost shouted, "you have to say more than that."

Dino responded, "Okay, Aram. Mr. Petrosian, I fell in love with a young woman who I'm going to marry. I love her with all my heart. You know the expression—or maybe you don't—I fell head over heels in love. That means I wasn't thinking like a businessman. I was thinking like a teenager. Aram, I'm sure you remember running from the Heights down to Inwood in pouring rain so you could tell Annette that you acted like a jackass. Everyone in George Washington High School is probably still laughing about that story. It was so funny people didn't believe it was true. But it was true, wasn't it? Well, my story is true, too. Only I didn't get soaking wet for love. I betrayed your father. Your excuse? You were just a kid. My excuse? I don't have one. We both acted foolishly for the same reason. I hope you can understand why I did what I did."

"He ruined my bathrobe," said Dr. Nazarian. "I still don't think that was funny."

"I don't know about Aram getting wet," said Mr. Petrosian. "Tell me that story."

"Ask Aram," Dino said. "I just want to say that I love the woman I'm going to marry at least as much as Aram loved Annette. I went overboard and bought a beautiful house for us to live in in New Rochelle, and that's where most of the money went. I'll take out a mortgage on the house to help repay it. You're all invited to the wedding. It will be in St. Elizabeth church here in the Heights. Bernie Heller will be my best man. We haven't set a date yet, but it will have to be before Sean Flaherty leaves for spring training. Stay tuned. That's all I have to say."

Dino stood up and headed to the door.

"Don't leave yet," Aram said. "I need to talk with you."

"Some other time, Aram. I'm all talked out."

"No, please, Dino, I have to talk to you. Please."

"I really am exhausted, so make it quick."

"I didn't have anything to do with how this thing was set up today. It was entirely organized by Annette's father. My father was very nervous about having a confrontation with you. He asked Nazarian to take charge. This was a travesty. It's all his fault. He arranged the seating. That stupid kitchen chair you were made to sit in. I so wish you had asked for the money. I'm certain he would have agreed to give it to you. Dino, my father is not in good shape. He had another ministroke. He is gradually losing his memory. Actually, he was more focused today than the last time I was with him, about a month ago. I think seeing you is good for him. That's ironic, isn't it?"

"Why is that ironic?" Dino asked.

"Dino, I have a lot of stuff that I need to confess to you. To get off my chest. I want you to know that I wanted to go to the police when I learned about what I was calling your embezzlement. The irony today is that my father was the victim of your crime. Yet seeing you is good for him."

"You really wanted me to go to jail?"

"Yes, I did, and it was Bernie and Sean and your sister who talked me out of it. The Infielders saved your ass. I'm so glad you weren't at the worst meeting we had about you and the missing money. Your sister called Annette a bitch. I was afraid she would attack Annette physically. Sean had to grab Terry and pull her out of Bernie's office. It was horrible. It certainly looked like the end of the 'capital *I*' Infielders."

Aram's eyes filled with tears. He continued to talk. "Tell me about your bride. Who is she? What's her name? Please tell me all about her, the whole story."

There was no response from Dino, who looked at his wrist-watch and then turned to the door out of the apartment.

"Forgive me, please, Dino," Aram said. "I am so ashamed that I even considered going to the police without talking to you first."

"I'll think about it." With that, Dino left the Petrosian apartment.

Chapter 61

Aram and Dino

A ram wasted no time in contacting Bernie to tell him the outcome of the "trial." He reported: "The so-called embezzlement is completely resolved. My father forgave Dino's debt. You would have been proud of your captain. My father-in-law acted like a total jerk, and Dino was beautiful. My father realized how much he owed Dino for all his years of work, and he no longer blames Dino for what he did. Dino said he's going to get married, but I don't know to whom. Bernie, you must know because he said you're going to be the best man."

Bernie said, "Slow down, Aram. I'm delighted to hear that the money thing is resolved. I'm not surprised that Dino handled himself well. He's our captain, after all. I met his fiancée last night up his house, where he introduced the girl and her mother to Mrs. Russo. She's quite beautiful. Hold on to your hat . . . she's colored. Very intelligent, quick-witted, and knowledgeable in modern art, works at the Museum of Modern Art. In the gift shop, but also as a guide. That's where Dino met her."

Aram interrupted, "In his statement today, at the so-called

trial, he mentioned that he loved a girl, I quote, with all his heart, and that he bought a house for them to live in. That's where most of the money went. Did you know that? I'm shocked to learn she's colored. Does his mother know?"

"She knows and has blessed them. I know all of that. If Sean is still in New York, we ought to reconvene the reunion party that Dino blew up. If you and Annette can be available, I'll call Sean and see if we can put it together."

"But wait. I asked Dino to forgive me, and he said he would think about it."

"I'm surprised to hear that. It's not like Dino to hold a grudge."

"Bernie, I told him everything. I had to get it off my chest. I told him I wanted to call the police and that you and Sean and Terry saved his ass. I told him what a terrible meeting we had. About Terry calling Annette a bitch."

"Please come to my office. We need to talk about this in person."

"I'll be there in a few minutes."

Alone in his office, Bernie thought, *Aram may have been first in our class, but he doesn't have half Dino's intelligence. He really has behaved stupidly in this whole thing. I think Dino would be within his rights never to forgive Aram, not when he was going to call the cops. I'm going to tell him that when he gets here.*

Bernie sat at his desk when Aram arrived. He didn't stand up or offer to shake hands. He nodded to Aram to sit in a chair opposite him. He told Aram exactly what he had just been thinking.

"What should I do?" Aram asked.

"There's nothing you can do but hope Dino decides to forgive you. The damage is done. My concern is whether the Infielders can survive without a second baseman."

"You're kidding, aren't you?"

"No fucking way I'm kidding. I've been giving a lot of thought lately to the idea of the Infielders. The idea that, no matter what, we stick together. That may have been an infantile notion, as Annette argued in this office. That idea was born at the time of the group hug after graduation. We were just boys, after all. But there was life in that idea. It endured. It influenced how we behaved—to one another, and for one another. Dino came close to breaking up with his colored girlfriend because he thought we—including you —wouldn't accept her. That may have been foolish, and he came to realize that, but he was thinking of the Infielders as if they mattered. I wish you had done the same. I've decided to reconvene the reunion. I'll call everyone. You and Annette should attend. Let's see what happens."

Chapter 62

Reunion

Second Try

Three evenings later, the Infielders were again gathering in the back room of the Tropical Gardens Pizzeria. As previously, the first to arrive were the Flahertys, Sean and Terry, at seven o'clock on the dot. Then Dino and Desi arrived. Dino said to Terry, "Desi is very nervous. Please stay close to her."

"I don't need a babysitter," Desi protested. "Besides, I want to stay close to you. And I'm not very nervous."

"As you wish. I find your closeness a comfort."

Bernie and Betsy arrived moments later. The casual conversation was mainly about Bernie's and Betsy's forthcoming wedding.

Aram and Annette arrived during that conversation. They were dressed as if they were going to a wedding and not merely a gathering of old friends in a pizza joint.

Sean started taking drink orders from everyone. He had hired a bartender. Desi asked for champagne.

Sean asked Dino if he could afford a girlfriend who drinks champagne. As soon as he said that, he knew it was a mistake. The subject of what Dino could and could not afford was fraught with scary implications.

Dino reacted with grace and did not take offense. "Aram and Annette, you've not yet met my fiancée, Desi Bradley. She's a serious baseball fan."

Annette shook hands with Desi with her arm fully extended as if she wanted not to be too close to her. Aram looked completely bemused as to what to do.

Annette requested a Pink Lady for her drink, and Aram said he would pass for the time being. "No drink." He appeared to be tense, and Sean brought him an unrequested whiskey sour.

Then Bernie clinked his glass, and the room became quiet. He spoke. "Fifteen years ago, the four men in this room formed the Infielders, which one of us called the most exclusive club in the world. It was intended to last a lifetime, and it would never admit new members. Today, it is on the verge of dissolving. Today may be its last day."

"No!" Sean shouted. "That can't be. It mustn't be."

"I know how you feel, Sean. I feel the same way. But it's not up to you or me. I want to give everyone here a picture of where we are. I'd like not to be interrupted. I think I know all of the relevant facts about Dino's relationship with Petrosian Motors, including his embezzlement. Aram's father has, in effect, retroactively authorized payment to Dino of all amounts paid to him. He decided it was only fair after all the money that Dino made for him through the business over the years. That matter is closed. Aram has, courageously in my judgment, told Dino everything he did and said when he learned that Dino had taken money from the dealership. Aram has apologized and has asked Dino to forgive him. Dino's response was . . . I think these were the words . . . 'I'll think about it.' That's where things stand at this moment. Dino or Aram, any comments?"

Aram said, "What you said is accurate."

Dino sat silently on a bar stool, holding Desi's hand. Everyone in the room expected Dino to say something. Finally, after a delay that was uncomfortable for most everyone, Dino stood up, holding a martini glass.

"I want to propose a toast to the Infielders, the men who played in the infield with me fifteen years ago, to Bernie, to Sean, and to Aram."

Shouts of "hear, hear" rang out.

Dino continued, "Wait, wait. There's more. I propose a toast to the Infielders, the idea—I repeat—the idea of a friendship that should last forever. An idea that four boys conceived and, now, that four men must work to preserve."

More cries of "hear, hear!" Dino took a long sip of his martini.

Dino continued to speak, and everyone in the room gave him their rapt attention. "Now that you know where my heart is, I need to talk about what's in my head, not my heart. I've done some really stupid things, monumentally stupid things. I've taken money from my employer without asking for it. If I had asked for it, he would have given it to me in a heartbeat. I broke up with Desi because I was afraid to introduce her to my mother, fearing that she'd reject her. When I finally worked through that fear, Mama embraced Desi in a heartbeat. I said ugly things to most of you the last time we were here, and I ran away from you. Hardly the behavior of an Infielder."

He paused for a sip of martini.

"I want you to know that that was the lowest point of my life, lower than when my Papa died. My rant that day occurred exactly one day—twenty-four hours—after I moved out of the house where Desi and I were living. I moved out because she wanted to get married, and I couldn't agree to do that because of her color—her color! Can you believe that? I broke off my relationship with this beautiful woman because I thought the color of her skin would be a barrier to her being accepted by my mother and my friends."

Dino paused to take another sip of his martini. He continued, "I was in excruciating pain from my self-inflicted wounds. After that, I learned that Aram and Annette wanted to go to the police to have me arrested for embezzlement. Hardly the behavior of an Infielder. Thank you, Bernie, Sean, and Terry, for heading that off. This is quite a party. We should have hired a psychiatrist, not a bartender.

"I said I was sorry to Mr. Petrosian, and he forgave me in the most tangible way. He gave me the money that I stole from him. I apologized to Desi, and she forgave me in the most tangible way by agreeing to be my wife and to bear my children—"

There was a burst of applause.

"And I think I said I was sorry to Aram, and he definitely said, 'I forgive you.' There's something tangible in that forgiveness. I assume the money I stole would have been part of his inheritance after his parents pass away."

Dino drained the glass and asked the bartender for a refill.

He continued to speak, his words cutting through the utter silence in the room. "And now we come to Aram and me and whether he is still my second baseman and I am still his short-stop and captain. He has asked me to forgive him for thinking and acting like I was a criminal. He said he was sorry, he asked me to forgive him, and I said I would think about that. I have to explain why. *Sorry* and *forgive* are just words, important words to be sure. I hope I can forgive Aram and preserve the Infielders, but I don't want to simply say 'I forgive you' because I'm not sure that I do. I don't want to utter empty words. Aram called me a thief, and, even worse, he believed I was a thief. There is no room in the Infielders for both a thief and his accuser. In order for me to forgive Aram, I need tangible evidence that forgiveness isn't just an empty gesture. I need something to make it honest. That can only happen over time. I'm not sure how. Perhaps by overt demonstrations of regret. Surely by overt demonstrations of the unconditional friendship that we had when we became the Infielders. I'd like to see you, Aram and Annette, taking pleasure in my choice of bride by showing her respect and affection for no reason other than she is my wife and I love her. Maybe paying me an occasional visit at the dealership or at my home. Inviting me and Desi to spend some time with you and Annette in Cambridge would help. Mostly by acting as if our friendship is valuable to you. That the idea we had fifteen years ago is still alive. I pray that you give me such reasons to forgive you and embrace you again as my friend and second baseman."

Dino finished the remainder of his second martini and asked the bartender for another as he sat back down on the stool.

After an unusually long period of silence in which a great deal of drinking took place, Aram stood up and walked to the center of the room. He cleared his throat and said, "Dino's remarks make me think of a great poem by Walt Whitman that begins with these lines:

> O Captain! my Captain! our fearful trip is done,
> The ship has weather'd every rack, the prize we
> sought is won.

"Well, dear friends, Dino has just told us—actually told me— that in his opinion, our fearful trip is not yet done. The prize we sought is not yet won. I regret that he feels that way. I think my request that he forgive me was appropriate. He thinks he can see into my heart. He has challenged me to prove that I have erased from my heart the anger that I felt when I learned about the missing money. To Dino, forever my captain, I have another couple of lines from that poem to offer.

> O Captain! my Captain! rise up and hear the bells;
> Rise up—for you the flag is flung—for you the
> 　　bugle trills.

"I may have some rough sailing ahead of me. I promise you I'll do it. You see what happens when you have a professor of literature in a club of baseball players."

Several simultaneous conversations ensued. Annette overheard Terry saying, "If you want to have someone be your lifelong friend, you should respect him enough to hear his side before deciding to go to the police."

Annette called across the room to Aram, "Did you hear what Dino's sister just said?"

He answered, "I think she's right."

Bernie clinked his glass several times. When the room grew quiet enough for everyone to hear him, Bernie said, "Betsy and I would like to talk about our wedding. I have no poem to recite."

Betsy added, "And I haven't been part of this group long enough to have lost my mind."

"Just you wait," said Terry.

Bernie, with some help from Betsy, described a Jewish wedding ceremony to the group and the role that they wanted all of the Infielders and their women to play. Betsy gave the group a lesson on how to dance a hora.

Dino, after leaving his third martini virtually untouched, approached Aram. "Hey, Aram," he said, determined to smooth things over as much as he could for the sake of everyone in the room. "Desi and I have been staying at my mother's house. We can't sleep together there. Mama thinks she's a virgin. Any chance we could sleep at your parents' house tonight?"

To Dino's relief, Aram smiled. "You bet. There's always been an extra bedroom in that apartment. I think my dad will be delighted to have you as a houseguest, depending—I regret to say— on the state of his mind right now. He was pretty good last night, but you never know. Let me phone him from here and tell him you're coming."

Chapter 63

An Armenian Breakfast

The pleasure on Mr. Petrosian's face when Dino arrived with Aram felt to Dino like a reward or a bonus. Mr. Petrosian showed the couple to the spare bedroom where they would spend the night.

Dino and Desi spent a comfortable night in the spare bedroom on Laurel Hill Terrace. In the middle of the night, Desi poked Dino in his ribs and said to him, in a whisper, "What you said about the Infielders was beautiful. I wish I could belong."

The couple awoke the next morning—Desi first, and Dino half an hour later—donned the clothing they had worn the previous evening, and walked quietly into the kitchen, which was empty.

From the dining room, Mr. Petrosian shouted, "Come in here for a breakfast like none you've ever had before."

Mrs. Petrosian had prepared an authentic Armenian breakfast for their houseguests. The table was loaded with fruits of all kinds. At every place setting, there was a stack of lavash, an Armenian flatbread baked during the night by Mrs. Petrosian from flour, olive oil, yeast, lots of honey, and whole milk. When Dino and Desi entered the dining room, Mrs. Petrosian began to fry a dozen eggs mixed with chopped tomatoes in an enormous pan sizzling with butter. Mrs. Petrosian couldn't welcome her guests in English, but she certainly could with food.

Annette was the first to give Desi a welcoming hug, which Dino understood to be a message of some sort to him. Mr. Petrosian's welcome was effusive. He was genuinely happy to have Dino in his home. Aram's greeting, on the other hand, was stiff and cold. *He must have had a bad night*, Dino thought.

Dino was still scarfing down the delicious scrambled eggs when Annette and Aram stood up and announced that they needed to get started to catch a train back to Boston. They kissed the parents, patted Desi and Dino on their backs, said goodbye to all, and left the room.

It was pleasant to be alone with the elder Petrosians. Mr. Petrosian, even after everything, felt like a father to Dino, and he was warmed to his soul by the older man's affections.

Chapter 64

Bernie and Betsy's Wedding

S hortly after New Year's Day 1963, Betsy composed the following notice to *The New York Times* for publication in its society column on January 29.

On Sunday, January 28, 1963, in the sanctuary of Yeshiva University synagogue, Elizabeth Weinstein, known to all who know her as Betsy, daughter of Benjamin and Ruth Weinstein of Riverside Drive, and Bernd Heller, known far and wide as Bernie, son of Herbert and Sadie Heller of Washington Heights, were married in a traditional Jewish wedding ceremony. The groom wore a traditional white robe called a kittel over his tuxedo, and the bride wore an elegant white gown with train

and veil. Immediately prior to the
ceremony, the groom delivered a
commentary on the portion of the Torah
to be read at that week's Sabbath
service. The rabbi commended him on
the quality and perceptiveness of his
comments. A traditional marriage
contract was witnessed and set apart
for delivery by the groom to the
bride.

With special permission of the
rabbi, the four poles holding the
wedding canopy were held by friends of
the couple, Aram Petrosian, Sean
Flaherty, Annette Petrosian and
Theresa Russo Flaherty. Bernardino
Russo, a friend of the groom, served
as best man, and Sarah Weinstein,
sister of the bride, was maid of
honor.

The couple will live in Washington
Heights, where the groom maintains a
law practice.

Bernie read Betsy's draft of the wedding announcement and said, "That's very nice what you wrote about me and the rabbi, but it hasn't happened yet, and I haven't even read the Torah portion, much less written a commentary on it. How can you send that to the *Times*?"

"No problem, I have great confidence in you."

"But won't the editors notice that the date has not yet arrived."

"No problem, I'm going to send it the day after the wedding. I just want to have it ready. Besides, the *Times* distorts the past, so why can't it predict the future?"

Bernie said, "My love, that's a conversation I'd like to have with you."

"Good, we'll have something to do for the rest of our lives."

"I can think of a few other things."

"Like what? Never mind. I know what your adolescent brain is thinking. Sunday night, January 28th."

"No practice sessions?"

"None," she said. "Bernie Heller is going to marry a virgin."

The wedding took place exactly as described except for a few additional traditional Jewish rituals, such as the groom running into a room where the bride is sitting in a throne-like chair wearing her entire wedding outfit plus a dark veil concealing her face. Bernie was followed by a long line of male attendants, each with his hands on the waist of the man in front of him. The groom approached the bride in her chair. He removed her veil and confirmed, "Yes! This is the woman I'm going to marry." At that moment, the men began to dance in a circle around the couple and the place erupted into an exuberant celebration.

There was a time when my Jewishness meant nothing to me, Bernie thought throughout the ceremonial rituals. *If my parents hadn't insisted, I might have missed all of this. If Betsy hadn't entered my life, I would have missed all of this. Whoever thought being a Jew could be fun? Sean goes to mass. Aram prays in Armenian! Dino's going to get married in a Catholic church. Being a Jew is who I am.*

After the formal wedding ceremony, a sumptuous dinner was served to the nearly one hundred guests. There was lively, happy music and dancing the whole time, men and women together. Betsy's father got permission from the rabbis for the dancing. *It's possible some money changed hands*, Bernie thought. *I don't want to know. I'm so happy. So are my friends.*

It was the Infielders and other members of the team who lifted Betsy and Bernie as they sat in plain wooden chairs. Everyone danced, holding the couple up high. For a moment, Bernie was scared he would fall ... until he saw Sean and Dino holding the chair.

Chapter 65

Dino and Desi's Wedding

The day before the wedding, Desi composed the following notice to send to the *New York Post, Washington Heights Edition.*

George Washington High School Baseball Captain Married in Lavish Ceremony

On Sunday afternoon, February 10, 1963, Dino Russo of Washington Heights and Desi Bradley were married in St. Elizabeth Roman Catholic Church in Washington Heights. Mr. Russo was captain of the only GWHS baseball team to ever win the city high school championship. Father Garrity, pastor of St. Elizabeth's and longtime friend of the Russo family, presided at the wedding mass. Bernie Heller, a dear *friend of the groom, served as best man, and the groom's sister, Terry Flaherty, was maid of honor. In attendance at the wedding mass and the following celebration party, held in the gymnasium of George Washington High School, were the mothers of the couple, Bianca Russo and Rose Bradley; Dino's four siblings; the other three Infielders from the 1947 city championship baseball team and their wives; retired baseball coach Art McCullough; and four other members of the championship baseball team. Also in attendance at were Carlie Metro, the Manager of the Chicago Cubs; two players from that team; and numerous residents of the Washington Heights neighborhood who knew the Infielders when they were boys. A total of 173 people reveled at the celebration.*

"That's very nice," Dino said, "but how do you know how many people will be at the celebration?"

"I made it up. No one will be counting."

"Oh, I thought you were an honest woman."

"You're going to make me an honest woman tomorrow."

"Also, there's something wrong with the punctuation."

"That's why the newspaper has editors."

Neither Aram nor Bernie had ever been in the St. Elizabeth Roman Catholic Church. They always felt that the imposing neo-

Gothic building on Wadsworth Avenue was out of bounds for them. Each wore his best suit and made sure his shoes were shined. They arrived together with their wives. They made sure to be early, for they expected a large crowd to come to Dino's wedding. That was a good idea. They found a space for the four of them in a third-row pew on the center aisle. Within a few minutes, the church was filled to capacity.

Powerful chords rang out from the organ. The congregation stood, and the priest and attendants walked to the altar. Next, Dino, escorted by his mother, walked down the aisle and sat in the first row. Then Desi walked down the aisle, escorted by her mother, and sat next to Dino. The two mothers sat together, holding hands. There was a hum of conversation as people recognized that the stunningly beautiful bride and her mother were Negroes.

The priest called for a reading from the Old Testament. "Bernie Heller, please."

Bernie had no idea what to do. Fortunately, an usher came and led him to a reading stand where, in large print, there was an excerpt from the Song of Songs. Bernie read in his best lawyer voice.

> Hark! my lover—here he comes springing across
>   the mountains, leaping across the hills.
> My lover is like a gazelle or a young stag.

The reading ended with:

> Let me see you, let me hear your voice,
> For your voice is sweet, and you are lovely.
> My lover belongs to me and I to him.
> He says to me:

"Set me as a seal on your heart, as a seal on
    your arm;
For stern as death is love, relentless as the nether
    world is devotion; its flames are a blazing fire.
    Deep waters cannot quench love, nor floods
    sweep it away."

The priest then said, "The word of the Lord."

"That was so beautiful," Betsy whispered to Bernie when he returned to his seat. "I wish it had been read at our wedding."

Sean was then called up to read from the New Testament. He read from Mark's gospel.

Jesus said:
"From the beginning of creation,
God made them male and female.
For this reason a man shall leave his father and
    mother and be joined to his wife, and the two
    shall become one flesh.
So they are no longer two but one flesh. Therefore
    what God has joined together, no human
    being must separate."

When Sean finished the reading, Dino pumped his fist and said, "Yes."

The priest said, "The gospel of the Lord."

Sean's face was glowing when he returned to his seat.

The wedding ceremony strictly followed the traditional Roman Catholic wedding rituals. After about an hour from the time the ceremony began, Father Garrity said, "Now let us humbly invoke God's blessing upon this bride and groom, that in his kindness he may favor with his help those on whom he has bestowed the Sacrament of Matrimony. In the sight of God and these witnesses, I now pronounce you husband and wife! You may now kiss!"

Even when he hit a home run, Sean never heard a roar as loud as the one that shook the church when Dino and Desi kissed.

Several people remarked about Desi's and her mother's color, and a few actually left the building when they walked down the aisle. The subject of race seemed to dissolve and disappear into the jubilance of the day.

The wedding was held on a Sunday rather than a Saturday in deference to Bernie and Betsy Heller's observance of the Sabbath on Saturday.

Fortunately, the day of the wedding was a sunny, crisp, and refreshingly clear day because the crowd that attended the wedding in the church had to walk about six blocks to the high school for the reception celebration in the men's gymnasium that was rented for that purpose, courtesy of Coach McCullough.

The reception was open to the public. People from all over Washington Heights stopped into the gym to sample the food at the buffet tables; some stayed to dance. Many—but not all—sought out the bride and groom for handshakes and hugs.

A six-piece dance band, hired by Mr. Petrosian, enhanced the celebratory atmosphere that filled the gym and spilled out onto Audubon Avenue. Youngsters took time out from playing stickball to try to find Dino and, especially, Sean in the crowd. Dino may have been the star of this show, but Sean Flaherty was the only major league ballplayer from the Heights. His autograph was a thing of value.

Desi was something of a curiosity. Lots of people sought her out to talk with her, wish her good luck, hug her, kiss her, dance with her, and welcome her to the Heights. Some people kept a

distance from her, as if her brown skin might have been conta-
gious. But they were very few.

She commented to Dino in one of their rare private moments
together, "You once said you were part of a movement. Well, the
movement's still got work to do."

He answered, "I want to get my mother involved. She's a
powerhouse. Have you watched her dancing? This has got to be
the happiest time in her life since my father died. Thanks to you."

The leader of the band gave Bernie a microphone and said it
was time for a toast by the best man. The drummer provided a
drum roll, and the bandleader introduced Bernie Heller to a crowd
that already knew him well.

This was his toast: "I have known Dino Russo since we were in
first grade at PS 189. He is my best friend. He is my shortstop—"
He was drowned out by cheering and applause.

He continued, "He is my captain. He has accomplished many
wonderful things. But the best thing of all, he has brought Desi
Bradley into the Russo family, and I know everyone here—which
seems like the entire population of the Heights—everyone here
joins me in wishing Dino and Desi Russo a lifetime together
filled with happiness, fulfillment of every goal they share, and,
God willing, a houseful of children. To Bernie and Desi: *l'chaim!*
To both Mrs. Russos, that means 'to life!'" There was much
cheering.

It wasn't one of Bernie's greatest speeches, but it fit the
occasion.

Sean and Terry were the first to thank Bernie for his toast.
Sean congratulated Bernie on its brevity.

Terry took Dino aside to tell him that Aram and Annette were
standing alone in a corner of the gymnasium. "This is a perfect
time for you to be alone with them and give Aram the opportunity
to make peace with you."

"I need Bernie and Sean with me. I don't want a one-on-one relationship with Aram. The Infielders are a four-on-four group."

"I give up," Terry said as she walked away from Dino, leaving him standing alone.

Noticing that the groom had no one to talk to, Desi rushed to be by his side. She was aware that there was some sort of problem between Dino and Aram. She thought the money problem had been resolved. Now, she thought that was not the case. She didn't want to think about that problem on her wedding day, and she didn't want Dino to be distracted by it either. She decided to do something about it.

"Let's find Sean and Bernie," she said to Dino. "I want you and them to fetch Aram away from Annette so the four of you will use your collective brains and solve the problem you have with Aram so that we can start our marriage without a shadow over it." Her voice was rising as she spoke. Dino just stood as if posing for a portrait. Desi resumed, barking into Dino's ear like an officer addressing a private, "Do that. Do it for me. Do it for yourself. Do it for us. And do it for the Infielders, whatever the hell that means."

She waived to Terry to join them. "Terry, please help me to find Bernie and Sean. Dino needs them to solve his problem with Aram. There's a chill in this room that's spoiling my wedding."

The two women, holding hands, waded into the crowd.

They found Sean surrounded by a crowd of teenage boys and men of all ages. Sean was a celebrity.

"Hey, Sean," Desi cried out as she pushed her way through the squadron of adoring baseball fans. "You haven't kissed the bride yet, and that makes me sad."

"I did kiss you. In the church. I was one of the first."

"Well then, your kiss has worn off. Come with me and Terry. I want another kiss, a proper one this time."

The three of them found Bernie and Betsy in the midst of a lively conversation with people from the neighborhood. Terry whispered to Bernie, "The women want you and Sean to accompany Dino when he goes to make peace with Aram."

"That's great," Bernie exclaimed. "Dino has agreed to do that?"

"Not yet, but he will. Desi's on the case."

The three Infielders huddled in a corner of the room. "This day has been ninety-nine percent perfect," Dino said. "I never thanked you for being the Bible readers at the wedding. You did beautifully. You know, I'm sure that the one percent that's not perfect was Aram's absence from this celebration."

Aram and Annette were at the wedding in the church, but at the reception, they'd been standing alone under the basketball backboard at the far end of the gym, talking to each other but to no one else.

Dino said, "I'm tempted to walk up to him and drag them into the party. I'm wondering whether one of you should do that. What are your thoughts?"

Sean said, "Terry will call Annette tomorrow. Are you going to be here, or are you and Desi going on a honeymoon?"

"Our honeymoon started two years ago. We did things backward. The honeymoon ended with the wedding."

"That is really funny," Sean said. "I'm going to tell Terry."

"When does spring training start?" Bernie asked.

"It already started for the pitchers and catchers. Terry and the kids will be going to Chicago on Wednesday, and I will be spending a day with my father. Then I'm flying to Florida. It's probably my last season."

The three Infielders talked about the championship game, Sean noting that Aram hit a single and a double in that game.

"Let's walk over to him now and tell him that we remember those hits," Sean said with enthusiasm.

"Nice idea," Bernie said. "All four of us have to get beyond the fact that he wanted to turn you over to the cops. Everyone makes a mistake now and then. You, Dino, made a whopper of a mistake when you neglected to get old man Petrosian's okay for taking the money. And Aram made the worst possible mistake when he let his concern about the money become more important to him than our promise of friendship. And more important than your life. Let's try to use today's joyous celebration to erase those mistakes."

Chapter 66

Ninth Inning

The first baseman, the third baseman, and the newlywed shortstop casually approached Aram and Annette. Dino said, "We were just talking about baseball. For some reason, we started to talk about the New Dorp game. I said, 'Aram's got to be part of this conversation.'"

"I think I'll leave," Annette said.

Utterly bemused, Aram said, "New Dorp? That was the championship game. That's what you want to talk about?"

"Yes," said Bernie. "More specifically, we want to talk about the two hits you got in that game."

"Why? Why now? Why on Dino's wedding day?"

"Looks like he doesn't want to talk about those two hits," said Bernie. "Sorry to have bothered you, Aram."

"Wait, don't go. I've been waiting fifteen years to talk about those two hits."

"Well, go ahead and talk," Dino said.

Aram began, "The first hit was in the second inning. We had already scored two runs on a homer by Sean after a walk to

Bernie. There were two outs and we had men on first and third. I hit a ground ball, not very hard, but their pitcher couldn't snag it, and it rolled into centerfield. The guy on third—he wasn't an Infielder—he came in to score. That was my first RBI of the season. I was in heaven. My other hit was a double. It was in the eighth inning, and we were ahead by a ton of runs. I led off the inning. The pitch was a fastball, and I swung late. But I managed to get the end of my bat on the ball and hit a weak line drive over the head of their first baseman. It landed just a foot on the fair side of the right field foul line and actually spun into foul territory. Their right fielder had to run a mile to retrieve the ball that had stopped rolling in front of the box seats along the right field line. It could have been a triple, but I was so excited about getting an extra-base hit that I virtually stopped running on my way toward second to look at where the ball I hit was lying against the fence in front of the seats. I didn't have to slide into second. I went in standing, and they never threw the ball to second. I eventually scored—for the second time that season—after our leadoff hitter grounded to second and I advanced easily to third. Then Bernie hit a line drive into right center, and I trotted home easily. When I went into our dugout—which was the dugout of the Brooklyn Dodgers for their home games—nobody said a word to me. Not a handshake, not a pat on the back. As if I had just struck out. Nothing from the coach or any of my teammates. And, most importantly, nothing from the Infielders. Bernie was on second base after hitting the double that drove me in from third base, but Sean and Dino were in the dugout, and they didn't even look at me after I scored that run. After Bernie scored from second on a fly ball that was dropped by their center fielder, that was when everybody started celebrating my double and the run that I scored. They were waiting for all the Infielders to be together to celebrate me. I later learned from Coach McCullough that it was

Bernie's idea to give me a cold shoulder until the four of us were together."

"Just like now," Bernie said.

Dino said, "I love how you remember every detail of that game."

"There was more to it than that," said Aram. "I also remember another detail in the ninth inning when we were on the field. Our pitcher was wild—probably from nerves. He got the first guy out on a foul pop-up that Bernie caught, but then he walked the next two batters. Then came the best fielding play of my life."

"Oh, yes," Dino said. "I know what you're going to say."

"Our pitching had fallen apart. The big lead that we had in the early innings was down to two runs. In the ninth inning, they were up with one out and the bases loaded. Their cleanup hitter, a big, strong lefty batter, stepped into the batter's box like he was Babe Ruth. I moved to my left because Coach told me he was a pull hitter. Our pitcher was still having trouble finding the strike zone. The count was two balls, no strikes. The guy swings and hits a bullet, not to my left but to my right. I moved toward second like a leopard going in for a kill, dove into the dirt behind second base, got dirt in my mouth, and caught the ball on a short hop in my bare right hand. I flipped it over my shoulder to Dino, who was ready for the ball at second base. Dino caught my flip in his bare right hand. He jumped in the air to avoid the runner sliding into second and made a perfect throw to Sean at first to complete a game-ending double play. We were champions."

"Because of you, Aram," said Sean.

"A thing of beauty," said Bernie.

"The best fielding play I ever saw," said Sean.

"The best we ever did," Dino said. "That play gave us our victory. Thanks to Aram."

The Infielders continued to share memories of the championship season until Annette interrupted them, saying, "All of your wives, including the newest bride, have been waiting for you to pay a little attention to them. I know whatever you've been talking about is extremely important, but President Kennedy will protect us from the Soviet Union while we celebrate Dino's and Desi's wedding. It's really time for you guys to resume your real lives. You've been talking for more than an hour."

"That can't be right," Dino said.

Of course it was right. The Infielders adjourned their meeting and returned to the celebration to redeem their wives.

After

The Infielders never again met as a group. From time to time, Dino and Bernie would meet for coffee at a diner on St. Nicholas Avenue.

Sean became the hitting coach of the Los Angeles Dodgers, and he and his family moved to Southern California. Aram never saw Sean again. Bernie and Dino saw him when he came to New York for his father's funeral.

Bernie and Betsy produced two children. Their productivity was surpassed by that of Dino and Desi, who became the parents of three. Their third child was a boy. They named him Frank. Sean phoned Dino from Los Angeles to congratulate Dino and Desi and to remind Dino that he and Terry also have a son named Frank. He said, "I hope your Frank Russo and his cousin, my Frank Flaherty, will be friends someday. And I hope that each can be a man like your father, bless his soul."

Many years later, Dino—now retired from the car dealership—said to his wife, Desi—now a grandmother and retired from the Board of Directors of MoMA—"I just realized that it was on this date exactly fifty years ago that we won the championship game. On that day, I really believed that the Infielders would be part of one another's lives forever. I was a naïve eighteen-year-old. But, you know, I am so grateful that we were the Infielders for many years and that I can still call up those memories. All these years later, I think of them, and they fill my heart with joy."

For the Infielders, the varied circumstances of their lives—the details, the occurrences, and the unique experiences of their lives —gradually overshadowed their friendship. But it didn't crash and burn. And it didn't fade away. It just became a memory, a memory of a beautiful thing.

Acknowledgments

As far as I know, no one has ever written a full-length novel alone. I have always needed input from intelligent readers, and I've been fortunate to have had that necessary help in writing *The Infielders*. I am especially grateful for the comments of Prof. David A. Stern of the University of Connecticut (UConn) Drama Department; Mitchell Rosen, a Washington Heights native with a prodigious memory; Ted Zupnick, a firm but not a caustic critic; Prof. (Ret.) Manny Lerman, UConn Math; and my beloved daughter, Karen, Columbia College English major, who writes better than I do.

The copyediting of the manuscript, a formidable task, was performed by Eva Kelly Hall of atxEva Editing Services with meticulous care and great enthusiasm.

The substantive editing of Molly Rookwood of Rookwood Editing transformed my rough manuscript into a fluent and coherent novel. She knows nothing about baseball but virtually everything about friendship. She was my partner in writing this book.

About the Author

At the end of 2023, Lew Segal retired from the practice of law after sixty-three years of assisting clients in their business transactions. His newfound free time enabled him to devote his energy to completing *The Infielders*, his third novel. Lew grew up in the Washington Heights neighborhood of Upper Manhattan and attended George Washington High School, where he played baseball but not nearly well enough to make the GW team. He then went on to Columbia University to be educated in the liberal arts, followed by Yale Law School. While attending Yale, he met and married Shirley, with whom he celebrated the sixty-fifth anniversary of their wedding and his eighty-ninth birthday in April 2024. They have two adult children and two adult grandchildren. Lew and Shirley have lived in Connecticut for over sixty years.

Also by Lewis Segal

With All Due Respect

The Brief and Glorious Reign of King Frederick the Brave

Printed in the USA
CPSIA information can be obtained
at www.ICGtesting.com
CBHW020849040824
12542CB00025B/48